# THE CANTELOWE ACCOUNTS

**Records of Social and Economic History** is a British Academy Research Project.

The British Academy, established by Royal Charter in 1902, is the national academy for the humanities and social sciences, promoting, sustaining and representing advanced research. As an academy composed of senior scholars throughout the UK, it gives recognition to academic excellence and achievement, and plays a leadership role in representing the humanities and social sciences nationally and internationally. As a learned society, the British Academy facilitates the research of individuals and groups of scholars.

More information can be found at *www.thebritishacademy.ac.uk*

RECORDS OF SOCIAL AND ECONOMIC HISTORY
NEW SERIES 64

# THE CANTELOWE ACCOUNTS

## MULTILINGUAL MERCHANT RECORDS FROM TUSCANY 1450–1451

EDITED BY
MEGAN TIDDEMAN

*Published for* THE BRITISH ACADEMY
*by* OXFORD UNIVERSITY PRESS

*Oxford University Press, Great Clarendon Street, Oxford OX2 6DP*



*First edition published 2022*



*British Library Cataloguing in Publication Data*
*Data available*

*Library of Congress Cataloguing in Publication Data*
*Data available*

*Typeset by Newgen Publishing UK*
*Printed and bound by CPI Group (UK) Ltd, Croydon, CR0 4YY*

*ISBN 978–0–19–726685–4*

# Foreword

Long-distance trade is especially prone to the 'principal agent problem', of the difficulties main traders have in managing their representatives. Good lines of communication and careful accounting are self-evidently important ways of addressing this. As previous volumes in this series show, historians have long valued commercial correspondence for shedding a powerful light on the nature of domestic and international trade, often in the process personalizing the operation of abstract market forces and the challenges of co-ordinating credit and debt. In contrast, account books have attracted less attention, in part because they can seem cold and inert, offering summaries without much of a human voice. In this meticulous edition Megan Tiddeman shows how wrong that is.

The accounts here were kept for Sir William Cantelow in London by his agent John Balmayn in Italy and concern the shipping and sale of English wool in Pisa and Florence. As such, they demonstrate the value of this raw material to manufacturers in one of the most economically advanced societies of its time. As well as showing ways in which this market worked, which has cultural, social as well as economic dimensions, it also helps to explain the prosperity of the great wool producing areas of medieval England, most obviously evidenced today by the surviving built environment of towns such as Lavenham in Suffolk. But as Dr Tiddeman powerfully shows, of no less interest is the ways the accounts show how linguistic barriers were bridged by Balmayn imaginatively employing several languages, including Middle English and Anglo-French. We get some sense here of the protean nature of language and of how developments can be enriched by relatively distant contacts and a search for common ground. All told, this is an edition which offers something to a wide range of specialists both of late-medieval Europe as well as those interested in the wider histories of international exchange.

Professor Phillipp Schofield shepherded this volume to the production stage, where Professor Harding, the general editor of the series, also helped. Geetha Nair, Portia Taylor and their colleagues at the British Academy saw the volume through the press with great care and skill. I am very grateful to them all for their considerable efforts.

Julian Hoppit, Chair, Records of Social and Economic History Committee
August 2022

# Contents

# Acknowledgements

An earlier version of this edition formed part of a longer doctoral thesis on Anglo-Italian language contact which I wrote at Aberystwyth University, under the supervision of the late Professor David Trotter. David was a world-leading Anglo-Norman specialist, lexicographer, and scholar of medieval multilingualism. He was not only a professional inspiration to me but a man of renowned wit, energy and integrity. David died in August 2015, just before the start of the final year of my PhD. The last time I saw him in person was at a meeting to discuss my chapters on the Cantelowe material, and he was typically enthusiastic and excited by this unique source. This book is therefore dedicated to his memory.

I would also like to thank Dr David Parsons and Dr Geert De Wilde, unflappable and meticulous both, who stepped in as my supervisors during my last year as a postgraduate. Without their support and guidance, my thesis, and consequently this edition, may never have reached completion. Special thanks must also go to Professor Phillipp Schofield for his advice and encouragement in preparing my submission to the RSEH series, and to Professors Vanessa Harding and Julian Hoppit for helping me improve my many drafts.

I am grateful to numerous academics in the UK and overseas for answering my queries and they are acknowledged in footnotes throughout the edition. However, two Italian scholars deserve particular mention here. Firstly, I would like to thank Professoressa Roberta Cella for welcoming me so warmly to Pisa back in 2012 and helping me navigate the bureaucracy of the Scuola Normale archives. Lastly, I must express my gratitude to Dottore Angelo Nicolini who has been unfailingly generous over the years in sharing his knowledge of all things historical, paleographical and toponymic. Several puzzles emerged during the transcription of the accounts which I may never have solved without his help, and for this I am greatly indebted to him.

# List of Tables

# List of Illustrations

# Abbreviations

**Languages:**

| | |
|---|---|
| AF | Anglo-French |
| BML | British Medieval Latin |
| CF | Continental French |
| Fior. | Florentine |
| It. | Italian |
| Lat. | Latin |
| ME | Middle English |
| OE | Old English |
| Ven. | Venetian |

**Dictionaries:**

| | |
|---|---|
| AND1 / AND2 | *Anglo-Norman Dictionary*, 1st / 2nd ed., www.anglo-norman.net. |
| DMF | *Dictionnaire du Moyen Français*, www.atilf.fr/dmf. |
| DMLBS | Ronald Edward Latham, David Howlett *et al* (eds), *Dictionary of Medieval Latin from British Sources* (Oxford: British Academy, 1975–2013). |
| FEW | Walther von Wartburg *et al* (eds), *Französisches etymologisches Wörterbuch: eine Darstellung des galloromanischen Sprachsatzes* (Bonn / Leipzig / Basel: Zbinden, 1922-). |
| LEI | Max Pfister, Wolfgang Schweickard *et al* (eds), *Lessico etimologico italiano* (Wiesbaden: Reichert Verlag, 1979-). |
| MED | *Middle English Dictionary*, quod.lib.umich.edu/m/med/. |
| OED2 / OED3 | *Oxford English Dictionary*, 2nd / 3rd ed., www.oed.com. |
| TLF | *Le Trésor de la Langue Française*, atilf.atilf.fr/tlf.htm. |
| TLIO | *Tesoro della Lingua Italiana delle Origini*, tlio.ovi.cnr.it/TLIO/. |
| VTO | *Vocabolario Trecanni*, http://www.treccani.it/vocabolario/. |

**Online lexical databases:**

AD *Archivio Datini: corpus lemmatizzato del carteggio Datini*, aspweb.ovi.cnr.it/.

LCC *Lexis of Cloth and Clothing Project*, lexissearch.arts.manchester.ac.uk/

OVI *Opera del Vocabolario Italiano: Corpus OVI dell'Italiano antico*, www.gattoweb.ovi.cnr.it.

**Other online resources:**

EIDB *England's Immigrants 1330–1550* project, www.englandsimmigrants.com.

VOH *Views of the Hosts of Alien Merchants, 1440–44*, online transcription by Helen Bradley, https://sas-space.sas.ac.uk/102/.

**Archives:**

TNA The National Archives, Kew, United Kingdom.

AS Archivio Salviati, Scuola Normale Superiore, Pisa, Italy.

# Introduction

> Contact between cultures is sometimes perceived in terms of shared literary, dramatic, musical and visual forms, and thought of largely as a question of the geographical spread of styles and ideas over time. However, there is another, entirely different, dimension to contact between cultures, one which is much more commonplace. It arises from trade, and considering this other dimension necessitates expanding our view to accommodate a wider community and, to match it, a wider sense of what we imagine 'culture' to be.[1]

The Salviati family archives, housed in a stunning Renaissance *palazzo* in central Pisa, contain a surprising gem for scholars of late medieval England. Hidden amongst thousands of registers, bills and letters detailing centuries of business is a short account book from 1450–1, written by a Londoner, John Balmayn.[2] This contains the earliest written evidence of an English merchant using Italian as a second language. Indeed, the author uses a unique mixed-language code, combining Tuscan, Middle English, Latin and Anglo-French, as well as a modern use of Arabic numerals that was decades ahead of his colleagues back home.

At first glance, the accounts may seem dull, even by the standards of medieval administration. There are none of the cutting-edge financial techniques for which Italians were famed, such as double-entry bookkeeping.[3] There are no exotic commodities, no silks and spices from distant shores, no fine wines and furs. All but three of the pages are devoted to the same large shipment of English wool

[1] Helen Bradley, '"Saluti da Londra": Italian Merchants in the City of London in the Late Fourteenth and Early Fifteenth Centuries', in Michele Campopiano and Helen Fulton (eds), *Anglo-Italian Cultural Relations in the Later Middle Ages* (Woodbridge, York Medieval Press, 2018), pp. 103–27 at p. 103.
[2] Archivio Salviati (AS) Serie I: 339.
[3] Modern double entry book-keeping was pioneered in Italy with the earliest fragmented examples being found in the Forolfi accounts in Florence in 1299 and the first complete system in the Messari accounts in Genoa in 1340 (Luc Lauwers and Marleen Willekens, 'Five Hundred Years of Bookkeeping: a Portrait of Luca Pacioli', *Tijdschrift voor Economie en Management (Katholieke Universiteit Leuven)*, 39, no.3 (1994), 289–304 at 300). There is no record of an English merchant employing the technique until Thomas Howell, a cloth merchant based in Seville, did so for his ledgers in 1517–28 (Trevor Boyns and John R. Edwards, A *History of Management Accounting: the British Experience* (Abingdon, Routledge, 2013), p. 86). However, we do know that the Venetian, Gabriel Corbizzi, who became Steward of Southampton in the 1440s, overhauled office accounting in the port along Italian lines: see Anne Thick, 'The Fifteenth-Century Stewards' Books of Southampton', Ph.D. thesis (King Alfred's College, University of Southampton, 1995), pp. 73–4; Tom Beaumont James, 'The Town of Southampton and its Foreign Trade 1430–1540' in Michael Hicks (ed), *English Inland Trade* (Oxford, Oxbow, 2015), pp. 11–25 at p. 13.

that arrived in Tuscany from Southampton around November 1450. Balmayn oversaw the sale of some of this valuable cargo in Italy on behalf of his master, Sir William Cantelowe, himself a business partner of the wealthy Salviati of Florence. The author also methodically records all the details of its delivery and purchase in Pisa and Florence by forty-four Italian buyers over a period of eleven months. Included are precise weights and deductions for each lot of wool, expenses incurred, the price paid in florins and a long list of bills of exchange[4] via Venice and Bruges, allowing payment to reach Cantelowe back in London.

This is not the first time the manuscript has been studied. The historian George Holmes visited the Pisa archives before 1993 and examined the accounts (along with others written by the Salviati themselves)[5] for a well-known article on the English wool export market in the mid-fifteenth century: 'Anglo-Florentine Trade in 1451'. Given the relative lack of information about Anglo-Italian trade in the fifteenth century, compared to the era of Tuscan Crown banking under Edwards I, II and III, the financial details in these sources provided vital new evidence. Holmes also transcribed several short sections of Balmayn's writing to include in his paper but (understandably, given the focus of his study) is not concerned with linguistic analysis.[6] His only comment on language use actually does the writer a disservice by underestimating his multilingual skills: 'At this stage the English

[4] The bill of exchange or *lettre de change* system was created by Italian merchants working across late medieval Europe and involved sending a written order of payment (detailing sum, payee and date) which authorised a company in another city or country to make a payment on a merchant's behalf. See De Roover for what are still considered the definitive articles on this financial system's development: Raymond De Roover, *Money, Banking and Credit in Medieval Bruges* (Cambridge, MA, The Medieval Academy of America, 1948); *Évolution de la lettre de change* (Paris, Colin, 1953). Rainer also gives a very useful diagram summarising the four parties typically involved in the transactions of a single bill: Franz Rainer, 'Le rôle de l'italien dans la formation de la terminologie cambiale française', *Revue de linguistique romane*, 78 (2014), 57–86 at 63.

[5] Holmes' other key source was the *Libro Grandi Rosso Segnato A,* the Salviati London book from 1448–51 (AS Serie I: 336). This lengthy set of Florentine records contains – not surprisingly – numerous examples of loanwords from Middle English and Anglo-French: see Megan Tiddeman, 'Early Anglo-Italian Contact: New Loanword Evidence from Two Mercantile Sources, 1440–1451', in Esther-Miriam Wagner, Bettina Beinhoff and Ben Outhwaite (eds), *Merchants of Innovation: the Languages of Traders* (Berlin, De Gruyter Mouton, 2017), pp. 217–34; 'Lexical Exchange with Italian in the Textile and Wool Trades in the Thirteenth to Fifteenth Centuries', in Robin Netherton and Gale R. Owen Crocker (eds), *Medieval Clothing and Textiles* 14 (Woodbridge, Boydell & Brewer, 2018), pp. 113–40. The 2,000-page accounts were transcribed in 1969 by Maura Cavallaro, an undergraduate student supervised by Federigo Melis at the University of Pisa. Despite some transcription errors, this document has proved incredibly helpful to me as a resource for both my own thesis and this monograph and, like Holmes before me, I would like to acknowledge its author: George Holmes, 'Anglo-Florentine Trade in 1451', *English Historical Review*, 108 (1993), 371–86 at 378, n. 2.

[6] There are six brief extracts of a sentence or so, as well as a list of wool names taken from f. 4v. Holmes also transcribed two longer sections – the two opening paragraphs to the accounts from f. 1r and some of Balmayn's letter asking for more wool on f. 64r. It goes without saying that these citations offered me an invaluable foothold into understanding the scribe's hand when I first began transcribing the text and for this, I am indebted to the late Professor Holmes.

accountant sometimes lapsed into Italian, presumably repeating what was said to him by his Florentine colleagues.'[7]

In reality, this document has not just economic but great linguistic and social worth. By its survival alone, it joins a very small group of Middle English private mercantile records from the first half of the fifteenth century. But, more importantly, Balmayn keeps switching language and writes in a fascinating mix of English, Italian[8] and Latin, peppered throughout with a small but consistent selection of Anglo-French abbreviations and expressions. The author writes in a clearly English hand but is a competent writer of medieval business Italian which, in itself, is an extremely rare example of early Anglo-Italian contact.

I have written elsewhere about the little-known presence of Italian borrowings in late medieval mercantile documents in England such as the Southampton Port and Stewards' Books, accounts of Durham Abbey and of the Worshipful Company of Grocers, and alien hosting accounts: e.g. *belendin* ('high-quality ginger'), *caffatin* ('high-quality sugar loaf'), *fangot* ('bundle of cloth'), *garble* ('to sift refuse from spices'), *maregon* ('galley carpenter'), *sportin* ('small basket'), *talany* ('Persian raw silk'), *yndigo* ('rich purple colour dye').[9] However, Balmayn's linguistic immersion goes far beyond the use of individual loanwords. Whilst it seems obvious that professionals who worked closely with Italian colleagues at home and abroad would have spoken Italian, concrete proof of such competence in the mercantile community has been elusive until this point.[10]

[7] Holmes, 'Anglo-Florentine Trade', 374.

[8] 'Italian' is obviously an oversimplified term as the reality of a single Italian language was centuries away – in the mid-twentieth century, some would argue: cf. Anna Laura Lepschy and Giulio Lepschy, *The Italian Language Today*, 2nd edn. (London, Routledge, 1988). However, it is employed here, as in other studies, as a useful catch-all for the diverse range of dialects from the peninsula. Balmayn's language use is clearly influenced by medieval Tuscan (and the Florentine dialect, in particular) which would go on to form the bedrock of modern Standard Italian as we know it. Note that it is not within the scope of the current work to include phonological or morphological analysis of Italian dialectal variants.

[9] Megan Tiddeman, 'Early Anglo-Italian Contact'; Tiddeman, 'Lexical exchange with Italian'; Megan Tiddeman, 'More Sugar and Spice: Revisiting Medieval Italian Influence on the Mercantile Lexis of England' in Laura Wright (ed), *The Multilingual Origins of Standard English* (Berlin, De Gruyter Mouton, 2020), pp. 381–410; Megan Tiddeman, '*Libri alienigeni:* Evidence of Anglo-Italian language contact from the fifteenth-century port of Southampton' in Alessandra Petrocchi and Joshua Brown (eds), *Languages and Cross-Cultural Exchanges in Renaissance Italy* (Turnhout, Brepols, forthcoming).

[10] Exciting new evidence of Italian use by non-native writers in England has recently been unearthed by Luigi Alessandro Cappelletti (Università di Cassino e del Lazio meridionale) as part of his doctoral research project. He has studied a roll of accounts from the Canterbury Mint which record the purchase of silver. The source dates from as early as 1291–4 when the Florentine, Lapino Roger, was in post as assayer. The text contains sections where two distinct hands, clearly belonging to English Exchequer scribes, write in a rudimentary but identifiable form of Italian vernacular, most likely Tuscan. The parchment was found in pristine condition alongside a standard Latin and Anglo-French version of the accounts and Cappelletti believes that an Italian merchant commissioned a copy in his native tongue but never received it. See Luigi Alessandro Cappelletti, 'Un testo in volgare italo-romanzo in un rotolo

Formal teaching and learning of Italian did not begin in England for another century when it became a popular aristocratic pursuit – one very much focused on literature and wider Renaissance culture.[11] The extensive mixing of Middle English and Tuscan business codes appears unique amongst known medieval texts, as is the extensive use of Arabic numerals, which is decades ahead of contemporary practice back in London.

The Cantelowe accounts are therefore deserving of a full edition in their own right. Their contents may initially appear dry and functional, but they offer extraordinary insight into the merger of English and northern Italian commercial worlds. In this, they provide a rare surviving example of a process that was probably happening in countless account books (and countless conversations) in late medieval merchant society as aliens and locals embarked on business ventures together.

---

della zecca di Canterbury (1291–1294)', *Studi linguistici italiani*, XLVI (2020), 163–200. I would like to thank the author for discussing his paper with me prior to its publication.

[11] William Thomas, a clerk in the Privy Council who had lived in Italy, published the first Italian grammar and glossary in England in 1550: *Principal Rules of the Italian Grammar with a Dictionary for the Better Understanding of Boccace, Petrarca and Dante*. This was eclipsed in scope and reputation by the Italian-English dictionary *Worlde of Wordes* (published in 1598 and again in 1611, in a longer format) by John Florio, an Oxford graduate and language tutor to the royal family. The son of a Tuscan protestant refugee, he also wrote manuals of Italian grammar and conversation such as the cheerily named *First Fruits, which yield Familiar Speech, Merry Proverbs, Witty Sentences and Golden Sayings* from 1578. For in-depth studies of Italian language learning in early modern England, see Jason Lawrence, *Who the Devil Taught Thee So Much Italian? Italian Language and Literary Imitation in Early Modern England* (Manchester, Manchester University Press, 2005) and John Gallagher, *Learning Languages in Early Modern England* (Oxford, Oxford University Press, 2019).

# 1
# Italian trade with England in the late Middle Ages: an overview

The Cantelowe-Salviati wool venture is but one small example of sustained Italian influence on English economic life that lasted for over two centuries until the end of the 1400s. The surname *Lumbardus* first appears in documents from St Paul's Cathedral c. 1110 and c. 1140 and then in a Pipe Roll of 1162–63, but continuous evidence for Italian trade in England begins in the 1220s.[1] Florentine activity is documented in London from 1223 and that of the Sienese from 1228, and we know that traders from Lucca sold fine cloths and richly embroidered liturgical vestments (orphreys) to the king from 1245 onwards.[2] By the early fourteenth century, Northern Italians had set up shop in the heart of London's financial district – known to this day as 'Lombard Street'[3] – when Edward I granted land to their gold- and silversmiths.

From the later thirteenth and into the fourteenth century, we find a wealth of records of northern Italian *compagnie* with representatives in England.[4] Merchant societies from Genoa, Florence, Lucca, Piacenza, Pistoia and Bologna also appear in government records from the second half of the thirteenth century and from Padua, Pisa, Milan, Asti and Venice in the fourteenth century. In addition,

[1] 'Lombard' was used generically in late medieval England to refer to natives of Genoa, Venice or Tuscany. In this early case, the men were probably Genoese (Pamela Nightingale, *Trade, Money and Power in Medieval England* (Aldershot, Ashgate Variorum, 2007), ch. VIII, p. 125).

[2] Roberta Cella, 'Anglismi e francesismi nel registro della filiale di Londra di una compagnia mercantile senese (1305–1308)', in Serge Vanvolsem *et al (eds), Identità e diversità nella lingua e nella letteratura italiana. Atti del XVIII Congresso dell'A.I.S.L.L.I.* (Firenze, Cesati, 2007), pp. 189–204 at p. 191; Richard Kaeuper, *Bankers to the Crown: the Riccardi of Lucca and Edward I* (Princeton, Princeton University Press, 1973), p. 5.

[3] This is itself an adaptation of Langbourne Street, by which the street was originally known: Henry A Harben, 'Lombard Street', in *A Dictionary of London* (London, 1918), http://www.british-history.ac.uk/no-series/dictionary-of-london/lodbury-lodingeberi-london-bridge-waterworks [accessed 13 October 2019].

[4] The early emergence of the *compagnia* was a key feature of Italian trade, originally 'a small family partnership – between father and son, or brothers – men who lived in the same house, who broke the same bread (as the word *compagno* implies)' (Iris Origo, *The Merchant of Prato: Francesco di Marco Datini* (Harmondsworth, Penguin Books, 1963), p. 109). The system allowed merchants (who were often literally 'in the same boat') to pool commodities and borrow cash within a close circle of mutual acquaintance. See Robert Lopez (ed), *The Dawn of Modern Banking* (New Haven, Yale University Press, 1979), p. 8.

there were, of course, numerous private merchants from the peninsula (some of whom acquired English citizenship) who worked on behalf of several companies or none.[5] The extensive London accounts of the Gallerani of Siena (now housed in Belgium) date from 1304 and are of great interest to scholars of Tuscan historical linguistics.[6] There are several examples of Italian marginalia scribbled on the edges of Anglo-French Exchequer warrants from 1324–1326 and 1339–1345 in the UK National Archives at Kew.[7] Also in the National Archives is a small but invaluable collection of Tuscan documents confiscated by the Crown during a period of recurring financial crisis between the King and his foreign bankers:

- sixteen letters to the Ricciardi, sent from the company head office in Lucca to its London branch between 1295–1301.[8]
- a section of Frescobaldi accounts relating to business in London from 1311–13.[9]
- nineteen letters to the Frescobaldi, sent from London, Florence, Bruges and Avignon between 1311 and 1313.[10]
- a letter from 1313 by Biagio Aldobrandini (factor to the London Gallerani company), to the Frescobaldi in Avignon.[11]

This bounty of documentary evidence reflects Tuscany's place at the forefront of commercial innovation in late medieval Europe and as the birthplace of the merchant-banking corporation. Its cities prospered through foreign trade: Pisa,

[5] Terence Henry Lloyd, *Alien Merchants in England in the High Middle Ages* (Sussex, The Harvester Press, 1982), pp. 173–4.
[6] The Gallerani material was edited in Georges Bigwood and Armand Grunzweig, *Les livres des comptes des Gallerani* (Bruxelles, Palais des Académies, 1961). Newly discovered sections were added in Roberta Cella, *La documentazione Gallerani-Fini nell'Archivio di Stato di Gent (1304–1309)* (Firenze, SISMEL edizioni del Galluzzo, 2009). For discussions of English and French loanwords in the accounts, see Roberta Cella, *I Gallicismi nei testi dell'italiano antico (dalle origini alla fine del sec. XIV)* (Firenze, Accademia della Crusca, 2003); Cella, 'Anglismi e francesismi'; Megan Tiddeman, 'Mercantile Multilingualism: Two Examples of Anglo-Norman and Italian Contact in the Fourteenth Century', in *Present and Future in Anglo-Norman: La Recherche Actuelle Et Future Sur L'Anglo-Normand* (The Anglo-Norman Online Hub, 2012), pp. 91–9; Tiddeman, 'Early Anglo-Italian Contact'.
[7] TNA, E 101/127/19-22 and E 101/127/36. These marginalia are discussed in Emilio Re, 'Archivi inglesi e storia italiana', *Archivio Storico Italiano*, 71 (1913), 249–81 at 266–72; Adrian R. Bell, Chris Brooks and Tony K. Moore, *Accounts of the English Crown with the Italian Merchant Societies, 1272–1345* (London, List and Index Society, 2009), p. 268; Tiddeman, 'Mercantile Multilingualism', pp. 92–4.
[8] TNA, E 101/601/5 and SC 1/58/20. These letters are edited in Arrigo Castellani and Ignazio Del Punta, *Lettere dei Ricciardi di Lucca ai loro compagni in Inghilterra (1295–1303)* (Roma, Salerno, 2005).
[9] TNA, E 101/127/10. See edited sections in Armando Sapori, *La compagnia dei Frescobaldi in Inghilterra* (Firenze, Leo S. Olschki, 1947), pp. 85–136.
[10] TNA, SC 1/49/121, 164, 165, 177; SC 1/58/13; SC 1/63/184 and E 30/1488. These letters are partially translated in Richard Kaeuper, 'The Frescobaldi of Florence and the English Crown', in William M. Bowsky (ed), *Studies in Medieval and Renaissance History*, Volume 10 (Lincoln, University of Nebraska Press, 1973), pp. 45–95.
[11] TNA, SC 1/58/6. The letter is edited in Ignazio Del Punta, 'Una lettera da Londra ad Avignone del 1313,' *Bollettino dell'Opera del Vocabolario Italiano*, 13 (2008), 351–69.

with its great port, Lucca, the centre of silk manufacture, Siena, home to the earliest banks and Florence, a European capital of commerce, banking and industry.[12] The Italians' financial strength, with its access to ready coin and sophisticated currency speculations, 'lay in the multi-faceted nature of their European trade, the capital which their partners and shareholders contributed in Italy, and the links of their numerous branches with the bullion and money market which had developed in the Champagne fairs'.[13]

In England, this Italian expertise was widely used in exchange and coinage[14] and new Italian book-keeping techniques can be seen to influence the recording of Wardrobe accounts in the fourteenth century.[15] However, the best-known involvement of Italians in medieval English financial life was through their large loans to a succession of monarchs, a subject which has inspired a considerable academic literature.[16] The reigns of Edwards I, II and III (1272–1377) ushered in a new era of Anglo-Tuscan interaction, with vast sums of money borrowed to cover a huge range of regal expenses. Members of the Ricciardi of Lucca and the Frescobaldi, Peruzzi and Bardi of Florence moved at the highest level of Court

[12] Cf. Richard Goldthwaite, *The Economy of Renaissance Florence* (Baltimore, John Hopkins University Press, 2009), pp. 14–15. Genoa and Venice would also follow as economic innovators: see Michele Fratianni and Franco Spinelli, 'Italian city-states and financial evolution', *European Review of Economic History*, 10 (2006), pp. 257–78 for the Florentine, Genoese and Venetian contributions made to 'financial evolution', such as commitment mechanisms, social insurance systems and the establishment of public banks. For a wider social examination of the shift of wealth and power from feudal lords to urban guilds and merchant families in medieval Italy, see Katherine L. Jansen, Joanna H. Drell and Frances Andrews (eds), 'The Commercial Revolution', in *Medieval Italy: Texts in Translation* (Philadelphia, University of Pennsylvania Press), pp. 77–110.

[13] Pamela Nightingale, 'Alien Finance and the development of the English economy, 1285–1311', *Economic History Review*, 66 (2013), 477–496 at 479.

[14] Several Italians were promoted to Warden of the Royal Mint in either London, Canterbury or Durham (an exceptional privilege for an alien merchant at the time): Orlando da Pagio and James Orlandi in 1279, Amerigo Frescobaldi in 1307 and Walter Bardi in 1377. Mint records also seem to show that, in some cases, official positions were exploited to quickly exchange bullion for sterling on behalf of their fellow merchants (Nightingale, 'Alien finance', 479).

[15] See Michael Prestwich, 'Italian Merchants in Late Thirteenth and Early Fourteenth Century England', in Lopez (ed), *The Dawn of Modern Banking*, pp. 77–104 at p. 83. He also makes the case (p. 99) that Italian influence in these areas would have been even more marked if exceptionally firm royal control had not stifled English banking development at this stage. This opinion is shared in James Bolton, *The Medieval English Economy, 1150–1500* (London, Dent, 1980), p. 348 and Nightingale, *Trade, Money and Power,* ch. I, p. 373.

[16] The bibliography is too vast to cite here but some key examples include: Edward A. Bond, *Extracts from the Liberate Rolls Relative to Loans Supplied by Italian Merchants to the Kings of England in the 13th and 14th Centuries* (London, The Society of Antiquaries of London, 1840); Robert J. Whitwell, 'Italian Bankers and the English Crown', *Transactions of the Royal Historical Society,* New Series 17 (1903), pp. 175–233; Emilio Re, *La compagnia dei Riccardi in Inghilterra e il suo fallimento alla fine del secolo XIII.* (Roma, R. Società Romana di storia patria, 1914); Ephraim Russell, 'The societies of the Bardi and the Peruzzi and their dealings with Edward III, 1327–45', in George Unwin (ed), *Finance and Trade under Edward III: the London lay subsidy of 1332* (Manchester, The University Press, 1918), pp. 93–135; Armando Sapori, *La crisi delle compagnie mercantili dei Bardi e dei Peruzzi* (Firenze, Leo S. Olschki, 1926); Sapori, *La compagnia dei Frescobaldi*; E. B. Fryde, 'Italian merchants in Medieval England

society, alleviating the king's 'perpetual cash flow problem'.[17] In return, they enjoyed lucrative favours such as hidden interest payments,[18] tax exemptions, rights to custom duties and grants of wool monopolies.

Wool was England's most precious commodity in the late thirteenth and fourteenth centuries, the lifeblood of its export economy and the lynchpin of Anglo-Tuscan trade. Sheep-farming was common to many countries, but England[19] and Spain dominated as producers of the highest-quality grades of raw wool. Estimates of peak English exports at the time vary from 30,000 to 45,000 sacks per annum;[20] this equalled the clip of around eight to twelve million sheep[21] being shipped from England every year to sustain the Flemish

c. 1270–1500', in *Aspetti della vita economica medievale: atti del Convegno di Studi nel X Anniversario della morte di Federigo Melis, Firenze-Pisa-Prato, 10–14 marzo 1984* (Firenze, Monte dei Paschi di, Siena 1984), pp. 215–32; Michael M. Postan, 'Italy and the economic development of England in the Middle Ages', *Journal of Economic History*, 11 (1951), 339–46; George Holmes, 'Florentine Merchants in England, 1346–1446', *Economic History Review*, 13 (1960), 193–208; Kaeuper, 'Frescobaldi of Florence'; Kaeuper, *Bankers to the Crown*; Richard Goldthwaite, 'Italian bankers in medieval England', *Journal of European Economic History*, 2 (1973), 763–71; Prestwich, 'Italian Merchants'; Lloyd, *Alien Merchants*; Edwin S. Hunt, 'A New Look at the Dealings of the Bardi and Peruzzi with Edward III', *Journal of Economic History*, 50 (1990), 149–62; Ignazio Del Punta, 'Italian Firms in Late Medieval England and their Bankruptcy: Re-reading an Old History of a Financial Crisis' in Michele Campopiano and Helen Fulton (eds), *Anglo-Italian Cultural Relations in the Later Middle Ages* (Woodbridge, York Medieval Press, 2018), pp. 67–86; Bell *et al.*, *Accounts of the English Crown.*

17 Hunt, 'Dealings of the Bardi and Peruzzi', 152.

18 To the medieval mind, money was unavoidably connected to usury. Italians gradually replaced Jews as England's moneylenders but with the role came a long tradition of the taint of sin (Derek Pearsall, 'Strangers in Late Fourteenth-Century London' in F.R.P. Akehurst and Stephanie Cain Van D'Elden (eds), *The Stranger in Medieval Society* (Minneapolis, University of Minnesota Press, 1997), pp. 46–62; Bolton, *Medieval English Economy*, p. 336). The adjective *lumbart* is used in *La vie de Saint Thomas Becket* (c. 1174) to mean 'characteristic of a usurer, greedy for money' (see AND2 sub **lombart**). Until the late thirteenth century in England, Italian creditors faced regular expulsion from the realm on charges of usury – in 1240, 1245, 1251, 1253 and 1263, for example (see Lloyd, *Alien Merchants*, p. 171) – but a personal grudge on the part of the king, or just a wish to avoid repayment, seem more likely causes than genuine moral outrage. The Third Lateran Council of 1179 had prohibited interest but not credit itself: the solution was usually to resort to hidden interest payments, levied as 'gifts' or 'damages' for late payment (cf. Prestwich, 'Italian Merchants' and Bell *et al.*, *Accounts of the English Crown*) or concealed as the price of a bill of exchange (cf. Raymond De Roover, *The Rise and Decline of the Medici Bank, 1397–1494* (New York, Norton, 1963), pp. 11–14).

19 In his merchant handbook, the *Pratica della mercatura* (c. 1339–1343), Francesco Balducci Pegolotti (who worked as a Bardi factor, amongst other things) details yields and guide prices for 173 wool-producing ecclesiastical estates in England. In contrast, only fifteen are mentionned in Scotland and twelve in Wales: Allan Evans (ed), *La Practica della Mercatura* (Cambridge, Medieval Academy of America, 1935), pp. 258–79. There is some evidence that Welsh and Irish wool was exported to Florence but it was used for cheaper fabrics because of its coarseness: Eileen Power, *The Wool Trade in English Medieval History* (London, Oxford University Press, 1941), pp. 12–15. However, it should be noted that in the Irish case the sums involved could be significant, with the Ricciardi advancing £200 and £70 to the earl of Ulster in 1285 and the lord of Offaly in 1292, respectively: Adrian R. Bell, Chris Brooks and Paul R. Dryburgh, *The English Wool Market: c. 1230–1327* (Cambridge, Cambridge University Press, 2007), p. 22.

20 Terence Henry Lloyd, *The English Wool Trade in the Middle Ages* (Cambridge, Cambridge University Press, 1977), p. 311.

21 A sack (364lb) is estimated to contain the wool shorn from 260 sheep: E. M. Carus-Wilson, and Olive Coleman. *England's Export Trade 1275–1547* (Oxford, Clarendon Press, 1963), p. 13.

and Florentine cloth industries. These two major centres of cloth manufacture were reliant on the import of Spanish merino wool and the softer English variety for the production of their famed fine cloths, aimed at the international luxury market. It was in medieval Florence that the great guilds of cloth-making and finishing, the *Arte della Lana* and the *Arte di Calimala*, were born: the former was the largest buyer of English wool in Italy.[22]

The major monastic orders in England at the time, the Cistercians, Augustinians, Benedictines and Knights Templar, were wool producers, as were large numbers of aristocratic estates, and the Italians invested considerable time and money in order to secure a reliable supply. A study of 203 wool contracts from 1200 to c. 1300 confirms that northern Italian firms bought more than any other nationality and usually paid the full value of the future crop in advance. Tuscan firms competed against each other to secure long-term partnerships, especially with the Yorkshire monasteries whose wool enjoyed a particularly high reputation. Rievaulx Abbey, for example, became one of medieval Britain's wealthiest through the links it forged with no fewer than six separate Italian merchant societies.[23] Nevertheless, by the second half of the fourteenth century, raw wool exports began to dip in the face of increasingly draconian customs impositions in England.[24] At the same time, the total volume of English cloths shipped abroad increased steadily. By the 1440s, the domestic cloth industry was flourishing and the wool market that remained was no longer monopolized by Tuscans but by English merchants, following the establishment of denizen privilege at the new Staple port at Calais in 1363. The success of English cloth making was still very much tied to Italian trade, however, given its heavy reliance on Genoese-imported dyes and the dye-fixer, alum, which arrived on huge carracks into the Southampton docks.[25] The same vessels were then used – along with the Venetian galleys – to transport the finished cloths for sale across the Italian trading empire, to as far away as North Africa and Asia Minor.

In his examination of the Cantelowe accounts, Holmes is keen to emphasize their value to economic historians. Scholars had often concentrated on the enormous sums and dramatic events involved in royal loans and the wool trade from 1280s to the 1350s, as recorded in Exchequer sources, as the main facet of Anglo-Italian relations. He concludes his article by saying:

[22] Alwyn Ruddock, *Italian Merchants and Shipping in Southampton, 1270–1600* (Southampton, University College, 1951), p. 17.
[23] Bell *et al.*, *English Wool Market*, pp. 22–4, p. 117.
[24] Bell *et al.*, *English Wool Market*, pp. 9, 13.
[25] Cf. Megan Tiddeman, 'Alum' and 'Southampton and the Later Medieval Textile Trade' in Gale R. Owen Crocker, Elizabeth Coatsworth and Maria Hayward (eds), *Encyclopedia of Dress and Textiles in the British Isles c. 450–1450*, Volume 2 (2018), https://referenceworks.brillonline.com/browse/encyclopedia-of-medieval-dress-and-textiles.

> The commercial empire of the various Italian cities in the fifteenth century was a vast system, of which England formed only a fraction, which is largely hidden from the student of English records, apart from memories of it remaining in the customs accounts. The Salviati–Cantelowe story shows much more clearly than any English sources, which indeed abound in xenophobic hostility to the Italians, how important they were in providing the technical skill and the financial investment needed to promote English business, long after the Bardi and Peruzzi period for which they are famous.[26]

Recent academic attention has indeed focused more on uncovering the full extent of commercial activities of Italians in fifteenth-century England: alien subsidy (or tax) records, hosting accounts[27] and other documents such as letters of denization and protection have been found to contain 1,616 instances of Italians living in England, of which 1,327 date from the period 1440–71. Nearly all were based in the established immigrant communities of London (around 86 per cent) and Southampton (around 10 per cent) with only a handful of 'pioneering individuals' venturing into other English towns.[28] Overall whilst these figures are useful, total Italian numbers in the English capital were undoubtedly higher than the surviving paperwork indicates, not least because of the peripatetic nature of the Italian merchant population. Contemporary records for alien subsidies and Views of the Hosts do not always tally up, with notable absences in either one or the other. Many Italians would stay regularly in England but for short periods of time, escaping either tax assessment or hosting legislation, depending on the timing of their visit.[29] Furthermore, the Genoese are mainly absent from the Views as they boycotted the government's hosting rules at the time. Overall, there was still enough concern about the general levels of Italian profit accrued on English soil that the Crown increased alien subsidy rates in 1449 and 1453,

[26] Holmes, 'Anglo-Florentine Trade', 386.

[27] In a short-lived bureaucratic experiment (1439–44), alien merchants were legally obliged to live with a native English host and submit bi-annual reports of their imports and purchases to the Exchequer: see Helen Bradley, *The Views of the Hosts of Alien Merchants, 1440–1444* (London, London Record Society 46, 2012). The printed edition contains a modern English translation of the Views. The author's transcription of the original Anglo-French and Latin text is available online: https://sas-space.sas.ac.uk/102/. Citations below from this online transcription are prefixed by the abbreviation VOH.

[28] Francesco Guidi Bruscoli and Jessica Lutkin, 'Perception, Identity and Culture: the Italian Communities in Fifteenth-Century London and Southampton Revisited', in W. Mark Ormrod, Nicola McDonald and Craig Taylor (eds), *Resident Aliens in Later Medieval England* (Turnhout, Brepols, 2017), pp. 89–104 at pp. 89–91.

[29] Bruscoli and Lutkin, 'Perception', pp. 94–5. This paper analysed the online databases compiled by the *England's Immigrants 1330–1550* project: www.englandsimmigrants.com. References below to this database are prefixed by the abbreviation EIDB.

with specific mentions of merchants who were 'Venetian, Italian, Genoan, Florentine, Milanese, Luccan, Albertine (i.e. of the Alberti of Florence) or Lombard' in the legislation.[30]

An earlier study by Bradley of merchant populations in London from 1350 to 1450 also challenges the traditional assumption that Italian influence was no longer significant in England after the collapse of the Crown banking firms and the drying up of the liquid capital they had poured into the wool trade.[31] She presents a changing community (one which was gradually more Genoese or Venetian than Tuscan) which not only continued to provide loans, luxury textiles and spices to nobles and royal household but played an essential role in the burgeoning English cloth market. The extensive London ledgers of the Borromei of Milan for 1436–8, for example, testify to a healthy volume of outgoing trade in English woollen cloth, as well as incoming luxury satins, velvets, jewels and spices.[32] Out of the sixteen Venetians documented in the Views of the Hosts from 1440–4, fifteen made most of their profits from exporting various types of English cloths and only one made significant purchases of wool.[33] The Lucchese community in London may have been small but it dominated the silk trade there (in partnership with members of the Mercers' Company) and continued to lend money to the merchants and nobles until well into the fifteenth century.[34] However, it would be wrong to assume that English wool held no more interest for Italian *compagnie* in the late fourteenth and fifteenth centuries.

Bradley's more recent article on trade routes between London and Southampton between 1430 and 1540 maintains that wool remained an important export to Italy in the early fifteenth century; Florentine agents, such as Paolo Morelli and Bartolomeo Marmora, were permanently based in Southampton and also attended

[30] Bruscoli and Lutkin, 'Perception', pp. 92–3.

[31] Helen Bradley, 'Italian Merchants in London, c1350–1450', Ph.D. thesis (Royal Holloway and Bedford New College, University of London, 1992).

[32] The Borromei Bank project is an online resource which began in 2001 and aims to calendar and translate the company's London and Bruges ledgers. However, as these sources are housed in a private family archive in Como, a transcription of the original Italian text is not available, although there are indexes given of customers, currencies, ship names, place names and commodities. See Francesco Guidi Bruscoli and James Bolton, 'The Borromei Bank Research Project' in Lawrin Armstrong, Ivana Elbl and Martin M. Elbl (eds), *Money, Markets and Trade in Late Medieval Europe: Essays in Honour of John H. A. Munro* (Boston, Brill, 2007), pp. 460–90.

[33] E. B. Fryde, *Studies in Medieval Trade and Finance* (London, Hambledon Press, 1983), ch. XVI, p. 348.

[34] See Bart Lambert, '"Nostri fratelli da Londra": the Lucchese Community in Late Medieval England' in Michele Campopiano and Helen Fulton (eds), *Anglo-Italian Cultural Relations in the Later Middle Ages* (Woodbridge, York Medieval Press, 2018), pp. 87–102.

the Cotswold wool fairs, paying cash advances to suppliers.[35] Similarly, Pandolfo dei Benvenuti was the Salviati's long-term factor in Southampton and accompanied wool from the port back to Tuscany.[36] The *Libro Grande Rosso* (1448–51) of the Salviati's London branch offers evidence of a wide volume of trade mainly in raw wool, cloth and tin.[37] Furthermore, the same commodities are found listed in the incomplete business records of the Villani of Florence who were also based in the capital in 1420s.[38] Similarly, a Florentine state galley left Southampton in 1430 loaded with a huge 1,028 pokes of wool, sixty-three large bales of local cloth as well as tin and lead.[39] Such evidence (along with the Cantelowe accounts) suggests that while Tuscan merchants no longer eclipsed their rivals from Genoa and Venice in terms of influence on English soil after 1350, they still carried out considerable amounts of trade there. Indeed, we know of seven merchant societies from Florence alone who established longstanding businesses in London during the 1420s to the 1460s: the Alberti, Bardi, Villani, Strozzi, Medici and Frescobaldi, as well as the Salviati.[40]

[35] Helen Bradley, 'Southampton's Trading Partners: London', in Michael Hicks (ed), *English Inland Trade, Southampton and its region* (Oxford, Oxbow, 2015), pp. 65–80 at p. 72.
[36] Matthieu Scherman, 'Apprenticeship of Florentine merchants-bankers: the example of the 15th century London Salviati bank', paper given at the European Social Science History Conference, Vienna (2014), *Learning and Training Patterns of Skilled Labour Force in Preindustrial Europe (14th-18th Centuries)* session, https://salviati.hypotheses.org/315 [accessed 1 November 2019].
[37] Maura Cavallaro, 'La compagnia di Jacopo di Alamanno Salviati di Londra negli anni 1448–51'. Undergraduate dissertation (Università di Pisa, 1969).
[38] Francesco Guidi Bruscoli, 'Un frammento inedito di un libro di conti di Domenico Villani e compagni di Londra, 1422–24', in *Storia Economica*, 13 (2010) 375–409.
[39] Michael Mallett, *The Florentine Galleys in the Fifteenth Century* (London, Oxford University Press, 1967), p. 138.
[40] Guidi Bruscoli and Lutkin, 'Italian Communities', p. 99. That is not to say, however, that Italians were not adversely affected by declining mercantile credit and economic recession in England in the 1440s to the 1460s. See Pamela Nightingale, *A Medieval Mercantile Community: the Grocers' Company and the Politics and Trade of London, 1000–1485* (New Haven, Yale University Press, 1995), pp. 461–89.

# 2
# William Cantelowe and Jacob Salviati

Sir William Cantelowe (d. 1464) had a successful career in business and in civic administration and featured regularly in contemporary records. We know that he became, for example, King's Victualler at Calais, alderman of Cripplegate, sheriff of London, master of the Mercers' Company, an MP and finally, a knight in 1461. Given his status, he was almost certainly also a host to visiting Italian merchants, along with his brother, John, in the early 1440s, although none of his hosting accounts survive.[1]

As a wealthy mercer, Cantelowe banked with the Milanese Borromei bank in London. He lent money to the Crown regularly between 1433 and 1452 (an exceptionally high £1,000 on one occasion) and was a well-known figure in court circles.[2] His connections with both the Crown and Italian fellow businessmen are well represented in the large Southampton wool shipment of 1450. In return for several advances to Henry VI in the 1440s, Cantelowe was allowed to freely export wool out of London, without subsidy, from October 1449. Even more generously, a Treaty Roll of November 1450 exempted him and 'his deputies or attorneys, native or alien' from custom duties on shipping 300 sacks of wool from Southampton through the Straits of Gibraltar.[3] This is precisely when Cantelowe and Jacob Salviati, of the Salviati London branch, embarked on their ambitious and lucrative joint wool venture. In *The Mercery of London*, Sutton says this of the enterprise:

> Cooperation brought far more profit than one-sided ventures [....] Salviati arranged the voyage and the sales, and the whole was done under a licence from the king obtained by Cantelowe. Cantelowe's servant, John Balmayn, went with the galley and kept the accounts. The total profit of over 22,300 florins was transferred back by exchange to London and Bruges via Italian companies in Venice; Cantelowe received his money in July 1452 and Balmayn stayed on in Florence as Cantelowe's representative.[4]

[1] Bradley, *Views of the Hosts*, pp.174–5.
[2] Anne F. Sutton, *The Mercery of London: Trade, Goods and People, 1130–1578* (London, Ashgate, 2005), p. 232.
[3] Holmes, 'Anglo-Florentine Trade', 377.
[4] Sutton, *Mercery of London*, p. 227.

In fact, the accounts make it clear that Balmayn arrived in Italy long after the wool. He states in his opening paragraph (2a),[5] which is headed '1451', that the *wolle and othyr marchauntyse* left England in 1450 but no month is given. The first wool sale in Italy is recorded on another folio as the 13th November 1450 (12b). Balmayn then writes that he was sent to Florence in 1451 leaving London on 13th May and arriving some six weeks later, on the 24th June (2b). This suggests that he arrived to oversee the end of the sales (from late June to October 1451) and, presumably, to compile records of the transactions for his master back in London. He wrote a letter to Cantelowe on the 27th of August of that summer (33a), asking him to send more high-quality wool to Tuscany. We do not know when (or if) Balmayn returned home afterwards; the last item surviving that he wrote is dated 11th October 1451 (28a).

Cantelowe's partner, Jacopo di Alamanno Salviati (1417–58) came from a prominent family of Florentine merchant bankers with close ties to other 'corporate giants' of the day, such as the Medici, the Bardi and the Borromei. The Salviati were part of the fabric of Florentine public and religious life for centuries, with sixty-three priors, five cardinals, twenty-one *gonfalonieri* (holders of a prestigious civic office) and dozens of commissioners, ambassadors and mercenary captains recorded amongst their ranks from 1293 to 1533.[6]

Jacob was the third son of the company patriarch, Alamanno Salviati (1389–1456), and part of a successful money-making dynasty. His eldest brother Piero (b. 1410) set up banks in Florence and Pisa; two other brothers, Francesco (b. 1412) and Giovanni (1419–72),[7] worked there, as well as in the Salviati branch in Bruges. The youngest brother, Averardo (1424–96) was, like Jacob, an expert in English wool who traded in England and Flanders before settling back in Tuscany. We know that in 1457 Jacob was living in a house on Via del Palagio in Florence with his widowed mother, Caterina, and three of his brothers and their wives, and that he had an illegitimate daughter in Flanders.[8]

Thanks to the wealth of private records in the Salviati archives, we also know several details about Jacob's training and his years in London.[9] He was an apprentice at both the Florence and Pisa branches, as well as holding a public office

[5] This and subsequent page numbers refer to those I have allocated to the original folios in the transcription (cf. Table 1, below), with an additional letter indicating the paragraph or section of text.
[6] Cavallaro, 'Jacopo di Alamanno Salviati', p. 66. Inexplicably, the typed thesis (over 2,000 pages) has no page numbers. Cited page numbers have therefore been allocated by me.
[7] As already noted, many Salviati descendants became embroiled in the politics of Renasisance Florence but one stands out in particular. Giovanni's son, Jacopo Salviati (1461–1533), married Lucrezia de' Medici, daughter of Lorenzo the Magnificent and sister of Pope Leo X. This lucrative match brought him great personal wealth and influence, as well as ten children.
[8] Holmes, 'Anglo-Florentine Trade', 380.
[9] Scherman, 'London Salviati Bank'.

(no doubt due to his father's connections) as accounts-keeper for the town of Volterra. He was sent to open a London office in 1444 at the age of twenty-seven, where he was closely assisted by a partner and chief cashier, Giovanni degli Albizzi, who is recorded as *Johan de Albycys* in Cantelowe's accounts.[10] The company also employed Jacob's personal servant, Giovanni di Prussia, several *garzoni* (or errand boys) and an apprentice, Niccolo d'Antonio de Rabatta,[11] who would go on to take over the running of the company when Jacob moved back permanently to Florence. Although the period of obligatory hosting had ended, the company rented a house from the London draper Robert Clopton,[12] and several entries in their accounts from 1448–50 record paying rent to Robert's wife, *Monna Margherita Cloppetone, nostra ostessa.*[13]

The London Salviati company exploited its connections with fellow Italians in England and Bruges to create an effective commercial network that dealt not just in money-lending but in raw wool, woollen cloth, luxury fabrics, dyes, hides, wine and tin.[14] They also – as we have seen – were happy to collaborate with local entrepreneurs when profit beckoned. Holmes gives us some further key details about the Cantelowe-Salviati partnership in 'Anglo-Florentine Trade':

> The account book[15] of the London Salviati records a debt of £4277 9s. 9d. from him which was balanced by a payment of £3728 4s. 1d. on 8 July and two previous receipts of £122 10s. and £426 14s. 8d. The debt had been gradually built up since the autumn of 1450 by a number of payments made on Cantelowe's behalf by the London Salviati [....] The Salviati has also borne the cost of the transport by galley of the 466 pokes from Southampton, £347 14s. 10d. being paid to Raffello Doria, Antonio Doria and Giovanni Ambrogio [....] The impression is that Cantelowe used Salviati as a bank which would make payments to him or for him in London

[10] Holmes ('Anglo-Florentine Trade', 379) speculates that it was actually Albizzi, not Salviati, who handled most of the business in the London branch. Albizzi was clearly a prominent member of the local Italian community; he is recorded as consul of the Florentine nation in London in 1450. See also EIDB 'John de Albys'.

[11] Bradley ('Southampton's Trading Partners', p. 126) suggests that this was the same *Nicholas de La Bate* who requested burial in Southampton (where there was a large Italian community) and left money to a church there in his will.

[12] Clopton had previously been assigned as a host to Leonardo Cattano and Gregorio Pinelli of Genoa in 1440 (Bradley, *Views of the Hosts*, p. 33).

[13] AS Serie I: 336, carte 4, 30, 43, 94, 229.

[14] Cavallaro, 'Jacopo di Alamanno Salviati', p. 164–89. The London business seemed to be declining by 1457, following several years of absence on Jacob's part; however, Holmes ('Anglo-Florentine Trade', 381) speculates that the firm exaggerated claims of their demise to avoid tax payments in Florence. Jacob and Piero da Rabatta also set up a new company in Bruges in 1456 which ran for at least three years: 'a testimony to confidence in northern European business prospects' and evidence of 'a steady and lively activity concerned largely with the day-to-day commercial affairs of north-west Europe and connections with the Mediterranean' (383).

[15] Holmes is referring here to AS Serie I: 341, carta 67, one of several unedited books from the Salviati London branch: *Debitori e creditori, segnato C* (1451–55).

> or Bruges and, presumably in agreement with Salviati, built up a considerable debt which both of them knew would be repaid by the sale of the wool at Florence.[16]

Examination of the relevant entry in the main Salviati London book shows that these galley transport costs were paid on the 4th December 1450.[17] This is useful as it is not made evident in Balmayn's records when exactly in 1450 the shipment arrived in Italy but it seems to be in November 1450 from details in the sales records and expenses. The December payment for the galley corroborates this evidence.

Just five years after these accounts were written, in 1456, Anglo-Italian relationships soured in England and Cantelowe suffered a temporary career set-back. As Master of the Mercers' Company, he was imprisoned for three months in Dudley Castle at the end of 1456 for failure to control anti-Italian violence, perpetrated by some of the younger men of the Mercery. In the spring of that year, a Lucchese merchant, Alessandro Palastrelli, had been assaulted and the next day, other Italian merchants had their houses looted in organised raids. A plot to murder a Genoese wool trader, Galiot Centurion, was also uncovered and the London mayor had to send out street patrols to keep the peace for weeks.[18] Given that Cantelowe had built his fortune on foreign trade and collaboration with alien colleagues, it is unlikely that he personally felt much ill will towards the 'Lombards'.[19] He was, nevertheless, given an exemplary punishment by the authorities but went on to regain royal favour and received a knighthood under Edward IV.

Overall, we know a relatively large amount about Cantelowe's professional life, his collaboration with the Salviati and the amounts of money and merchandise

[16] Holmes, 'Anglo-Florentine Trade', 378.

[17] AS Serie I: 336, carta 161. The same details are repeated in another section of the accounts (carta 175).

[18] Sutton, *Mercery of London*, p. 230–1; Nightingale, *Grocers' Company*, p. 504.

[19] Anti-Italian sentiment in late medieval England flared up regularly, fuelled by the emergence of what Bradley (*Views of the Hosts*, p. xii) calls a 'rampant new Englishness'. The Middle English version of the romance *Bevis of Hampton* (c. 1324) sees the hero slaughter a group of Italian merchants in the streets of London, an episode which, interestingly, does not occur in the work's earlier Anglo-French source text (cf. Ruddock, *Italian Merchants*, pp. 164–5; Pearsall, 'Strangers', p. 53; Robert Allen Rouse, 'For King and Country? The Tension between National and Regional Identities in *Sir Bevis of Hampton*,' in Jennifer Fellows and Ivana Djordjevic (eds), *Sir Bevis of Hampton in Literary Tradition* (Cambridge, D. S. Brewer, 2008), pp. 114–26 at p. 123. John Gower's morality poem *Le Mirour de l'Omme*, from the 1390s, pins his nation's political and economic woes on the deceitful 'Lombards', who not only empty the realm's coffers in return for shoddy goods but also act as spies: cf. Roger Ladd, *Antimercantilism in Late Medieval English Literature* (New York, Palgrave Macmillan, 2010), pp. 49–76; Jonathan Hsy, *Trading Tongues: Merchants, Multilingualism and Medieval Literature* (Columbus, The Ohio State University Press, 2013), pp. 50–1, 99–105). The London Mercers had already been directly involved in brutal attacks on two Lombards in 1357 and in the murders of a Lucchese silk trader, Nicholas Sardouche, in 1370 and a Genoese merchant, Janus Imperial, in 1378 (Sutton, *Mercery of London*, pp. 115–17).

involved. In marked contrast, we know nothing about John Balmayn, his representative and the writer of these accounts, who travelled out Italy on his behalf. There is no mention of him elsewhere in English records, not even in the London Mercers' archives.[20] He is, however, recorded on several occasions as *Giovanni Bolmanno, servante di Ghulglielmo Chantalo, aldermanno* in the Salviati London accounts (1448–51), carrying out banking transactions on behalf of his master.[21] The general lack of information about Balmayn is far from unusual for the period but frustrating, as details of his career and education would have been helpful in understanding his language use.

[20] Sutton, *Mercery of London,* p. 227, n. 135.
[21] For example: AS Serie I: 336, carte 222, 229, 234, 236.

# 3
# The manuscript and its contents

The extant manuscript (AS Serie I: 339) consists of thirty-five folios, followed by dozens of blank pages, assembled into a folder at some unknown later date. The accounts begin as follows:

> M*emorandum* that this boke ys for the rekenyng of resceyvyng of my mayst*er* Wyll*iam* Cantelowe ys wolle and othyr march*a*untyse send fro London and fro Hampton*e* to Pyse and Florens, the yere of oure Lorde God a*nno* m[ll] iiij[c] l and for the ret*or*ne agayn*e* of the seyd woll*e*, made by Jacob Salviatis and by me, Joh*an* Balmay*n*, s*er*vaunt of the seyd Will*iam* Cantelowe (2a).

The pages are foliated (recto only) by their author but are not consecutive and some sections of the accounts appear to be missing. This has little impact on the lexical value of the source and all the details relating to the unusually large consignment of 466 pokes seem to be present. Seven pages have been cancelled with lines drawn through them, indicating that they are drafts; these are a letter to Cantelowe on f. 64r., two isolated account entries on f. 64 *bis*, some rough calculations on f. 64v., and ff. 65r.-66v. of the wool buyers' entries. In addition, ff. 64r.-v. are written on loose leaves of paper which have been inserted into the main folder. Four of the folios (ff. 2v.-3v., 64v.) consist entirely of columns of Arabic numerals (see Part 5, below) and three others (ff. 2r., 4r., 5v.) also contain large amounts of figures, tallying up the weight of the wool in sacks, pokes and cloves.[1]

The quality of the folios is excellent, they are entirely undamaged and the ink is barely faded. Balmayn writes in a cursive hand with remnants of Anglicana, specifically making frequent use of a long, forked 'r' and more rarely, a double-decker 'a' (see Fig. 1, below, as an example). The neatness of his writing varies

[1] 'Sack' and 'clove' were precise measures of weight (364lb and 7lb *avoirdupois*, respectively) whereas 'poke' and 'sarpler' (the latter not used in the accounts) were more variable (cf. Holmes, 'Anglo-Florentine Trade', 373). At the time, a poke weighed roughly half a sack (182lb) and those in Cantelowe's shipment all weighed over 200lb each, before deductions for tare. Earlier the poke seems to have been larger, weighing closer to the equivalent of a sack. Customs accounts (TNA E122/71/25) record the galleys of Nicholas Bragadyn' and Andrea Gise leaving London on 7 September 1398, carrying 154 sacks and twenty-five cloves of wool in 138 pokes, and 120 sacks and three and a half cloves in 111 pokes.

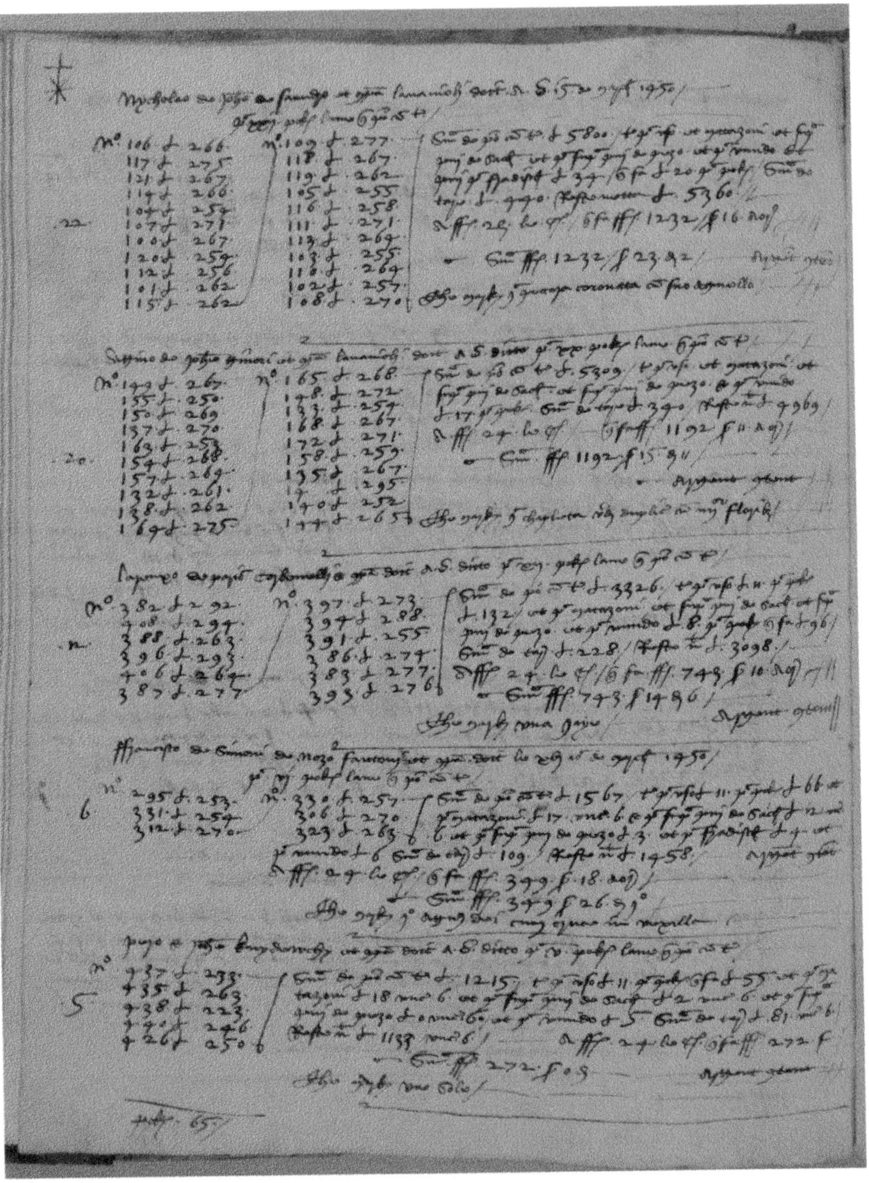

**Fig 1.** Sample page from the accounts: Archivio Salviati, Serie I: 339, f.67v

greatly, from a careful and clear hand in an 'official' version to a more hurried scrawl in drafts.

The surviving accounts can be divided into five main sections, as follows in Table 1, below. As mentioned above, the page numbers refer to those allocated as reference points within the body of the main transcription. I have also indicated the language(s) used in each section: Middle English (ME), Anglo-French (AF), Italian and Latin. However, as I discuss in detail in Part 4 (below), categorisation of individual words is not always straightforward.

**Table 1** Summary of the manuscript's contents

| Page ref. | Folio | Contents | Language |
|---|---|---|---|
| 1 | | Cover page of folder with William Cantelowe's merchant mark. Dated 1451. | ME |
| **Weights of the wool sacks** | | | |
| 2 | 1r. | 466 pokes of wool left Southampton on a Genoese carrack (patron, Antonio Doria) and were delivered to Francesco and Giovanni Salviati in Pisa.[1] Dated 1450. | ME |
| 3–7 | 2r.-4r. | The precise weight of each poke of wool is carefully recorded and tallied up in sacks and cloves. The final net weight (after deductions) is 251 sacks, 8½ cloves. | Arabic numerals + ME |
| 8–9 | 4v.-5r. | The number of pokes of each wool type in the shipment is recorded plus a description of the merchant countermark, used to identify the woolsacks. Dated 1450. | Latin with Italian and ME lexemes |
| **Expenses incurred at Pisa and Florence** | | | |
| 10 | 41r. | Including all duties and subsidies, unloading and storage at the port of Livorno,[2] carriage to Pisa and weighing at the customs house, porter fees, mending of torn sacks, and Jacob Salviati's ride to Pisa to see the wool. Dated 16th November 1450. | ME matrix with Italian lexemes<br>Italian matrix with ME lexemes |

(*continued*)

**Table 1** (*cont.*)

| Page ref. | Folio | Contents | Language |
|---|---|---|---|
| 11 | 41v. | Including all duties and subsidies, transport from Pisa to Florence, clerical fees, weighing at the customs house and storage costs. Dated 28th September 1451. | |
| **Sale of lots of wool to Italian buyers** | | | |
| 12–27 | 65r.-72v. | Each lot lists the Italian buyer, the numbers of the pokes bought, their gross and net weights after various types of tare are deducted. The countermark on the woolsacks is described at the end of each entry. Balmayn tallies up the 448 pokes sold from 13th November 1450 to 28th September 1451, which have sold for a total of fl. 22359. s.6. d. 9, after expenses.[3] | Italian with AF abbreviations and formulae and ME segments. Latin can appear in the description of the merchant marks. |
| 28 | 73r. | On 11th October 1451, Balmayn records an extra seventeen pokes sold for fl. 707 s. 5 d. 9, bringing the final total up to 465.[4] | |
| **Bills of exchange** | | | |
| 29–30 | 130r.-130v. | Careful record of exchange transactions to pay for the wool, from Florence to Venice and then on to Bruges or London.[5] List 1: 30th January to 6th October 1451. Bills of exchange which were paid by several Florentine firms to the Rucellai and Strozzi of Venice. | ME matrix with Italian lexemes<br>Italian matrix with ME lexemes |
| 31 | 131r. | List 2 (incomplete): 6th February to 9th June 1451.[6] Bills of exchange paid by the Rucellai and Strozzi of Venice to Jacob Salviati in London and Bruges.[7] | |
| **Miscellaneous documents** | | | |
| 32 | f. 5v | Another shipment of 104 pokes of wool left Southampton in April 1451 on a Genoese carrack (patron, Maurizio Cataneo)[8] and were delivered to Francesco and Giovanni Salviati in Porto Pisano.[9] | ME |

**Table 1** (*cont.*)

| Page ref. | Folio | Contents | Language |
|---|---|---|---|
| | | Some weights are listed but final calculations, wool types, merchant marks and expenses are absent. | |
| 33 | f. 64r. | A draft letter, from Balmayn in Florence to his master Cantelowe, encouraging him to send more high-quality wool over for sale. Dated 27th August [1451]. | ME |
| 34 | f. 64 *bis* | Two unrelated account entries, recording loans of £14 s.8 to John Bertrem and 80 ducats to Thomas Bedford in August and October 1451. | ME with Italian and AF lexemes |
| 35 | f. 64v. | Undated rough calculations, meaning unknown. | Arabic numerals |

[1] No month is given for the wool's arrival in Italy but we know that the first lot is recorded as being sold on the 13th November 1450 (12b) and the last on the 11th October 1451 (28a). Eleven months was apparently quite a quick turnaround for such a sale, according to Holmes. Commenting on the relative importance of the wool trade, as opposed to burgeoning domestic cloth exports he says, 'The relative ease with which Cantelowe's wool appears to have been sold at Florence indicates that there was still a substantial market for it, though of course much smaller than it had been a century earlier' (Holmes 'Anglo-Florentine Trade', 385). No record of any customs paid in England on the shipment has been found.

[2] A port on the Tuscan coast, also known as Leghorn in English.

[3] The same fl. 22359.s. 6. d. 8 [sic] for 448 pokes of wool on the 28th September 1451 is also recorded as credited to the Jacob Salvati of London in Alamanno Salvati's accounts in Florence (Holmes, 'Anglo-Florentine Trade', 375).

[4] The fate of the elusive 466th poke remains a mystery as its sale is not recorded. See also Table 4, below.

[5] Holmes ('Anglo-Florentine Trade', p. 373) notes that 'the interesting features of this section of Balmayn's book are the central position of Venice in the European exchange system through which went all the transfers from Florence to North West Europe, and the close association of agents in London and Bruges which made it possible for them both to be suitable for paying the London Salviati'.

[6] In fact, Cantelowe would not receive full payment for his wool (£4,277 9s 9d) until July 1452: the London Salviati records three instalments paid to him of £3,728 4s 1d, £122 10s and £426 14s 8d (Holmes, 'Anglo-Florentine Trade', 378).

[7] Most of the merchants listed in this section as payers in London are known from English records: *Umfrido Justyane* (Umfredo Giustiniani, Venetian merchant), resident in Broad Street ward in London in 1443 and 1449 and recorded in tax assessments in 1457 (see EIDB, 'Humphrey Justinian'); *Lowes Strossy* (Ludovico Strozzi, Florentine merchant), resident in Broad Street ward in 1449 and 1451 (see EIDB, 'Lewis Stroos'; De Roover, *Rise and Decline*, pp. 359–360; Holmes, 'Anglo-Florentine Trade', 385); *Filice de Fagniano* (Felice da Fagnano, merchant of Milan and Lucca), resident in Broad Street ward in 1441 and 1444 (see EIDB, 'Felix de Fanyan / Felice Famean'; Bradley, *Views of the Hosts*, p. 282); *Leonard Cattano* (Leonardo Cattaneo, Genoese merchant), resident in Bishopgate ward in 1441 (see EIDB, 'Leonard de Catayne'; Bradley, *Views of the Hosts*, p. 275);

*Vittore Capelle and his brotherys* (Vittore Capello, Venetian galley patron and his brothers, Albano and Giovanni), 'all three well known in London and Bruges' (see Bradley, *Views of the Hosts*, pp. 274–5). The Venetians *Sebestyane et Jerolimis Bawdwere* (Sebastiano and Girolamo Badueri) and *Antonio Partini* are not listed in EIDB but feature in numerous exchange transactions in the Salviati London Book (1448–51): see, for example, AS Serie I: 336, carte 28, 147, 193, 197, 241 and AS Serie I: 336 12, 13, 82, 83, 88, 224, respectively.

8 Resident in Bishopgate ward for tax assessment in 1441 and 1443, see EIDB 'Maurice de Catayne'.

9 No arrival date in Porto Pisano is given but this is possibly the same wool shipment as the ninety-one pokes recorded in the Port Book of Southampton in William Cantelowe's name which left on 3rd April and arrived on 24 June 1451 (Holmes, 'Anglo-Florentine Trade', 372–3).

# 4
# Language use

The Cantelowe accounts are recorded in the Salviati Archive catalogue as a 'libro di conti della detta ragione in lingua inglese'.[1] Holmes went slightly further and declared that it was 'written in English apart from technical terms in other languages'.[2] As we shall see, the reality is more complex. Like most administrative documents, it is highly repetitive, re-using certain phrases and formulaic expressions time and time again, but it does contain a mix of four languages with frequent lexical overlap. The matrix language can be Middle English (ME), Italian or Latin. Embedded lexemes, or phrases, can be any one of these languages or Anglo-French (AF). We frequently find three (and occasionally four) languages in a single sentence, so-called intra-sentential switching, but the switch points are certainly not restricted to those typical of medieval business practice such as commodities, professions, currencies and units of measurement.

There are some parallels between Balmayn's writing and the mixed-language, administrative text types analysed by Trotter and Wright. Trotter remarks that:

> The incidence of AF and ME words [in a Latin-matrix, fifteenth-century will] is striking and the way in which they are deployed is revealing. They are unmarked and (or so it seems) unconsciously incorporated. What this looks like is not a writer who is actively jumping between languages which he perceives as distinct but a writer who happens to have a range of lexical items at his disposal.[3]

Balmayn too very rarely signals his language shift and there are only four instances of a word being prefixed by *callyd* or *vocato*, for example:

> It*em* for cariours the which*e* be callyd victura for the bryngyng*e* fro Pise to Florens (11c)
> Et in num*ero* Cxxx[e] su*n*t lane vocat*e* flese woll*e* que ponderant cl*oves* vij (8i)

[1] See the Salviati Archive's online inventory: http://salviati.centroarchivistico.sns.it/index.php?id=73 [accessed 16 February 2019].
[2] Holmes, 'Anglo-Florentine Trade', 371.
[3] David Trotter, 'Death, Taxes and Property: some Code-Switching Evidence from Dover, Southampton and York', in Herbert Schendl and Laura Wright, (eds), *Code-Switching in Early English*, (Berlin, De Gruyter, 2011), pp. 155–89 at p. 175.

Below are two examples of the much more common unmarked intra-sentential shift; firstly, an ME entry with embedded Italian (underlined) and AF (bold) phrases and secondly, a Latin entry with Italian (underlined), AF (bold) and ME / AF (italic) lexemes:[4]

> Mayster Thomas Bedford, parson of Lubbenham in Lestetyrschyre, **doit le iiij jour de octobre pour** 80 doc. de camera remisse a [Pe]rogia, **a iiij moys** a pagare a gr. 52 ½ **pour** doc. and to rescyve hit of Nycholas Bedford, marchaunte of Caleys. (34b)
>
> De n° xxxvi ad numerum xli: *pokes* vj de juvene lana **de la Marche,** contrasignata de una ancella ut supra cum uno **pere precius** duplice de *coralle vermoille: pokes* vi (8c)

The writer moves seamlessly from one language to another, drawing from, as Trotter suggests, a large lexical reserve of commercial vocabulary. Several key words or phrases appear in several languages throughout the accounts – this reveals not only an underlying flexibility in language skills but also the fact that code-switching is not reliant on a term's absence from matrix-language lexicon.[5] Examples include:

- *le dyd jour / a dì ditto / the daye aboveseyd* (AF / It. / ME)
- *a dì 15 a vista da lettera / at xv dayes after the seyth of the letter* (It. / ME)
- *payer / pagare / to paye* (AF / It. / ME)
- *papavery / popeis* (It. / ME)
- *lanaiuoli / clothemakers* (It / ME)
- *ancilla / donzella / maydyne* (Lat. / It. / ME)
- *manipulum / mazzo / hand* (Lat. / It. / ME)

In 'Code-intermediate phenomena', Wright focuses on the bilingual and trilingual business codes in accounts such as the London Bridge Wardens' annual accounts (1460–61) or the Petty Customs Accounts (1480–81).[6] These supra-regional varieties were characterised by the use of 'visual diamorphs' i.e. multi-purpose abbreviations which could be expanded in either BML (British Medieval Latin) or ME / AF. In a minority of cases, however, abbreviations were carefully distinguished by language, such as the scribe's 'subtle' graphic distinction between Latin *saccus* and ME *sak* in the Bridge Wardens' accounts.[7] Similar

[4] Cf. Part 4.i, below, 'Categorising languages'.

[5] Cf. Louise Sylvester, 'Semantic field and text-type approach to multilingualism' in Päivi Pahta, Janne Skaffari and Laura Wright (eds), *Multilingual Practices in Language History: English and Beyond*, (Berlin, De Gruyter Mouton, 2018), pp. 77–96 at p. 94.

[6] Laura Wright, 'Code-intermediate phenomena in medieval mixed-language texts', *Language Sciences* 24 (2002), 471–489.

[7] 'Clerks could be very subtle in their integrating of the two languages. […] the scribe graphically distinguished between Latin and English lexemes which had the same form. The Latin word for a sack (L. *saccus*, *-i* 'a sack') lines 5–8, was always spelt with a <cc> graph: *saccis*, *sacc*, *sac*. The only

features, on a smaller scale, can also be found in the Cantelowe accounts. Balmayn differentiates between ME and Italian shorthand for *pok-* (ME *pokes*) / *poch-* (It. *poche*) and *sack-* (ME *sackes*) / *sach-* (It. *sachi*) but other examples are harder to label linguistically. The abbreviations *cu-* (*cum*), *q-* (*que*) and *tar-* (*tare*) remain translingual even when expanded: *cum* can be read as either Latin or Italian, *que* can be read as either AN, Latin or Italian, *tar-* could be *tare* (plural of *tara*) in Italian or an assimilated borrowing, *tare*, in ME. Wright's earlier analysis of mixed-language medieval business texts suggested a link between code choice and specificity of reference: a 'micropragmatic motivation' meaning embedded lexemes were more likely to be restricted in meaning in that context, i.e. more technical.[8] We can, at times, argue for a similar tendency in Balmayn's writing, such as the appearance of Tuscan civic terminology in the middle of an AF phrase: *Item pour sensaria de le dyd 448 pokes / Item pour averia pour consely de mare pour le dyd 466 pokes*. Nevertheless, it is difficult to distinguish clear patterns when the matrix language changes so frequently and switching points can, at times, can be difficult to identify or are seemingly random. The following entry from the accounts provides an apt example:

> It*em* for the custom*e* of Florens for the seyd 466 pok*es*, weyng lb 123067 a fl. uno, s.16 de pezoly le C. q*ue* fa fl.1230. Et po*ur* le s.16 q*ue* fa £987 s.4 d.3 de p*ez*., de le valeuta de £ a s.73 d.4 po*ur* fl. q*ue* fa fl.269, £- s.17 d.7 de p*ez*. S*um*ma in toto fl.1499, £- s.17 d.7 de p*ez*. Et po*ur* duodesimo, þe whych*e* ys uno p*ar*te de xij p*ar*te de le maiore. S*um*ma ut sup*ra* q*ue* fa fl.124, £4 s.- d.8 de p*ez*. Et po*ur* la p*ar*tita to the clerkys, £2. S*um*ma to*ta*le fl. 1623 …. po*ur* solid*i*, £6 s.18 d.3 de p*ez*, valeuta de grossy: fl.1624 s.18 d.4 (11d).

Overall, the contact phenomenon presented by the Cantelowe accounts is, so far, unique. We have no known equivalent to compare it to. The multilingual documents edited so far are all based on the three 'native' varieties of English administration, offering insight into the ever-changing interplay between AF, ME and BML and its contribution to the evolution of Standard English.[9] Isolated foreign loanwords can, of course, abound in these indigenous records but with this source, we are adding a new fourth element to the well-known trio: an entirely foreign matrix language that the author has (presumably) learnt from alien colleagues. Lastly, whilst company accounts in England certainly changed

exception is when the lexeme appeared in the English compound *sakclothe* (OE *sac*, 'a sack'), when a <k> graph was used. […]. Thus the scribe went to considerable lengths to indicate the Englishness of the compound element, as opposed to the Latinity of the simplex lexeme' (Wright, 'Code-intermediate phenomena', 473).

[8] Laura Wright, 'A hypothesis on the structure of macaronic business writing' in Jacek Fisiak (ed), *Medieval Dialectology* (New York, De Gruyter Mouton, 1995), pp. 309–21 at p. 318

[9] Cf. Laura Wright, 'The Contact Origins of Standard English' in Daniel Schreier and Marianne Hundt (eds), *English as a Contact Language* (Cambridge, Cambridge University Press, 2013), pp. 58–74; Wright (ed), *The Multilingual Origins of Standard English*.

their matrix language, this was a gradual process over some years that depended, in many ways, on the individual scribe at work.[10] Here, we have a single author who alters the template of his language-mixing from one page to another, or even from one sentence to another, in records which were written within the space of a few months.

Ultimately, we will never know how 'imported' words and phrases were perceived in Balmayn's mind. In modern linguistic theory, borrowings (or non-adapted ones, at least) are nearly always considered recognisable as blatant 'foreignisms' in the recipient language[11] but several scholars have argued that the medieval mind did not rigorously separate languages or consciously distinguish borrowings, especially technical terms, from other lexis.[12] Sylvester has recently suggested that multilingual medieval writers did not perceive several languages as a single repertoire but, rather, were using an emerging technolect

[10] The shift from Latin to vernacular and from AF to ME in English business accounts has long interested historical linguists. ME features heavily in the AF accounts of Gybon Maufield (or Gilbert Maghfelt) from 1390–94, an early bilingual code first discussed in Edith Rickert, 'Extracts from a Fourteenth-Century Account Book', *Modern Philology*, 24 (1926), 111–19. The text has been analysed more recently in Wright, 'Code-intermediate phenomena'; Laura Wright, 'Standard English and the lexicon: why so many different spellings?' in Mari C. Jones and Edith Esch (eds), *Language Change: the Interplay of Internal, External and Extra-linguistic Factors* (Berlin, De Gruyter, 2002), pp. 181–200. The *Views of the Hosts* were predominantly written in AF, almost certainly because they were considered public, legal documents rather than private business accounts. For the shift to ME-matrix in the 1420s to the 1440s in the trilingual administration of the London livery companies, such as the Merchant Taylors, Goldsmiths, Grocers and Drapers, see Jose Miguel Alcolado Carnicero, 'The Dates of the Shift to English in the Financial Accounts of some London Livery Companies: a Reappraisal', *Multilingua*, 34, no.3 (2014), DOI: 10.1515/multi-2014-0068; Jose Miguel Alcolado Carnicero, 'Bridges of innovation and change: the English language around the networks of the Mercery of London' in Esther-Miriam Wagner, Bettina Beinhoff and Ben Outhwaite (eds), *Merchants of Innovation: the Languages of Traders* (Berlin, De Gruyter Mouton, 2017), pp. 40–67. The Mercers chose to write their official accounts in AF-matrix until the late 1450s: see Lisa Jefferson, *The Medieval Account Books of the Mercers of London: an Edition and Translation* (Farnham and Burlington, Ashgate, 2009). This perhaps explains the persistent use of AF expressions throughout Balmayn's writing – his master was a Mercer and he may have trained as a scribe with the company (although he is, as we have noted, absent from records in the Mercers' Company archives).

[11] Martin Haspelmath and Uri Tadmor, *Loanwords in the World's Languages: a Comparative Handbook* (Berlin, Walter de Gruyter, 2009), pp. 42–3.

[12] Benedek Elemér Vidos, *Prestito, espansione e migrazione dei termini tecnici nelle lingue romanze e non romanze: problemi, metodo e risultati* (Firenze, Leo S. Olschki, 1965); William Rothwell, 'Lexical Borrowing in a Medieval Context', *Bulletin of the John Rylands University Library of Manchester*, 63 (1980), 118–143; Laura Wright, 'Bills, Accounts, Inventories: Everyday Trilingual Activities in the Business World of Later Medieval England', in David Trotter (ed), *Multilingualism in Later Medieval Britain* (Woodbridge, D. S. Brewer, 2000), pp. 149–156; Wright, 'Code-intermediate Phenomena'; David Trotter, 'Bridging the Gap: the (Socio)linguistic Evidence of Some Medieval English Bridge Accounts', in Richard Ingham (ed), *The Anglo-Norman Language and its Contexts* (Woodbridge, York Medieval Press, 2010), pp. 52–62; David Trotter, 'Italian merchants in London and Paris: evidence of language contact in the Gallerani accounts, 1305–08', in Dominique Lagorgette and Tim Pooley (eds), *Le changement linguistique en français: études en homage au professeur R. Anthony Lodge*, (Chambéry, Presses de l'Université de Savoie, 2011), pp. 209–26; Trotter, 'Death, taxes and property'.

where nouns were used because they encompassed usefulness (i.e. precision) and universality (i.e. comprehensibility).[13] This throws up interesting parallels with the Cantelowe accounts in which the fourth language of use was very much consciously learned by a non-native speaker. Balmayn was surely aware of language separation but seemed to develop his own technolect for the text which gave him access to wide range of content-laden vocabulary from all four languages. Of course, we are very much restricted by the lack of data in this regard and are unable to compare Balmayn's specific business code with others to see if overall patterns emerge.

A final point must be noted about the timing of the accounts' production. It was assumed by Holmes[14] and consequently by Sutton[15] that Balmayn travelled out with the wool shipment in the autumn of 1450. Yet, as we have seen, he actually arrived in Florence in June 1451 and was there in person only for the last third of the wool sales. This must mean that he wrote some of the accounts retrospectively and it is not clear where or how he got the information regarding previous transactions. His idiosyncratic mix of ME and Italian throughout the entire document shows that he did not ignorantly approximate what Italian colleagues dictated, as Holmes suggests, or copy verbatim, line by line, from the Salviati's own records.[16] Mysteries still remain, therefore, as to why he chose to adapt the information he was given in Florence in a mixed-language format and not write it entirely in ME (or Latin, or even AF) for his master.

## i) Categorising languages

Unsurprisingly, in a text that contains Latin, two forms of Romance and a Germanic language heavily influenced by Latin and French lexis, it is not always possible to tell which language(s) Balmayn is employing.

One of the main problems upon first analysis is distinguishing between Italian and Latin lexemes and short phrases. It is important to remember that *et*, *cum*, *uno* and *sine* are all frequently used medieval Italian forms and should be considered as such within Italian matrix sections. *Summa* can be Italian or Latin (or indeed considered a neutral, Europe-wide business term). *Ancilla* can be Latin or Italian whereas *ancella* is an Italian variation. *Campana*, *coronata*, *cruce*, *depincta*, *herba*, *libra*, *manipulo*, *medio*, *numero*, *pavo*, *rosa*, *scriptura*, *stella*, *unce* and, of course, *lana* are more examples of words that belong to both Italian and Latin lexis and it is, at times, challenging to differentiate between them.

[13] Sylvester, 'Semantic field and text-type', pp. 93–94.
[14] Holmes, 'Anglo-Florentine Trade'.
[15] Sutton, *Mercery of London*.
[16] Holmes, 'Anglo-Florentine Trade', 374.

Clearly when Balmayn writes an inflected phrase such as *quilibet poche cum duobus signis sine contrasignis* (9e), he is writing in Latin. The phrase *depincta de una manu cum uno manipulo rosarum de tribus foliis* (8o) could also easily be labelled as Latin whereas *depincta de uno pecore coronato cum suo agnello* (8g) seems entirely consistent with medieval Italian. Do we assume, therefore, that *depincta* is a Latin word in 8o and an Italian word in 8g? Given the frequency with which Balmayn switches language mid-sentence, it could well be that he has just inserted Latinised segments (*manipulo rosarum de tribus foliis*) into an Italian phrase. In the following example, it is easier to track Balmayn's shift back and forth between Latin and Italian and he even repeats the same noun (*peccore / pecus*) in both languages in the entry:

> De nº Cxxij ad num*erum Cxxx:* pok*e* ix de lana juv*ene* de Cotyswold*e* fine depincta de uno pecor*e* coronat*o* cu*m* suo agnello et pecus h*ab*et modicu*m* de una herba in ore (8h).

Ultimately, however, it is impossible to fully disentangle Balmayn's Italian and Latin vocabulary and, indeed, to attempt it may well be artificial and fruitless.[17] Nor should one underestimate the amount of Italian present in these documents, especially as a reader used to the trilingual model of most English accounts in which Latin features heavily. Given the circumstances of these documents' production, it seems perverse to assume that our author is using badly inflected Latin when he is almost certainly using sound Tuscan vernacular.

A related issue is the range of 'intermediate' AF / ME vocabulary which is notoriously difficult to label neatly as French or English in a specific text. Given the lateness of this medieval source and the fact there are no extended AF-matrix sections, it has been assumed for the purposes of this analysis that such lexemes have been absorbed and naturalised in ME and only unequivocally French features are classed as AF. In the case of originally French verbs with an anglicized morphology (e.g. *abatyd, delyvered, rebatyd, resceyved*), this is an uncontroversial decision. However, it is not a flawless solution for numerous nouns in the accounts (e.g. *borage, cariours, caryage, coralle, costs, credens, creditour, dettour, ennemyis, exchaunge, floryne, graunt, harneys, marchaunt, marchauntyse, mitre, offycyall, ospytalle, parcelle, parson, persone, plee, poke, portour, pye, quantite, remenaunt, usaunce, valewe*) and the adjectives *asur, diverse* and *vermoille*. We can only speculate as to what extent our scribe was actively conscious of this massive lexical overlap, but still need to bear in mind the AF origin of such vocabulary and AF's continued influence on commercial writing, even as late as 1450. However, all that being said, one of the defining

[17] It seems reasonable to suppose that a native medieval Tuscan speaker (whose language Balmayn is emulating) would not be able to consistently label his vocabulary as either Latin or Italian vernacular.

features of the Cantelowe accounts is the sheer amount of ME rather than AF that is present in the text, as is discussed below.

Finally, there is a small sub-group of words in Balmayn's writing which result from many decades of established Anglo-Italian contact in the field of trade and finance. These include originally Italian borrowings, widely found in English mercantile sources, which passed into ME directly or via French.[18] As we would expect, we find countless examples of the *florin* (the Florentine coin, *fiorino*),[19] and two maritime loanwords, *carryk*[20] and *patron*,[21] both of which are

[18] I believe that the lexical legacy of the Italian mercantile presence in late medieval England has been overlooked and that language contact between Italian dialects and insular French was very much a reality. Whilst some Italianisms undoubtedly entered England via the agency of Continental French (CF) dialects, many others entered insular French directly and then passed into ME. The case for contact is also strengthened by the presence of specifically AF borrowings in the writings of Italian merchants connected to English trade from the thirteenth century onwards. See Tiddeman, 'Mercantile Multilingualism'; Tiddeman, 'Early Anglo-Italian Contact'; Tiddeman, 'Lexical Exchange with Italian'; Tiddeman, 'More Sugar and Spice'.

[19] Together with the later Venetian ducat, the florin was a gold coin of Italian origin whose name was quickly adopted by many other European countries in the fourteenth century, such as England, France, Austria, Holland and Hungary. Given the extent and power of the Florentine banking network, the coin was the nearest thing Western Europe had to an international currency in the later Middle Ages. In England, *florinos* ('papal florin') is recorded in a BML text in 1277. *Florin* emerges in CF in 1278 in the Angevin material written in Naples and the coin name appears in AF and ME around a quarter of a century later. See TLIO sub **fiorino** / AND2 sub **florin** / DMF sub **florin** / TLF sub **florin** / OED2 sub **florin** / MED sub **floren** / DMLBS **florenus** and Klaus Dietz, 'Die frühen italienischen Lehnwörter des Englischen', *Anglia*, 123 (2005), 573–631 at 580.

[20] The *carraca* was a large, armed merchant vessel with three or four masts, built from the fourteenth century onward. The word spread from the original Arabic (*harrāqa*, 'fire ship') throughout Italy, probably via Genoese (it is attested in the Latin of Genoa as early as 1157), and then into wider European maritime lexis. *Karaque* appears in CF in the writings of a traveller in the Holy Land as early as c. 1245, meaning 'a small Saracen vessel' and then resurfaces in 1391 in the Italianising text, the *Gestes des Chiprois*, with the newer meaning 'large ship with sails' (cf. Lorenzo Tommasin, 'Sulla diffusione del lessico marinaresco italiano', *Studi Linguistici Italiani*, 36 (2010), 263–92 at 268; Benedek Elemér Vidos, *Storia delle parole marinaresche italiane passate in francese: contributo storico-linguistico all'espansione della lingua nautica italiana* (Firenze, Leo S. Olschki, 1939), pp. 290–1). The Genoese were at the forefront of medieval shipbuilding technology and developed the carrack to carry over three times as much cargo as a standard medieval galley – the earliest mention of a Genoese *carrake* in English records (the *Saynte Marie*) seems to be in the Latin customs accounts of Southampton from 1380 (Angelo Nicolini, 'Commercio marittimo genovese in Inghilterra nel Medioevo (1280–1495)', *Atti della Società Ligure di Storia Patria*, 47, no.1 (2007), 215–327 at 227 and 292). Near contemporary attestations can also be found in Chaucer, Foedera and the AF *Black Book of the Admiralty*: see OED2 sub **carrack**, MED sub **carik(e)**, AND2 sub **carrak**, DMLBS sub **carraca**. Note that a case involving a cargo of cloth stolen at sea and relating to a ship called 'la Carrak of Cateloigne' (freighted by merchants of Aragon and Spain) was heard in London much earlier in the fourteenth century, in 1338: see A. H. Thomas, *Calendar of the Plea and Memoranda Rolls of the City of London: Volume 1, 1323–1364* (Cambridge, Cambridge University Press, 1926), p. 172.

[21] A ship's *patron* was its captain or master. This semantic loan seems to have been transferred into medieval French via Genoese, initially. The specific maritime use of the term is first attested in the Latin of Genoa in 1246 and then appears in a bilingual CF / Latin shipping charter drawn up between the French Crown and Genoa in 1264: this source is absent from the major dictionaries and its early use of *patron des naves* is highlighted by Fennis (Jan Fennis, *Trésor du langage des galères: dictionnaire exhaustif, avec une introduction, des dessins originaux de René Burlet et des*

attested in texts in England from the 1380s. Borrowings in the opposite direction are represented by *poche* ('pokes of wool, 182lb each')[22] and *lochy* ('locks or inferior quality wool'),[23] commercial loanwords of AF or ME origin, first attested in Tuscan documents from 1291 and 1305 respectively. In these cases, language contact has gone full circle, with lexemes originally borrowed from England into Italian now being used in Italianised form by an Englishman.

## ii) Anglo-French lexis and abbreviations

Overt AF use is restricted to a few key features which nevertheless occur throughout the entire source and serve as a strong reminder of Balmayn's English scribal background. The first is his continuous use of the AF $p^o$ abbreviation for *pour*, found countless times in the accounts, in both ME and Italian-matrix entries:

> It*em* for to have hit owte of Pyse, s.1 ***pour*** pok*e* at the gate (10j).
> It*em* ***pour*** la deminuc*ione* del *con*tento de pok*es* 466 ***pour*** lb.123067 a s.1 d.8 a or*o* le C.[24] (11e).

---

*planches de Jean-Antoine de Barras de la Penne, un relevé onomasiologique et une bibliographie* (Tübingen, Niemeyer, 1995), pp. 1365–7). The *patron* of a visiting Genoese carrack (the same ship identified by Nicolini in 'Commercio marittimo genovese', above) is mentioned in the AF Parliament Rolls in 1380 (AND2 sub **carrak**, see also AND2 sub **patron**), and an earlier BML Close Roll from 1338 records *patronis Johanni Dorye* [Genoese] *et Nicholao Blaunk* from a galley ship (DMLBS sub **patronus**). A century later, the *patrone* of the *caryk of Jene* which carried the Cantelowe wool shipment is clearly identified by Balmayn as *Antoni de Aurea de Jenua* (3a).

[22] *Pocca* is most likely borrowed from AF *poke* (AND2 sub **pouche**). It is of uncertain ultimate origin but is one of several English wool terms borrowed into Italian (notably, it is used over seventy times in the Salviati London Accounts): see Tiddeman, 'Mercantile Multilingualism', p. 96; Tiddeman, 'Lexical Exchange with Italian', p. 128, p. 138; Roberta Cella, 'Prestiti nei testi mercantili toscani redatti di là dale Alpi. Saggio di glossario fino al 1350', *La Lingua Italiana: Storia, struttue, testi*, 6 (2010), 57–99 at 68 and TLIO sub **pocca**. The first attestation of *pocca* dates from 1291 in a letter sent from the merchant Consiglio de' Cerchi in Florence to his colleague, Giachetto Rinucci, in London. The letter's editor glossed this hereto unknown loanword as 'balla di lana' and suggested either the Flemish or Old Frankish *poke* as an etymon (Arrigo Castellani, *Nuovi testi florentini del Dugento* (Firenze, G.C. Sansoni, 1952), vol. 2, p. 900). Castellani's theory is also repeated in the FEW entry sub ***pokka**, p. 641a.

[23] The ME term *locks* referred to the lowest grade of professionally prepared English wool and appears in civic administration from 1232 onwards (DMLBS sub **locca**), including dozens of attestations in the advance wool contracts drawn up between English monastic orders and (mainly) Italian buyers and submissions of wool accounts sent to the Exchequer on behalf of Italian companies (transcribed in Adrian R. Bell, Chris Brooks and Paul R. Dryburgh, *Advance Contracts of the Sale of Wool, c. 1200-c. 1327* (Chippenham, List and Index Society, 2006)). The Italianised *locchi* is first attested in two citations in the Sienese accounts of the Gallerani London branch from 1305–08 and is identified by Cella in her two mercantile loanword glossaries (Cella, 'Anglismi e francesismi', p. 195; Cella, 'Prestiti nei testi mercantili', p. 82). Like *pocca*, the loanword endured in Tuscan dialects for at least 150 years, with the Salviati London books containing over thirty attestations from 1450–51. See Trotter ('Italian merchants in London', pp. 214–15); Tiddeman, 'Lexical Exchange with Italian', pp. 136–37; TLIO sub **locchi**.

[24] This graph recurs dozens of times throughout the accounts and consists of a capital C followed by a generalised, flourished abbreviation sign. Holmes ('Anglo-Florentine Trade', 385) left it as a blank space in his transcription excerpt. It is probably an abbreviation for *centum* or hundredweight

On ten occasions, we do find a distinct *per* abbreviation (with a line through the tail of the *p*), showing that the writer can distinguish between the two if he chooses:

> ***Per*** *con*to signato G for money send by exch*a*unge to Joh*an* Russelaye and Vanni Francisco de Strossy et *compagni*a de Ve*necia* **per** Alaman*o* Salviati in Florens, as hit apperyth in the tothyr syde of this leve (30a).

Sometimes, the two forms appear in the same entry. It seems that whilst *pour* can be used before an ME or Italian lexeme, *per* only appears before or within an Italian segment:

> It*em* ***pour*** taratura q*ue* fa le tare de le lana s.2 d.6 de p*ez.* ***pour*** pok*e* q*ue* fa pok*es* 448 come appare ***per*** vendute q*ue* [fa] £56 de p*ez*., valeno: fl.13 s.5 d.2 (11i).

The most concentrated area of AF presence is found in the opening lines of each of the buyers' entries over pp. 12–28 which stick closely to a fixed formula:

> Juncta Ibindo de Will*ia*mo Juncta et *compagni*a, lanaiuoli, doit le xxiij jo*ur* de novembr*e* po*ur* iiij pok*es* q*ue* po*ise* cu*m* t*are* [...]
> S*um*ma de po*ise* cu*m* tare [...] (12c).
> Leonardo de Angelo de Balioni et *compagni*a, doit le xiij jo*ur* de fev*er*ell*e* po*ur* viij pok*es* lane q*ue* po*ise* c*um* t*are* [...]
> S*um*ma de po*ise* cu*m* tare [...] (15b).

Every entry begins with the buyer's company name and then the AF verb *doit.*[25] The date is expressed by the format *le* + Roman numeral + *jour* abbreviation. This is sometimes replaced by the Italian equivalent (*a dì ditto*) or an Arabic numeral is used. The AF abbreviation *po-* (with a suspension line and dot) is expanded as *poise* and used both as a verb (cf. AND2 sub **peiser**) and a noun (cf. AND2 sub **peis**[1]). Both forms occur consistently in each account entry following the relative pronoun *que*[26] and the construction *summa de.*[27]

---

*avoirdupois*, equal to 112lb today. In the case of these accounts, it is a measure of wool but it was widely used for other commodities as the MED entry sub **c.** shows, e.g. *And ȝif it be such maner merchaundyse that be seld and weyen by the c, as brasyle, alom, almondys, rys, or other such maner merchaundyse, for every c, iiij d.* (c. 1436). There are currently no examples in the AND corpus but several examples of *le C* can be found in the *Views of the Hosts* e.g. *lij sackez de savone vendeus a Robert Aylward pris le C xx s.* (VOH, p. 119, att. 1442–3). It appears less likely (given that all the other units of weights used in the accounts are English) that the *C* stands for *cantaro*, the rough Italian equivalent of a hundredweight, widely used for bulky shipments transported by sea such as wool and varying regionally from 100 to 250 *libbre* (cf. Ronald Edward Zupko, *Italian Weights and Measures from the Middle Ages to the Nineteenth Century* (Philadelphia, American Philosophical Society, 1981), p. 71; Florence Edler, *Glossary of Mediaeval Terms of Business. Italian Series 1200–1600* (Cambridge, MA, The Mediaeval Academy of America, 1934), pp. 59–61).

[25] See AND2 sub **deveir.**

[26] This is represented by a curly, rounded 'q', rather like a back to front @ sign. Balmayn uses it in both an AF formulaic expression (*que poise* [+ weight]) and an Italian one (*que fa* [+ sum of money]).

[27] There are numerous similar constructions in the AND corpus e.g. sub **grain**[1]: *La karke du greine qe poise ccc livers deit a Escawenge xl deniers* (Lib Alb 230, att. 1419). See also the dozens of late AF examples in the *Views of the Hosts* e.g. *Item le xj*[me] *iour de Janever lan suisdit a Rauf Stokes*

There are several other notable instances of AF use in the accounts. By far the most common is the phrase *argent content* which is found over eighty times at the close of a buyer's entry to indicate that they had paid in cash.[28] On one occasion, this is written in full as *a payer argent content* (12b) and on another, *a payer a un anne* (19f) is recorded instead. The other widely used Gallicism is *le dyd* which appears to be an unconventional rendering of *ledit* ('the said').[29] It too occurs over eighty times, nearly always before personal names or AF *jour* but can also be found preceding Italian *conto*, ME / AF *pokes* and It. / AF *lane*. The form remains grammatically 'inactive' throughout and no plural or feminine variations are given:

> It*em* le **dyd** Bernardo, doit le **dyd** jo*ur* po*ur* iiij pok*es* lane (19c).
> [...] send all*e* this p*ar*cell*es*[30] as folowyth to Jacob Salviati et *compagni*a de Londra et de Brugis po*ur* le **dyd** *con*to (31b).
> Et po*ur* spago po*ur* *con*sare le **dyd** pok*es* (11j).
> It*em* po*ur* magasino[31] de le **dyd** lane (11k).

There are a couple of further AF lexemes which occur in one section only. When Balmayn tallies up how many pokes of wool are recorded on p. 27 towards the end of the accounts, he clearly uses the AF demonstrative pronoun, *ceste*[32] referring to the *levys* (or leaves) of his book:

> Thys ys the rate þat *con*taynyth in this viij levys, what in pok*es* and what in florynys:

| | |
|---|---|
| Cart*a* p*ri*ma | þe whych*e* ys f. 65 de **ceste** c*ontaynth* in pok*es* 45 |
| Cart*a* 2 | þe whych*e* ys f. 66 de **ceste** c*ontaynth* in pok*es* 60 |
| Cart*a* 3 | þe whych*e* ys f. 67 de **ceste** c*ontaynth* in pok*es* 92 |
| Cart*a* 4 | þe whych*e* ys f. 68 de **ceste** *contaynth* in pok*es* 45 |
| Cart*a* 5 | þe whych*e* ys f. 69 de **ceste** c*ontaynth* in pok*es* 69 |
| Cart*a* 6 | þe whych*e* ys f. 70 de **ceste** c*ontaynth* in pok*es* 67 |
| Cart*a* 7 | þe whych*e* ys f. 71 de **ceste** c*ontaynth* in pok*es* 57 |
| Cart*a* 8 | þe whych*e* ys f. 72 de **ceste** c*ontaynth* in pok*es* 13 |

> S*um*ma of this viij levys þat *con*taynyth in pokes ys 448 [...] (27d).

---

*xviij bales dates que poise ultra mille mille mille viijC iij quarts* (VOH, p. 2; att. 1441–2) / *Peris de le Reype Florenteyne dischargy lij sackys de savone blanke que poysse net iijxxxixC & xxvij libres* (VOH, p. 119; att. 1442–3).

[28] See AND sub **argent**: '*argent contant*, cash, money, coin(s)'.

[29] Versions of *ledit* are always attested as a single word in the AND corpus. See AND sub **dire**, p.p. as adj.: e.g. *aucunes raisons & requestes proposeés por ledict Roy d'Angleterre par maistre Jehan Louvel* (Foedera i 898, att. 1256); [...] *de semblable drap comme lesdites tables* (Bedford Inventories, B36, att. 1433).

[30] See AND2 sub **parcele** / MED sub **parcel** / OED3 sub **parcel**: 'an item or entry in a financial account'.

[31] See TLIO sub **magazzino** 'Edificio o locale destinato al deposito e alla conservazione di merci e materiali vari'. Balmayn later uses an anglicized version of the same lexeme: *magasyne* (see Part 4.viii, below).

[32] See AND sub **cest** e.g. *felonies, faites devant la date de cestes* (Stats i 194 vi, att. c. 1275).

Two unrelated records of small exchange transactions (p. 34)[33] seem to include the AF *pour amont presté* and *iiij moys*, and the AF *pere precius*[34] apparently features in a mixed-language wool-mark description:

> Joh*an* Bertrem doit le xi j*our* de auguste **pour amont**[35] **presté**[36] a xliiij d. le doc., ster. xiiij s. viij d. [...] (34a).
> [...] **a iiij moys**[37] a pagar*e* a gr. 52 ½ po*ur* doc. and to rescyve hit of Nycholas Bedford, march*aun*te of Caleys (34b).
> De n° xxxvi ad num*erum* xli: pok*es* vj de juvene lana de la March*e*, co*ntra*signat*a* de una ancella ut supra c*um* uno **pere precius** duplic*e* de corall*e* vermoill*e*: pok*es* vi (8c).

Finally, there is an intriguing case where Balmayn's stay in Italy seems to have affected his spelling of an AF word: *savacondyd*[38] ('safe-conduct'). The form could simply be misspelt or, more likely, be influenced by its medieval Tuscan equivalents, *salvacondotto.*

> It*em* le dyd for a **savacondyd** po*ur* le robe de Will*ia*m Cantelowe duryng*e* a yere (30n).

## iii) Middle English-matrix sections

As has already been mentioned, the Cantelowe accounts contain a large amount of ME. One point of immediate note is the use of the graphs thorn (*þ*) and yogh (*ȝ*). These forms are certainly not unheard of in late ME but were increasingly unusual by 1450 and so they have been maintained in the transcription. Balmayn's graphic choices offer a small snapshot of a period of transition as modern letter forms took over. He favours *th* overall but thorn does occur fifty-seven times at the start of the words *þe*, *þat* or *þere*, as well as once in *boþ*. The scribe's thorn is, typically for the fifteenth century, almost indistinguishable from his letter *y*, contrary to the conventional typographical character of *þ* used here. There seems to be no pattern to his usage and often, *th* and *þ* are found in

[33] This is one of the hardest of all the folios to read and appears to have been written in haste.
[34] Cf. AND2 sub **pere**[2] / **precius**.
[35] Attestations of the noun *amount* are actually very rare in AF (and ME). The AND2 entry sub **amunter** has some attestations of the present participle used nominally e.g. *amontant* or *amuntant* (with one variation of *amunte* from 1174–75). The MED entry sub **amounten** only has verbal forms e.g. *A somme of gold..Þat amounted a c Ml marc of money* (in the ME Prose Brut, att. c. 1450) and the OED2 sub **amount n.** does not record *amount* as a noun until 1710.
[36] See AND sub **prester**[1] and also sub **rade**[2].
[37] See AND sub **meis**[1]. It seems less likely that this is the ME *mois* (att. 1435), always found in a construction with 'Easter 'or 'Michaelmas' and referring to law terms (cf. OED3 sub **mois**), but it certainly cannot be ruled out given the code-switching nature of the text.
[38] See AND sub **conduit**[1]: e.g. *rumpours des treux & save conductes du* Roy (*Rot Parl* 1 iv 452, att. 1279–1377), MED sub **conduct:** e.g. *To Schewe thair Saufconduct* (GRed Bk Bristol p2 p62, att. 1462). See also OVI sub **salvacondotto**.

the same short phrase or even in consecutive words, suggesting that the author is switching between them randomly:

> It*em* for **the** ryȝth of **the** Offycyall*e* of **þ*e*** See **þe** whych*e* was juge bytwex us and **þ*e*** patron*e* for div*erse* harneys of **the** woll*e* (10m).
> And so I dowȝt not of the otterawnce w*ith* **that þat** there com*e* no quantite but yo*ur*s (33c).[39]

Yogh appears consistently in the ME words *broutȝh*, *dowȝt*, *freyȝth*, *rytȝh* and *weyȝht*. In nearly all other instances, a modern *g* is used in ME / AF and Italian, e.g. *borage*, *botega*, *sage*, *spago*. The key exception is *macaȝoni* ('damage, imperfection' < Ital. *macagne*, see Part 4.iv, below) in which Balmayn chooses yogh to approximate the *gn* sound of the Tuscan lexeme. The yogh character is near indistinguishable from the scribe's *z*, as used in *pezo* and *pezoly*, again a normal trait in the mid-fifteenth century.

ME is used to open new sections within the accounts, with the Latin-matrix description of merchant marks on pp. 8–9 being the only exception. The only embedded 'foreign' words here are standard Latin business abbreviations and two well-established maritime borrowings of Italian origin, discussed above (*caryk* and *patrone*).

> M*emorandum* þ*at* by the g*ra*ce of God here bygynnyth the wh weyȝth*s* of iiij$^{C}$lxvj pokys wolle aftyr the rate of þ*e* weyȝth*s* of Engeland*e*, schippyd in a caryk of Jene at Southeh*a*mpton*e* a*nno* m$^{ll}$ iiij$^{c}$ l in the name of Joh*an* de Albycys, for to be delyv*e*red by the g*ra*ce of God at Pyse to Frawnsis et Joh*an* Salviat*is*, or to suche as schall*e* be ther in theyr name. And þ*e* patron*e* ys name ys Antoni de Aurea de Jenua (3a).

Occasionally, Balmayn also adds a closing paragraph to a section using an ME-matrix, for example:

> The whych*e* makyth in sackys CC$^{o}$ lxiiij$^{o}$ s*emis* and v clo*ves* s*emis*, of the whych*e* ys rebatyd for the Tare of ev*e*ry poke j clo*ve* s*emis*. Þ*e* whych*e* s*umma* ys xiij s*ac*kys et xxiij clo*ves*. And so reste clere n*e*t: cc$^{o}$ lj s*acky*s clo*ves* viij s*emis* (7a).

The longest continuous piece of ME in the accounts is to be found on p. 33, a rough draft of a letter on a scrap of paper, inserted into the main folder. Balmayn informs Cantelowe that he has been successfully selling his wool for 25 florins per hundredweight, beating even the Strozzi and the Medici, who made 24 florins per hundredweight. He passes on the advice of Jacob Salviati to send a further hundred or two hundred sacks of the finest wool over to Tuscany.

[39] In this example, one might be tempted to suggest that there is a link between form and function and that Balmayn is writing *that* for demonstrative pronouns and *þat* for conjunctions. However, he does not maintain this distinction elsewhere in the text.

> And s*o* ther*e* ben*e* x pok*es* of þe mark*es* of þe sage I solde for redy money at xxv fl. le C. Et ij pok*es* of theme ben*e* delyv*er*ed and S*er* Jacob woll*e* avyse you and s*o* he woll*e* send to you a le*ttr*e þ*at* ye scholde by a C or ij^C^ sack*es* woll*e* but ye moste bye of þe beste and sorte ev*er*y colour by hymselffe; for x flysse in a pok*e* schall*e* distroye þe remenaunt[40] as in þe sale and s*o* the [S*er*] Strossys and the Medyc*is* hathe not solde as yet past*e* lx pok*es* and yet ther w[oll*e*] ys ryȝth gode and they selle hit for xxiiij fl. le C. the beste[41] (33b).

He alludes to several other letters that have been delayed and one can imagine that he is used to a regular flow of correspondence between London, Bruges and the Italian Salviati offices, of which this draft is just a small remnant. Only the date (*a dì 27 augusto*) and a footnote of *scrito* (to show that the proper version had been written) are in Italian. Yet it is worth noting that even in a monolingual letter back home, there are still small Italian administrative features such as these in Balmayn's work.

> Also ye schall*e* undyrstand howe that the le*ttr*es þat were made at London the xvij and xviij daye of J*une* were send fro Brugous to Venic*e* and theyr the le*ttr*es of þe Medyc*is* Anton de Rabatt*is* and the Salviatys were et ben*e* taryed and so as yet we have them*e* not (33d).

In the main section of the accounts, pp. 11–12, we find lists of expenses incurred. These begin with the *costes of Pise*, signed in November 1450, covering arrival at Livorno, weighing and 'piling up' of the pokes, their storage by a local 'host', all taxes and transport to Pisa. This is then followed by the *costes of Florens,* completed in September 1451, which cover the time taken to sell the wool. Over these pages, the scribe regularly changes language but the amount of Italian increases most dramatically in the second list where he shifts into Italian-matrix halfway through (see Part 4.iv below).

Some of the items of expenses are therefore entirely in ME, such as:

> It*em* to the man þ*at* sawe the harneys of the woll*e* (10n).
> It*em* for the portou*r*s for pylyng*e* up of þ*e* seyd wolle et for ou*re* pylyng (10o).
> It*em* for the mendyng*e* of the pockys wher*e*as they were ibroke[42] (10p).

Other ME-matrix entries in these lists contain an Italian(ised) term for which Balmayn gives an English equivalent or explanation:

> It*em* for cariours the which*e* be callyd **victura**[43] for the bryngyng*e* fro Pise to Florens the for*e*seyd 466 pok*es* woll*e* (11c).

[40] See MED **remenaunt** / OED3 **remanant** / AND1 **remanant**: 'the rest, remaining part or quantity'.
[41] Holmes ('Anglo-Florentine Trade', 385) comments on this section of the letter: 'This is presumably an indication, not unexpected, that the market for English wool was very dependent on quality, which Cantelowe was able to supply'.
[42] This is apparently *ibroke*. The English past participle sometimes retained the Germanic *ge-* prefix, rendered as *i-*, cf. German *gebrochen*. By 1450, this would seem to be a rather outdated feature; the latest attestation I can find in the OED / MED corpora is 1398: see OED2 sub **weft**: *ȝif þe wefte is ibroke þei begynneþ to amende it.*
[43] *Victura* is a rare Tuscan variation of the commonly used term *vettura*, meaning 'cart or wagon'. There is currently only one example in the OVI corpus of this spelling from 1219: *si debia avere ogne*

> It*em* s.1 po*ur* poke for the ryȝth of the schipe house þat ys for to saye the **arsinà** of Lyvorn*e* (11f).[44]
> It*em* for the **avery**[45] of the galley or schippe the whyche ys to saye þ*at* eve*ry* march*a*unt shall bere his p*ar*te aft*er* the rate of his march*a*untyse for all mann*er* of cost*es* don*e* upon þe galleys or schippe for cause of ennemyis to the savacon*dyd* of the godys: Nothyng*e* payd (10l).

Et po*ur* **duodesimo**, þe whych*e* ys uno p*ar*te de xij p*ar*te de le maiore (11d).[46]

Towards the end of the accounts, Balmayn records some merchant marks in a ME-matrix paragraph. However, he mainly switches back to the Italian-Latin mark descriptions he has employed elsewhere in his records.

> [...] and viij pok*es* yong*e*, I markyd w*ith* borage and iij pok*es*, I markyd w*ith* **signo** ***contra*****signo** of the marke of all*e* the balys and j pok*e*, I markyd w*ith* **j pecora coronat*a* cu*m* *e*rba in ore**. The s*um*ma ys xviij pok*es* (27f).

The obvious exception is the 'mark of the maiden' (described elsewhere as *una donzella / ancella*) and her coral jewellery:

> The mark*e* firste viij pok*es* w*ith* a hand of borage, vj pok*es* yong*e* March*e* w*ith* **a maydyn*e* his head w*ith* a peyr of corall*e* bedis abowte her neke**, ij pok*es* w*ith* signo † *contra*signo and anothir pok*e* þat hadd*e* neyther nombyr nor marke (28b).

In the list of exchange transactions most of the entries contain a mixture of ME with Italian (underlined) and AF (bold) segments of varying lengths and it is, at times, difficult to designate a matrix language:

> It*em* a d*ì* 13 ditto **po*ur*** £80 s. 4 d. 0 p*ez*. 12 de gr. send by usaunce a Venec*ia* a ditti da lloro midesimi, a £15 st. 17 d.10 a fl. **pour** libra de gr. For hit was delyv*er*d here to the seyd *compagnia* **de le dyd** Russelay et Strossy: fl. 878 s.28 d. 7 (29f).
> It*em* a d*ì* ditto **po*ur*** £148 s. 1 d. 7 de ster. send to Jacob Salviati et *compagnia* de Londra, a pagare a d*ì* 15 da vista da l*ett*era, for to resceyve of Pero de Medici and Jeros de Pili, **po*ur*** fl.886 s. 7 d. 3 (30l).

---

*die ii s. p(er) feo, e pagare le victure* (OVI, Doc. montier, 49.34). See also OVI sub **vettura** for over 350 fourteenth- and fifteenth-century citations.

[44] This is a variant of *arsenà* or 'dockyard'. The Italian is derived from the Arabic *dâr assinâ'a* ('workshop / factory'), as is the variant *arsenale:* TLIO sub **arsenà**. *Arsenal* is first attested in CF in 1266, most likely borrowed from Venetian (Fennis, *Trésor du langage des galères*, p. 268; Vidos, *Parole marinaresche italiane*, pp.198–206; Thomas Edward Hope, *Lexical Borrowing in the Romance Languages: a Critical Study of Italianisms in French and Gallicisms in Italian from 1100–1900* (Oxford, Blackwell, 1971), p. 23). It does not appear in English records until 1511, however: OED2 sub **arsenal.** Note that Holmes ('Anglo-Florentine Trade', 374) transcribed this word as *dysma* i.e. a subsisdy known as 'the tenth' (cf. TLIO sub **decima**[1]). However, following reexamination of the manuscript and discussion with Dr Angelo Nicolini, *arsinà* seems to be the correct transcription.

[45] This was a duty (< Tuscan *averia*) imposed to cover potential loss or damage during a sea voyage: TLIO sub **avarià**. It is not currently attested in this form in a Middle English matrix text (see Part 4.viii below).

[46] *Duodesimo* = *dodicesimo*. This seems to be another sort of Florentine duty called 'the twelfth' but I have been unable to find details of it.

It*em* **le dyd** for a **savacondyd** ***pour*** le robe[47] de Will*ia*m Cantelowe durynge a yere: fl. 30 s. 19 d. 4 (30n).

## iv) Italian-matrix sections

An extended series of Italian-matrix buyers' entries is contained within pp. 12–28. As noted above, the first and last lines always contain some AF abbreviations and fixed expressions. Balmayn meticulously records the precise weight of each numbered poke of wool[48] and adds up a total for each lot. He then lists various kinds of tare: amounts of weight deducted from the gross to calculate the net weight for which the buyer will be charged in gold florins. These sections are formulaic and repetitive but nevertheless include some important vocabulary. The following two examples show the main structures used in the majority of the entries:

Brancho Costantino da Perosa et *compagni*a, doit a d*ì* ditto po*ur* x pok*es* lane *que* po*ise cum tare*:

| | | | | | |
|---|---|---|---|---|---|
| N° | 336 | lb 260 | N° | 324 | lb 250 |
| | 311 | lb 260 | | 314 | lb 274 |
| | 308 | lb 280 | | 345 | lb 281 |
| | 334 | lb 256 | | 388 | lb 276 |
| 10 | 309 | lb 279 | | 335 | lb 257 |

S*umm*a de po*ise* cu*m* *tare*: lb 2673
T*ara* po*ur* uso: lb 11 po*ur* sach*i* *que* fa lb 110
Et po*ur* maca3oni:[49] lb 30
Et po*ur* supr*a*più de sach*i*: lb 20 unce 6
Et pour sup*ra*più de pezo: lb 7 unce 6
Et po*ur* umido: lb 10
Et po*ur* fradysch*o*:[50] lb 4

[47] Given the sense, this must be Italian *robe* as in 'goods, possessions' rather than 'robes' (cf. VTO sub **roba**). It is not entirely clear whether the scribe is using the Italian feminine plural article here or the generic *le* which he frequently uses before AN, ME and Italian nouns: see Part 4.vii below.
[48] As mentioned previously, all of the pokes weighed over 200lb before deductions for tare, with the heaviest at 299lb (poke no. 379) and the lightest at 223lb (poke no. 338).
[49] *Maca3oni* = *macagne*, a Tuscan variant of *magagna* meaning 'blemish / damage / imperfection'. See TLIO sub **magagna** 'Imperfezione o guasto, spec. non manifesto, che altera la struttura o dimiuisce il pregio (specif. di un manufatto)'.
[50] *Fradyscho* = *fradicio*, a Tuscan variant of *fràcido*, meaning either 'very wet, soaked' or 'damaged, rotten, putrefied'. Indeed, it is this form which has persisted in modern Italian in both meanings. I am very grateful to both Professor Francesco Guidi Bruscoli of the Borromei Bank Project and to Professor Matthew Davies now of Birkbeck, University of London, for discussing this lexeme with me. See also VTO sub **fràdicio:** 'agg. metatesi di *fracido*: Assai bagnato, inzuppato d'acqua / Marcio, guasto, putrefatto'. The TLIO entry sub **fràcido** has numerous citations from the 1290s onwards but none of them have either the *frad-* stem or are used overtly in the 'wet' sense. However, there is a reference to a soaking process in cloth-making used by Arte della Lana: *Li quali siano sopra vedere*

S*umma*: lb 182
Rest*e* n*et* lb 2491, a fl. 24 le C. monta fl. 597 s. 16 a or*o*
S*umma*: fl. 597 s. 23 d. 2, argent *con*tent (18b).

Laurenxo de Paris Chorbenelli et *compagni*a, doit le dyd jo*ur* po*ur* v pok*es* lane q*ue* poi*se* cu*m* t*are*:

| | | |
|---|---|---|
| N° | 32 | lb 272 |
| | 10 | lb 272 |
| | 1 | lb 277 |
| | 16 | lb 278 |
| 5 | 23 | lb 260 |

S*umma* de poi*se* cu*m* t*are*: lb 1355
T*ara* po*ur* uso: 11 po*ur* pok*e*, lb 55
Et po*ur* macaȝoni et sup*ra*più de sach*i*: lb 20
Et po*ur* umido: lb 5
Et po*ur* intyngim*ent*o[51]: lb 11 unc*e* 6
Et pui lb 2 po*ur* poch*e* d'achordo
S*umma* de tar*e*: lb 101 unc*e* 6
Rest*e* n*et* lb 1253 unc*e* 6, a fl. 26 s.10 a or*o* le C. q*ue* fa fl. 332 s.3 a or*o*
S*umma*: fl. 332 s. 4 d. 4, argent *con*tent (25b).

Occasionally, there are further variations in the second half of the entry such as:

T*ara* po*ur* uso et po*ur* toti altri tar*e*: lb 15
Rest*e* n*et* lb 265
Et lb 154 po*ur* lana juvene, a fl. 18 le C.
Et lb 111 de lana bona, a fl. 24 le C. q*ue* fa in toti fl. 54 s.7 a or*o*
S*umma* fl. 54 s. 10 d. 0, argent *con*tent (22f).

Rest*a* netta[52] lb 1032, a fl. 28 le C. q*ue* fa fl. 288 s. 19 a or*o* (19f).

Et pui lb 2 de tar*e* po*ur* sachy de canevas q*ue* era duply[53] (24c).
Et po*ur* lochy:[54] lb 2 unc*e* 6 (25c).

*et extimare tutte le questioni delli danni di lane sucide et lavate, et di boldroni sucidi et lavati, et d' ongn' altro lavoro che ad arte di lana apertegna che fusse sì di fracido come di bagnato, et di roctame ch' avesse per sacco oltra libbre XV di lana, u vero che non seguitasse la mercatantia, secondo le conventione che fusseno state tra le parti* (Stat Pis. cap. 63, p. 698.18, att. 1304).

[51] *Intyngimento* = *intingimento*, 'dipping or immersion (in liquid)'. See VTO sub **intingimento,** '*l'atto di bagnare leggermente, tuffando in un liquido*'. There are no attestations of this noun in the OVI / Datini corpora. We do find several versions of the root verb *intingere* from the 1350s onwards but none of the sources are mercantile. Together with *fradischo* above, the Cantelowe Accounts could provide important evidence for these lexemes in medieval Italian, albeit in a text written by an Englishman.

[52] In six entries, Balmayn writes Italian *netta* out in full, rather than then abbreviation *nt.*

[53] This would seem to be *duplie* from the verb *doppiare*, 'to double'.

[54] This is *locchi* < ME *lockes* (see Part 4.i above). *Lochy* also appears in entry 23c but in 15a, the ME *lokes* is used.

Only one buyer's entry contains an ME phrase:

> Et pui lb 10 in le pok*e* de nº 377 for hit was not sewyng*e* (18c).

The precise meaning of all the various tare – the names of which are carefully written out in full – is not immediately evident. *Tara pour uso* refers to a standardised fee for 'wear' and is given as 11lb per poke in every single entry.[55] S*uprapiù de pezo / de sachi obviously* refers to 'surplus' weight or sacks but what this actually means in practical terms is unclear. The same is true of the *poche d'achordo* or 'agreed / contracted' pokes. *Macaȝoni, umido, fradischo* frequently occur as separate deductions (e.g 15b) in the same entry. However, *fradischo* and *intingimento* never occur in the same entry apart from 28a: *Et pour fradyscho et intyngimento*: *lb 60*. This suggests that Balmayn may be using the words as synonyms in this instance for the same kind of tare and means that *fradischo / intingimento* are both used to mean soaked rather than damaged wool. A tentative summary of these four tare might therefore be:

- *Pour macaȝoni*: for damaged or low-quality wool
- *Pour umido*: for damp wool
- *Pour fradischo / intingimento*: for soaked wool

I have found very little information about the practice of deducting weight from wool based on its wetness, let alone about gradations of dampness and how they are measured. Edler does, however, gloss *tara* in some Florentine accounts from 1442 as follows: 'tare, allowance made in weight for container or wrapping (or goods, humidity in wool, etc.)'.[56] Furthermore, in *Medieval Super-Companies*, Hunt discusses the 'agonizing slowness' that Italian companies had to endure in obtaining permission to export wool they had already bought in England. The following refers to an entry in Edward III's Close Rolls of 1339–41:

> The many transfers and formalities afforded almost unlimited opportunities for delays. Ships that turned back to ports in England to escape piracy or bad weather were sometimes held up for customs examinations all over again [....] The latter entry shows that London customs even had to be ordered to release wool for export on the basis of the first lading, ignoring the extra weight caused by the 'damp' when the ship carrying the wool returned to port after a storm at sea.[57]

[55] Cf. Edler, *Mediaeval Terms of Business*, p. 288.
[56] Edler, *Mediaeval Terms of Business*, p. 288.
[57] Edwin S. Hunt, *The Medieval Super-Companies: a study of the Peruzzi Company of Florence* (Cambridge, Cambridge University Press, 1994), p. 66.

Questions still remain as to the precise nature of tare system and wool weighing practices but, overall, the topic offers another good example of the value of the Italian-matrix section of these accounts (ignored in Holmes' article) and how they could still hold useful information for economic historians and wool market specialists, as well as for linguists.

Balmayn's Italian is much more varied and spontaneous in the lists of expenses and bills of exchange where he includes a sizeable amount of Tuscan bureaucratic vocabulary. As discussed, he shifts frequently from ME and back again, apparently at will. Italian entries in the costs of Florence include:

> It*em* pou*r* pisare[58] a comperatory et pou*r* portare a lor*o* botega[59] s.3 d.4. de p*ez.* pou*r* poke q*ue* fa pok*es* 448 come appare p*er* vendute q*ue* fa £174 s.13 d.4 de p*ez.* u*no*, Fl: fl. 17 s.16. d.6 (11g).
> It*em* pou*r* taratura[60] q*ue* fa le tare de le lana s.2 d.6 de p*ez.* pou*r* pok*e* q*ue* fa pok*es* 448 come appare p*er* vendute q*ue* [fa] £56 de p*ez.*, valeno: fl.13 s.5 d.2 (11i).
> It*em* pou*r* farle styvare et restivare più volte quando sono mostro a chomperatore. Et pou*r* spago pou*r* c*on*sare[61] le dyd pok*es* non se mitte nulla, q*ue* seribbino più di [due] fl. : fl.- d.- (11j).
> It*em* pou*r* retenc*ione*[62] de denar*i* 2 de p*ez.* pou*r* fl., lo damno mownta pou*r* toto ¼ de fl. pou*r* C. q*ue* fa fl.63 s.23 d.5 de fl.: fl.63 s. 23 d.6 (11l).

The following entries appear in the last two folios:

> It*em* pou*r* senceria[63] de ditt*i* denari cambiati p*er* sencyale:[64] fl. 3 s. 16 d. 4 (30o).
> Item pou*r* sensaria de denari cambiati a questo *con*to a sensiale: £-. 8.4 (31aa).
> It*em* pou*r* nostra p*r*ovisione a doc. ij pou*r* m*i*ll*e* et pou*r* Gatico,[65] doc. ij pou*r* m*i*ll*e*: £2. 2. 0. 12 (31bb).

[58] Presumably, Balmayn means *pesare*, 'to weigh'.

[59] *Bottega* (< Lat. *apotheca*) first attested in the Italian vernacular c. 1230, was a merchant's shop, workshop or studio. See TLIO sub **bottega** and LEI sub **apotheca**. It would enter English as a borrowing in the nineteenth century: OED3 sub **bottega.**

[60] *Taratura*, meaning 'calibration, adjustment', is still used in modern Italian. It derives from the Arabism *tara* (see below) and is not currently present in the OVI / Datini corpora, although the related forms *taratore* ('the person who calculated the tare') and *tarare* ('to calculate the tare') appear a handful of times. *Taratura* is found, however, in an account book entry from 1461: *per taratura alla vendita a s. 2 d. 6 per balla* (Copia di estratto-conto dell'11 marzo 1461, Firenze-L'Aquila) (Frederigo Melis, *Documenti per la storia economica dei secoli XIII-XVI: con una nota di paleografia commerciale a cura di Elena Cecchi* (Firenze, Leo S. Olschki, 1972), p. 258).

[61] This is apparently *conciare* ('to repair, adjust'), see TLIO sub **conciare** and Edler, *Mediaeval Terms of Business,* p. 83.

[62] Cf. Edler, *Mediaeval Terms of Business,* p. 248: '*Ritenzione*, deduction from a sale or purchase price, of fixed percentage, usually d.2 per sealed florin found in some Medici journals and ledgers of the 16th century.'

[63] *Senceria* = *senseria*, 'a broker's fee'. See OVI sub **senseria** and Edler, *Mediaeval Terms of Business,* p. 269.

[64] *Sencyale* = *sensale,* 'a broker' from Arabic *simsār* (Edler, *Mediaeval Terms of Business,* p. 269). There are over 500 examples in the OVI sub **sensale** from 1334 onwards.

[65] The *consolatico* refers to the consul office in medieval Florence, first attested in this sense in 1357. See TLIO sub **consolàtico**.

Holmes cites entry 11j, above, as proof that Balmayn has 'lapsed' into Italian and is merely scribbling down what his Florentine colleagues are saying.[66] Given the use of his language in the document as a whole, this is an unfair assessment. There does seem to be failure to make the past participle *mostro* agree and in any case, we would expect *mostrato* in its place.[67] We would also expect a slightly different spelling of the Tuscan third person conditional of the verb 'to be' (i.e. *sirebbino* or *sarebbino* rather than *seribbino*).[68] Nevertheless, the sense of the entry is more or less clear ('For the stowing and restowing [of the pokes] several times when they are shown to the buyer. And for string to repair the said pokes, we put nothing, it would be more than two florins').[69] Most importantly, all the other Italian-matrix entries in the accounts (none of which are cited by Holmes) are perfectly competent and understandable, even if his use of *y* for *i* (e.g *pezoly, comperatory, fradyscho, lochy, intyngimento, sencyale*) and yogh (*macaȝoni*) makes some spellings look oddly anglicized at first glance.

## v) Merchant mark descriptions

Every buyer's entry ends with a statement which identifies the merchant mark or sign for that lot of wool. These are intriguing snippets both historically (see Part 6, below) and linguistically: the frequency of Balmayn's language shift in these mark descriptions is notable. Following an Italian-matrix list of tare, these sentences always begins with ME *The marke* (*ys*). The description then continues in one of four ways:

a) Italian:
The marke una donzella (20e).
The mark*e* j$^{a}$ pecora coronata cu*m* suo agnello (17a).
The mark*e* uno sole (17e).
The mark*e* j$^{o}$ mazzo de 5 papavery cu*m* breve q*ue* dixe Laus Deo (16c).
The mark*e* una mitra cu*m* cruce de sup*ra* (21g).

b) talian / Latin mix:
The marke una chapleta verid*e* duplic*e* cu*m* quatuor florib*us* (12b).
The mark*e* uno garland*o* virid*e* duplic*e* et in medio dict*i* garland*i* una rosa. (13c).
The mark*e* de uno pavo et una campana ad pedem sinistrum (15a).

[66] Holmes, 'Anglo-Florentine Trade', 374
[67] It is worth noting, however, that medieval Tuscan past participles sometimes had the same form as the first person of the present tense: e.g. *cerco, porto, tocco, salvo* (see Martin Maiden, *A Linguistic History of Italian*, 2nd edn (Abingdon, Routledge, 2013), p. 123).
[68] I am grateful to Dr Ignazio Del Punta (University of the Republic of San Marino), for confirming this.
[69] Presumably, the payment for the string had already been settled. My particular thanks go to Dr Angelo Nicolini for sharing his thoughts with me on the meaning of this account entry.

The mark*e* una peccora coronat*a* cu*m* suo agnello et pecus h*ab*et modicum de erba in ore (25c).

c) an Italian / Latin mix with an ME lexeme:

The marke ys una manu cu*m* una manipulo rosar*um* de trib*us* foliis et degito ariculare **strawte** recto (13a).

The mark*e* j° manip*u*lo de quinq*ue* **popeis** cu*m* una sc*ri*ptura que dicit Laus Deo (18c).

The mark*e* una **jaye** cu*m* erba in ore (21f).

d) (rarely) ME:

The mark*e* una jaye (17c).

The mark*e* a abbot ys crowysse (23g).

It seems that he deliberately chose to write the opening paragraphs to his account section in ME or list the wool types in Latin-matrix but here things are less clear-cut. It is worth considering that Tuscan colleagues with whom the scribe spoke or whose accounts he read also mixed in Latin lexemes and they formed part of the dialect of the merchant community in which he was immersed.

## vi) Latin-matrix sections

The only section of the surviving accounts to be in extended Latin-matrix is found over pp. 8–9. The language here appears typical of that of many late British medieval accounts, adequate but simple, and full of vernacular lexemes. The hand is especially careful and neat and Balmayn meticulously groups the numbered 466 pokes of wool, according to their wool type and merchant mark:[70]

> Factura lana*rum* pock*es* cccclxvj signat*a*, num*erata* et depinct*a*, p*ro*ut inferius continet*ur*,[71] carigat*a* in carraca unde est patronus Antonio de Aurea de Janua, no*mine* Johan*nis* de Albic*is* consignand*o* in portu de Pis*e*, Francisco et Johan*ni* et sociis vel aliis qui fuer*a*nt pro ip*s*is (8a).
>
> De n° xxxvi ad num*erum* xli: pok*es* vj de juvene lana de la March*e*, co*ntra*signat*a* de una ancella ut supra *cum* uno pere preci*us* duplic*e* de coral*le* vermoill*e*: pok*es* vi (8c).
>
> De n° iiij$^{c}$ix ad num*erum* iiij$^{c}$ xxj: pok*es* iij de lana fine juv*ene* de Cotiswold, depinct*a* de uno pye: pok*es* iij (9b).
>
> Lane de le Marche constant hic quarte p*ar*ti plus q*u*am fine lane de Cotiswold*e*. Et juv*ene* lane de Costiswold*e* su*n*t peiori quarta p*ar*te q*u*am lane fine de Cotiswold*e*.

[70] Latin is only used in the accounts with reference to these merchant marks, although as we have seen, other languages are used to describe them further on in the accounts. Could this language choice result from a wish to confer more formality or pseudo-legality at this point?

[71] 'As is contained below' i.e. as is written below.

Hoc vobis dico, ad hoc ut h*ab*eatis attendere ad vendic*io*n*e*m. Et ut intelligatis ut vos gubernare habeatis[72] (9h).

Six different kinds of wool are recorded, but there are over twenty-six different merchant marks (see Table 4, below). By far, the most popular wool type is Cotswold with 314 pokes, then young Cotswold (eighty-five), March (thirty-five), Abbey[73] (twenty-four), young March (six) and young Abbey (two). Balmayn takes care to note if the colour of the wool is reddish (rather than white), referring several times to *lane vermoille / rubie*[74] and once to the cheaper 'fleece wool' grade.[75]

Lane **vermoile**: Nota q*uo*d in pok*es* in num*er*o lxx sunt lane **rubie**. Et in numero Cxxx[e] su*n*t lane vocat*e* **flese wolle** que ponderant cl*o*v*es* vij de lane fine de Cotyswold*e* de rac*ione*[76] yong*e* (8i).

Several pokes of wool are also described as *storo*, a term which is repeated later on in the buyers' entries:

De n° CCCClj ad num*erum* iiij[c]liiij: pok*es* iiij de lana Abbathie de illa sorte de pok*es* viij ut sup*ra*, depinct*a* de una sc*ri*ptura sup*ra*scri*p*to **storo**: pok*es* iiij (9d).
De no j ad num*erum* viij: pok*es* viij de lana de Cotiswolde fine, vocat*a* storo, depinct*a* de una manu quod tenet un*um* manipulu*m* de borage de trib*us* foliis: pok*es* viij (9f).
The mark*e* una sc*ri*ptura sup*ra*scripto **storo** (24d).

It seems that this refers to 'stock' wool, i.e. purer wool from a single flock rather than *collecta*, which was wool from various farms surrounding a monastic estate. Discussing the advance wool contracts for Pipewell Abbey in the late thirteenth and early fourteenth centuries, Bell *et al.* comment that '[...] some merchants frowned upon *collecta* and demanded wool *de stauro suo* (from his stock)'.[77]

[72] Here Balmayn explains that March wool should fetch four times the price of fine Cotswold but young Cotswold is only worth a quarter of it. He advises the reader to be patient (*gubernare* as in to 'govern oneself') and to wait for the right sale. As Holmes ('Anglo-Florentine Trade', 373) notes, the wool prices in the accounts are 'roughly in line with a parliamentary petition of 1454, where Shropshire march wool is priced at 14 marks the sack, Cotswold at 12½, young Cotswold at 8'.
[73] Referred to here generically as *lana Abbathie* throughout so we do not know from which particular abbey the wool came.
[74] The wool had probably been 'raddled' with red dye, a centuries-old practice of identifying particular sheep, such as marking out an ewe's lambs or that she had mated with a ram: see OED3 sub **raddle[1]**.
[75] Bell *et al.*, *English Wool Market*, p. 72: Fleece-wool is defined as that 'obtained from the living animal at the annual shearings'. This is in contrast to fell-wool which was wool that has been 'pulled from a sheepskin, rather than shorn from a live animal' see OED2 sub **fleece-wool / fell-wool.**
[76] It is not entirely clear what this word means or indeed which language it is in but it could be a variant of It. **ragione** ('sort, quality of a commodity'), see Edler, *Mediaeval Terms of Business*, p. 237.
[77] Bell *et al.*, *English Wool Market*, p. 78.

Like *poche* and *lochy*, *storo* is an example of a specifically English commercial term that has achieved currency amongst Tuscan merchants.[78]

A final interesting point about this Latin-matrix section is that it is the only one to contain glosses for non-technical terms. We have four instances, three written as insertions above the line and one in the main body of the text. One is preceded by the traditional Latin marker *anglice*:

> […] depincta de uno pavo, **a pecok*e*** (8l).
> […] depinct*a* de uno agn*us* Dei cum cruce in vexilla, **a baner** (8s).
> […] depinct*a* de uno pastorale, **an abbot*s* croyse** (9a).
> […] depinct*a* cu*m* uno sole, **ang*li*ce a sonne** (9c).

Given the range of vocabulary elsewhere, it seems unlikely that Balmayn was writing cribs for himself. We could suggest they are for his intended reader back in England who may not know the Latin / Italian terms *pavo* and *vexilla* and the Italian *pastorale* but this seems a tenuous argument too, especially given the everyday nature of the lexeme *sole* which too is glossed. More likely, as often appears to be the case with medieval glosses, these could be near subconscious products of the writer's train of thought. However, the fact remains that they only appear in this part of the accounts and this may not be entirely coincidental.

## vii) Use of articles

Balmayn's extended use of a generic, residual AF *le* is striking and, at times, seemingly indiscriminate. However, it does not seem to fit in with the patterns common to late English trilingual business writing where its use consistently signals a language shift mid-sentence, e.g. Latin / AF preposition + *le* + ME lexeme.[79] If there is a general rule to be applied, it is that *the* (or *þe*) only ever

[78] These theories are backed up by the presence of the wool type *story* (also *stery)* in the Villani London Book fragment (1422–4), although its presence attracts no editorial comment: *per chosto e spesse di sacha L q. ij cº vj di lana chontisgualda chonpratta per loro da diverse persone e fattone poche Lxx ly xLiij di story e xxvij chogliette* (Guidi Bruscoli, 'Domenico Villani', p. 404). In the same source, we can clearly see *story* wool being distinguished from the *choglietta* (i.e. *collecta* or wool from several farms on an estate): cf. Tiddeman, 'Lexical Exchange with Italian', pp. 128–9, 134, 139.

[79] E.g. *Omnia instrumenta et necessaria shopae meae ad le meltynghouse et ad countor meum spectantia* (Test. Ebor II 1.6) (Trotter, 'Death, Taxes and Property', p. 178). For more discussion, see also Trotter, 'Bridging the Gap'; Trotter, 'Italian Merchants in London'; Richard Ingham, 'Code-switching in the Later Medieval English Lay Subsidy Rolls', in Herbert Schendl and Laura Wright (eds), *Codeswitching in Early English* (Berlin, De Gruyter, 2011), pp. 95–114; Richard Ingham,'Language-Mixing in Medieval Latin Documents: Vernacular Articles and Nouns' in Judith A. Jefferson and Ad Putter (eds), *Multilingualism in Medieval Britain (c. 1066–1520): Sources and Analysis* (Turnhout, Brepols, 2013), pp. 105–21; Richard Ingham, 'Medieval Bilingualism in England: on the Rarity of Vernacular Code Switching' in Päivi Pahta, Janne Skaffari and Laura Wright (eds), *Multilingual Practices in Language History: English and Beyond* (Berlin, De Gruyter Mouton, 2018), pp. 319–37; Laura Wright, 'A Pilot Study on the Singular Definite Articles *le* and *la* in Fifteenth-Century London

precedes an ME lexeme whereas *le* is found before all three of the accounts' other languages: AF, Italian and Latin.

*Le* features most commonly by far in dates throughout the accounts: e.g *le xxx jour de june* (23a), *le primer jour de june* (31w), *le dyd jour* (13d), *le 17 de le dyd* (31t). The abbreviated Latin *centum* in the expression *pour le C.* ('per hundred-weight') also occurs dozens of times. There is no use of the form *lez* but we can argue that in examples such as *le costes de Pyse* (10u) and *pour le sackes* (12d) that the scribe's *le* should be read as the AF plural form, *lé*. There are only three clearly feminine AF articles, all in the expression *de la Marche* (8b, 8c, 9g).

Importantly, there are also several cases of *le* + Italian lexeme, even in the middle of an Italian-matrix segment:

> Et po*ur* le s.16 q*ue* fa £987 s.4 d.3 de p*ez*. de **le** valeuta de £ (11d).
> It*em* po*ur* taratura q*ue* fa **le** tar*e* de **le** lana (11i).
> [...] þe whych*e* ys uno p*ar*te de xij p*ar*te de **le** maiore (11d).
> It*em* le dyd for a savacondyd po*ur* **le** robe de Will*ia*m Cantelowe (30n).
> [...] send by usaunce to Lo*n*do*n* a st. 45¼ po*ur* **le** doc. (31c).

It seems that in examples 11i (*le tare*) and 30n (*le robe*) we are dealing with the Italian feminine plural definite article *le*. There one example of the Tuscan masculine definite article *lo* and several of the feminine *la*, as well as the partitives *de la* and *del*:

> It*em* po*ur* retenc*io*ne de denar*i* 2 de p*ez*. po*ur* fl., **lo** damno mownta po*ur* toto ¼ de fl. po*ur* C. q*ue* fa fl.63 s.23 d.5 de fl. (11l).
> Et po*ur* **la** p*ar*tita to the clerkys (11d).
> Estimate a fl.20 le C. **de la** lana q*ue* fa fl. 24614 (11f).
> [...] for to resceyve of Antonio **de la** Luna (29b).
> It*em* po*ur* **la** deminuc*ione* **del** *con*tento de pok*es* (11e).

There also seems to be an instance of an Italian direct object pronoun (feminine plural):

> It*em* po*ur* far**le** styvare et restivare più volte quando sono mostro a chomperatore. (11j).

As regards, indefinite article use, *a / an* are only found in ME segments, as we would expect. The Italian (or Latin) *uno* and *una* appear over sixty times each. The masculine and feminine articles are usually found in front of Italian and Latin nouns: e.g. *uno sole / una donzella, uno agnus / una manu*. They also appear occasionally in front of other vernacular nouns: we find both *uno jaye* and *una jaye*, as well as *uno pere* and *una pye*.

---

Mixed-language Business Writing', in Richard Ingham (ed), *The Anglo-Norman Language and its Contexts* (Woodbridge, York Medieval Press, 2010), pp. 130–42.

## viii) Commercial loanwords and semantic loans

The Cantelowe accounts are an excellent example of how lexical value and lexicographical usability are not necessarily one and the same. No one can deny that the text represents a compelling piece of early Anglo-Italian contact but, as is typical for such mixed-language sources, it does not always fit in with the (unavoidable) conventions of dictionary-making.

The obvious problem is matrix-language and its frequent shift. It would be inaccurate to declare this an 'ME source' in its entirety. As we have seen, Balmayn changes language on a line by line (or even word by word) basis at times and large sections are solely in Italian. This is a text written over the course of several months by one native ME speaker who has learned Italian, and the subtleties of his linguistic immersion are not easily quantified in lexicographical terms. There are countless commercial terms, such as *arsinà*, *accordo, botega, consolatico, macaȝoni* and *senseria*, that must have filtered into Balmayn's ME and that he used when speaking with English colleagues about his work. But as we only have proof of their existence in an 'Italian' sentence (albeit one written by an Englishman), they cannot be considered loanwords. Conversely, rare usages of forms such as medieval Tuscan *fradicio*, *intingimento* and *taratura* by Balmayn are of significant relevance to Italian historical lexicography, as is wool terminology borrowed from English commerce such as *pocca, locchi* and *storo.* Multilingual sources can be of value to multiple dictionaries but all too often they fall through the cracks and are exploited by none.

Table 2 (below) recapitulates six important Italianisms that appear in ME-matrix sections of the Cantelowe accounts. The coin types *grossy* and *pezoly* are not currently recorded in the MED or the OED (although variations of these same coin names are, see below). Two loanwords – *ditto* and *magasyne* – offer significantly earlier first attestations than those currently found in the OED which are from 1625 and 1583, respectively. The citations here offer noteworthy additions to the histories of these loanwords in English. Two further cases – *avery* and *tare* – provide a valuable new citation of a borrowing that is very rare in English prior to 1500. Even so, there are questions to be raised, however. Clearly, our source (with its use of *ditto* after AF and Italian words) offers an exciting illustration of the process by which loanwords flow from one language to another in a bi- (or multi-) lingual text. But could we include the *ditto* citations in a monolingual dictionary when the term only appears after *a dì* or *le [jour] + number* in the text, even if these segments are themselves embedded in a longer ME entry? Similarly, how do we catergorise the word *grossy* in its mixed-language segment (*at usaunce pour £100 de Grossy de Venecia to Johan Russelay*) and does it belong in the OED, the AND or both? Distinguishing use in English and use by an English writer can be a thornier problem than it first may seem.

**Table 2** Commercial loanwords in the Cantelowe accounts

| **Lexeme**[1] | **Freq.** | **Example** | **OED** | **MED** |
|---|---|---|---|---|
| **Avery** 'maritime tax to cover damage to ship or its cargo'[2] < It. *averia* (pl. *averie*) | 1 | *Item for the avery of the galley or schippe the whyche ys to saye þat every marchaunt shall bere his parte after the rate of his marchauntyse for all manner of costes done upon þe galleys or schippe for cause of ennemyis to the savacondyd of the godys* (10l). | OED2 sub **average**[2] (2) *Auerays* att. 1491 | X |
| **Ditto** 'in the aforesaid month'[3] < It. *ditto* | 31 | *Item le 11 ditto, send by usaunce to London a st. 45 le doc., a Sebestyane et Jerolimis Bawdwere, for here hadde hit Vittore Capelle and his brotherys: £10* (31d). | OED2 sub **ditto** (1) Att. 1625 | X |
| **Grossy** 'Silver coins from Venice'[4] < It. *grossi* | 3 | *Firste Alaman Salviati of Florens send by echaunge for the parte of the conto aboveseyd signato G le xxx jour de janever 1450, at usaunce pour £100 de Grossy de Venecia to Johan Russelay [...]* (29b). | X | X |
| **Magasyne** 'warehouse for merchandise'[5] < It. *magazzino* | 1 | *A item for weynge in the custome house of Florens and for the berynge to the magasyne, .2 de pez. pour poke que fa £46 s.12 de pez., valeno: fl. 10 s. 28 d.* (11n). | OED3 sub **magazine** (1a) Att. 1583 | X |
| **Pezoly** 'small, low value coin of copper-silver mix'[6] < Fior. *piccioli* / Ven. *pizoli* | 2 | *Item for the custome of Florens for the seyd 466 pokes, weyng lb 123067 a fl. uno, s.16 de pezoly le C. que fa fl.1230.* (11d). | X | X |
| **Tare** 'weight of packaging deducted from gross'[7] < It. *tara* (pl. *tare*) | 1 | *The whyche makyth in sackys CC$^{o}$ lxiiij$^{o}$ semis and v cloves semis, of the whyche ys rebatyd for the tare of every poke, j clove semis* (7a). | OED2 sub **tare**[2] (a) Att. 1486 | MED sub **tare**[2] Att. 1379–80 (Grocers' accounts, AF) Att. 1429 (Grocers' accounts, ME) |

[1] It is notable that three of these loanwords (*avery*, *magasyne*, *tare*) are ultimately from Arabic – testimony to the Italian peninsula's extensive trading empire in the late Middle Ages.
[2] See TLIO **avaria**. Genoese *avaria* (from Arabic *awwar*, 'to damage') was borrowed into CF and first appears in a commercial document in 1498 (DMF sub **avarie**); the word's history is described in detail by Vidos (*Parole marinaresche italiane*, pp. 218–24).

Table 3 summarises six semantic loans from the field of trade and finance which are present in the accounts. These are defined as the borrowing of a meaning from the donor language so that a pre-existing form in the recipient language develops a new use. At first sight, they may not seem as dramatic a signal of Italianisation as the loanwords above but on, closer inspection, the strong influence of the Tuscan commercial lexicon on Balmayn's writing becomes increasingly evident. In three of the cases – *exchaunge, net* and *usaunce* – the dictionaries include a handful of examples of the semantic loan in question in English texts prior to 1500 but they are extremely rare. *Provisione* is not recorded in Middle English and does not emerge until 1589. *Ostelage* is not currently found in the MED or the OED and *oste* is absent with the meaning Balmayn employs.

---

Here, Balmayn's *avery* is clearly borrowed from the Tuscan variant *averia* which he uses elsewhere in an Italian-matrix segment: *Item pour averia pour consely de mare* (11f).

[3] See OVI sub **ditto** – a Tuscan variant of the more common past participle *detto*, first used in this specific administrative sense in 1296. Balmayn's use of *ditto* is of great interest and an excellent example of Italian business language influencing an English writer's work much earlier than is documented at present. The current OED2 entry sub **ditto** records this commercial shorthand as entering English in 1625, 174 years after Balmayn wrote his accounts. In France, the Italianism *dito* makes its first appearance in Savary's *Dictionnaire du Commerce* even later, in 1723: see TLF sub **ditto** / FEW III: 70a sub **dicere** (cf. Hope, *Lexical Borrowing*, p. 360). In contemporary UK and US English, the term has persisted, especially in colloquial speech, to mean 'me too' (ironically, the modern Italian speaker would revert to Latin and say *idem*).

[4] See VTO sub **grosso** and Alan M. Stahl, *Zecca: the Mint of Venice in the Middle Ages* (Baltimore, Johns Hopkins University Press, 2000), pp. 16–27. A silver coin (literally *denaro grosso* or 'large penny'), introduced in Venice in 1202. Note that the diminutive form *grosset* (from *grossetto*) is found in the MED in a source describing Italian currencies by the traveller, William Wey: *Doketys, grotys, grosettis, and soldys of Venyse wyl go wel in Surrey* (MED sub **grosset**, att.?1458). The OED2 also has an entry sub **gross**[2] ('A name for various foreign coins (historically representing the medieval *grossus* or *groat*); e.g. the German *groschen* and the Italian *grosso*, worth about 3d') with earliest citation dating from 1638.

[5] See TLIO sub **magazzino**. This is another Italian commercial term of ultimate Arabic origin (from *makzan* / *makzin* or 'storehouse') and Balmayn repeats the Italian equivalent elsewhere in the accounts: *Item pour magasino de le dyd lane* (11k). The OED3's earliest example dates from 132 years later and the loanword is classed as an indirect Italianism which entered English via the Middle French, *magasin*. In the case of the Cantelowe accounts, however, the donor language is unequivocally Italian.

[6] See OVI sub **piccioli / picciolini / pizoli**. Note that the coin name variants *pechelyne and pychelyne* (derived from the Tuscan diminutive *picciolino)* are attested in two ME texts from c. 1440 – see MED sub **pecheline**.

[7] See TLIO sub **tara**. There is only one clear ME phrase which uses *tare* in the accounts. However, it appears hundreds of times in the Italian-matrix buyers' entries where it is frequently abbreviated to *tar*- or simply *t*-. *Tare* (ultimately from Arabic *tarah*, 'to throw away') is found in just two other sources in England prior to 1450, both with strong Italian links. These are the accounts of the Worshipful Company of Grocers (in AF-matrix in 1379 and in ME-matrix in 1429) and in several hosting accounts in the VOH from 1440–4 (see Tiddeman, 'More Sugar and Spice').

**Table 3** Semantic loans in the Cantelowe accounts

| Lexeme | Freq. | Example | OED | MED |
|---|---|---|---|---|
| **Exchaunge**<br>'bill of exchange (authorising payment on merchant's behalf')[1]8<br>< It. *cambio* | 7 | *Memorandum that this ys the money send by exchaunge fro Florens by Alaman Salviati to Venice and to London [...] for the whyche the seyd Alaman Salviati hathe wretyne to Johan Russelay et Vanni Francisco de Strossy et compagnia de Venecia for to rescyve of divers personis as folewyth* (29a). | OED2 sub **exchange** (5)<br>Att. 1485 | MED sub **eschaunge** (2b)<br>Att. c. 1447 |
| **Net**<br>'amount or weight remaining'[2]<br>< It. *netto / netta* | 1 | *Þe whyche summa ys xiij sackys et xxiij cloves. And so reste clere <u>net</u>: cc° lj sackys cloves viij semis* (7a). | OED3 **sub net[4] / adj.** (3a)<br>Att. 1418 (Grocers' accounts, ME)<br>Att. 1486 (Cely Papers) | MED sub **net adj.**<br>Att. 1418 (Grocers' acounts, ME) |
| **Oste**<br>'host: receiver of goods who stores them temporarily'[3]<br>< It. *oste* | 1 | *Item for the provysyone of the oste of Lyvorne and for the unlading fro the schippe s.10 pour poke: summa £233* (10e). | X | X |
| **Ostelage**<br>'fee paid to host for receiving and storing goods'[4]<br>< It. *ostellaggio* | 1 | *Item for house hyre where the wolle stodde and for ostelage: fl.4* (10s). | X | X |
| **Provisione**<br>'commission paid to a broker, host or official'[5]<br><It. *provisione* | 2 | *Item for oure provesyone the viij parte of a floryne pour le poke: fl.58.5* (10u). | OED sub **provision** (4b)<br>Att. 1589 | X |
| **Usaunce**<br>'period of time in which bill of exchange must be paid'[6]<br>< It. *usanza* | 30 | *Item le 19 de le dyd, we have wretyne to themeselfe to make credens for ij days length past the usaunce at Brugens a gr.52 ¾ and to make us dettours: £33* (31u). | OED sub **usance** (4)<br>Att. 1487 (Cely Lett.) | X |

[1] See TLIO *cambio* and Edler, *Mediaeval Terms of Business,* p. 56. *Cambio* was used to describe exchange of actual currency and also as a shortened form of *lettera di cambio* or 'bill of exchange', the written document authorising payment on a merchant's behalf by another party. Balmayn clearly states that the exchange transactions he records are carried out 'by exchange' (i.e. via a bill of exchange) with payment due within a usuance period (see below) of 15 days *a vista da lettera* (i.e. from receiving the bill). Employing *exchange* in this way is rare in ME and the OED2 has two citations of the semantic loan from 1485, both from William Caxton's translation of the French work *Paris and Vienne.* See also Rainer, 'Le rôle de l'italien', a study which amply demonstrates the heavy influence Italian exerted on CF terminology relating to the bill of exchange. He presents over eighty semantic loans calqued from Italian; most date from the 1500s and 1600s but CF *lettre de change* < It. *lettera di cambio* dates from 1400–01. The same term can be found in the AND2 sub **change** in the Port Books of Southampton in 1430, where the water bailiff, Robert Florys, worked frequently with resident and incoming Italian merchants: *iij letrez de change, come il apiert par j bille endenté.*

[2] See OVI sub **netto / netta** and Edler, *Mediaeval Terms of Business*, pp. 191–2. Like *tare* (see above), *net* only appears once in an ME-matrix phrase but appears frequently throughout the mixed-language text in abbreviated form (n$^{t}$). On six occasions, our author clearly writes the Italian version out in full – *netta* – at the end of a buyer's entry. ME had already inherited the word *net* from AF to mean physical or spiritual cleanliness: see AND2 sub **net**$^{1}$ / OED3 sub **net**$^{4}$ / MED **net** (adj.). The additional meaning of a 'clean' weight or sum of money (i.e. after deductions are taken from the gross) first appears in Italian accounts from the start of the fourteenth century. We find only one attestation of this financial usage in the OED and the MED prior to 1450: in the ME-matrix Grocers' accounts. To this can be added a new example from a hosting account of Florentine and Venetian merchants from 1442–3 (see Tiddeman, 'More Sugar and Spice').

[3] See OVI sub **oste** and Edler, *Mediaeval Terms of Business,* p. 198. The better-known meanings of host (i.e. a guest or the receiver of a guest) are, unsurprisingly, widely attested in late medieval England: see AND2 sub **oste**$^{1}$, OED2 **host**$^{2}$, MED sub **host(e)**$^{2}$, DMLBS sub **hospes**. Balmayn's specific use of *oste* to refer to the person who houses merchandise temporarily (which occurs frequently in Italian records) seems to be, so far, unique.

[4] See TLIO sub **ostellaggio** and Edler, *Mediaeval Terms of Business*, p. 198. There are no entries at all in the MED / OED / DMLBS for *ostelage* but is attested in the AND2 sub **[ostelage]** in 1330 in the sense of 'lodging, provision of overnight accommodation'.

[5] See OVI sub **prov(v)isione / privigione** and Edler, *Mediaeval Terms of Business*, p. 227. The specific financial use of the term to mean 'commission' is currently unattested in the OED3 until 1589: 'to receave the like sum in the currant money of that Cuntrie, without any manner of provision as the merchantes call it [...]' (OED3 sub **provision** 4b). Balmayn uses it four times in the accounts, twice in ME and twice in Italian: *Item pour nostra provisione* (11m / 31bb).

[6] See OVI sub **usanza** and Edler, *Mediaeval Terms of Business,* p. 306. *Usaunce* is used regularly in this specific financial sense by Balmayn throughout the lists recording the bills of exchange sent between Venice, Bruges and London. In the Cantelowe accounts, the official time period for payment seems to be fifteen days (see 30k, k–m). We find only one ME citation of this meaning for *usaunce* in the OED3 from the accounts of the wool-trading Cely family in 1487: *haue made yow over be exchaunge..an Ciiijxx nobullys sterlyng, payabull at vsaunce. Usuance* already existed in ME and AF to mean 'customary practice or use' from the mid fourteenth century onwards (see AND sub **usance** / OED3 sub **usance** / MED sub **usaunce**). The DMLBS entry sub **usancia** gives one attestation of the commercial sense (*ad. duplicem usanciam viz. ad finem duroum mensium*) but the source dates from the sixteenth century.

# 5
# Numeral use

Balmayn's immersion in Tuscan mercantile culture was not limited to the lexical. Another exciting feature of the Cantelowe accounts is their extended use of Arabic numerals, some fifty years at least, it seems, before they even started to gain wider acceptance in English accounts (for examples, see Fig. 2a and 2b below). Italy was at the forefront of mathematical advances in Europe, acting through its geographical and trade links as a bridge to the advanced civilisations and scholarly practices of the East. The earliest evidence of Arabic numerals in medieval Europe (or more correctly, Hindu-Arabic or Indo-Arabic numerals) is found in a tenth-century Spanish manuscript, followed by a Sicilian coin from 1138. However, it was the Latin treatise of Leonardo of Pisa, better known as Fibonacci, that would prove pivotal in introducing this new system to the West.[1] After spending several years in Algeria with his merchant father and travelling in Egypt, Syria, Greece and Sicily, Fibonacci returned home an enthusiastic convert to Arabic arithmetic. His famous and lengthy *Liber abaci*, written in 1202, opened with the nine Indian figures and the zero symbol, an entirely new concept in itself.[2] The mathematical historian Carl Boyer declared that the work represented 'a remarkable achievement', containing, amongst other feats, 'the most accurate European approximation to an irrational root of an algebraic equation up to that time or anywhere in Europe for another 300 years or more'.[3] Notably, Fibonacci

[1] See John W. Durham, 'The Introduction of "Arabic" Numerals in European Accounting', *The Accounting Historians Journal*, 19 (1992), 25–55.

[2] 'An idea of the puzzlement that the zero caused can be gained from a note in a late twelfth century manuscript now in Cambridge, in which, among the several names given to the new symbol, is the 'chimaera', the imaginary beast of mythology' (Charles Burnett, *Numerals and Arithmetic in the Middle Ages* (Aldershot, Ashgate Variorum, 2010), ch. IX, p. 16). Similarly, a mathematical treatise from the early thirteenth century, written by a monk at Tewkesbury Abbey, compares Roman numerals with the new Indian figures but includes errors which show the scribe misunderstood some key concepts (Burnett, *Numerals and Arithmetic*, ch. IX, p. 18). Note also that Arabic numerals can be found in a Latin translation of an Arabic treatise on astrology and alphanumerical notation from as early as 1160 which is housed in the British Museum. However, the work was written in Italy and even contains an annotation in a Tuscan dialect (most probably Lucchese). This extremely early example of the Italian vernacular has escaped the attention of the major philological authorities in Italy (Burnett, *Numerals and Arithmetic*, ch. X, p. 80).

[3] Carl Boyer, *A History of Mathematics* (New York, John Wiley & Sons, 1968), p. 282.

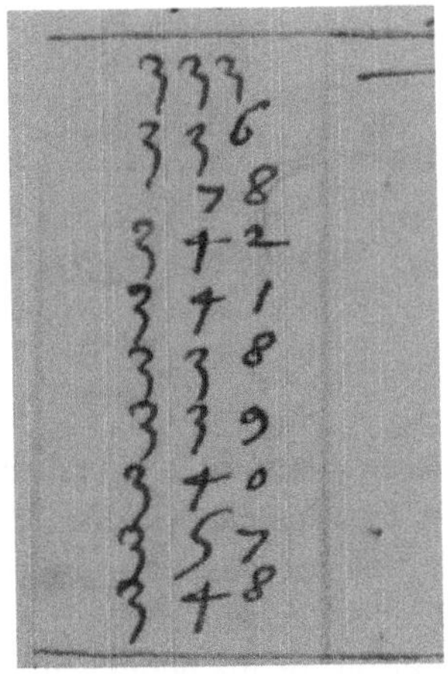

**Fig. 2a** Example of Balmayn's use of Arabic numerals

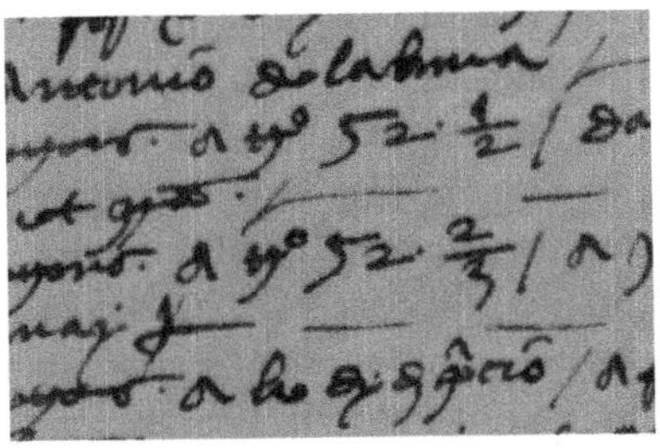

**Fig. 2b** Example of Balmayn's use of modern fractions

started out not as a scholar but as a merchant and the *Liber abaci* used numerous commercial examples such as currency conversions and interest calculations to present its theories.

Ground-breaking as it was, however, it took some time for Fibonacci's 'new' numerical notation to filter into widespread practice in Italy, and even longer in the rest of Europe.[4] The tradition of Roman numerals was deeply entrenched in the merchant world, in spite of the difficulties in using them for complex arithmetic, and suspicions were (rightly) aroused that Arabic figures could be more

[4] 'The introduction of 'Arabic' numerals in the West is much more complicated than is usually presented. [….] There is little doubt that 'Arabic' numerals were well known to academic circles by the eleventh century; the introduction of the new numeration system to bookkeeping seems to have occurred primarily in the late fifteenth century. The first examples are actually early fourteenth century from Italian sources. However, the introduction was slow, most fifteenth-century books of account use Roman numerals; 'Arabic' numerals are not standard until the late sixteenth century' (Durham, 'Arabic Numerals', 26).

easily falsified. The Florentine *Arte del Cambio* even famously forbade their use all public accounts in 1299 and issued fines for non-compliance, insisting that guild members 'write openly and at length using letters'.[5]

Whilst there was no English parallel for this express prohibition, 'it was not until the 16th century was well advanced that they began to be generally employed for the purposes of calculation; and even in their capacity of mere graphic alternatives for Roman figures they are not really common in English documents before about 1530.'[6] Whilst there are confirmed early specimens in non-academic, legal documents such as the Shropshire Eyre Rolls of 1256 and 1296,[7] it appears that the earliest examples of Arabic numerals in merchant records in England were written by Tuscans, as for example in the Gallerani London Book (1305–08)[8] or three annotations scribbled in Italian hand on BML / AF Exchequer Rolls concerning allowances claimed by the Frescobaldi in 1309 and the Bardi in 1339–45.[9]

From the 1380s in Italy itself, we find more numerous examples of Arabic numerals, alongside the Roman traditional notation, within the main body of Italian account entries in dates, weights and sums of money. The following example, from a list of accounts for a shipment of grain from Palermo to Pisa in 1386, clearly shows the scribe's dual use of Arabic (in bold) and Roman (underlined) figures:

> per ispese di mangare e di bere, da dì **9** d'ahgosto infino dì **21** novembre, per dare a 'Righo per beveraggo, che fu quegli fece vendere il grano, f.x: soma f. **29** et tt. **31** gr. v a tt. vi il f., sono f. **34** tt. 1 gr. v: f. **34** tt. **1** gr. **5**[10]

By the time Balmayn visited Tuscany in 1451, the new notation was spreading rapidly in business writing there and certainly within the Salviati's own accounts.[11] Arabic numerals form an extensive and integral part of the Cantelowe accounts,

[5] Alexander Murray, *Reason and Society in the Middle Ages* (Oxford, Clarendon Press, 1978), p. 84.

[6] Leonard Charles Hector, *The Handwriting of English Documents*, 2nd edn (Dorking, Kohler & Coombes Ltd, 1980), p. 43.

[7] It is difficult to date the earliest Arabic numerals used in government records accurately as they were nearly always used to number the folios or rolls and added at a much later date (Hector, *Handwriting*, p. 43; Hilary Jenkinson, 'The Use of Arabic and Roman Numerals in English Archives', *The Antiquaries' Journal*, 6 (1926), 263–75 at 266).

[8] In Bigwood and Grunzweig, *Les livres*, all figures are transcribed with Arabic numerals and the footnote 'en chiffres arabes dans l'original' is added to signal a departure from Roman numerals. Overall, there are more than fifty instances in the Gallerani *Libro di Londra* where the newer Arabic notation is used, principally (but not always) for writing dates.

[9] Bell *et al.*, *Accounts of the English Crown*, p. xvi.

[10] Melis, *Documenti per la storia economica,* p. 280 (*Estratto-conto del luglio 1386, Palermo-Pisa, da Ambrogio Bini all'azienda Datini*). Melis does not differentiate between the two systems in his transcription and uses Arabic numerals throughout. I have re-inserted Roman numerals based on the facsimile of the corresponding manuscript (p. 281).

[11] Cf. Cavallaro, 'Jacopo di Alamanno Salviati', p. 33.

being used to record all amounts paid in florins and pounds sterling and their totals, all weights of the pokes of wool and tare to be deducted and nearly all the poke numbers. Opening paragraphs in ME contain examples of both systems.[12] Roman numerals feature most heavily (unsurprisingly) in the Latin-matrix sections on pp. 8–9 and in dates throughout the document. One intriguing point is that the writer nearly always writes an AF date with Roman figures and an Italian one with Arabic figures, e.g. *le xiij jour de novembre / a dì 13 novembre.*[13] This would suggest that at some level, Balmayn associates the new style of numbers with the Italian language and the traditional method with his English scribal background. Furthermore, the manner in which he actually forms the figures also deserves attention, in particular his clearly upright number four (which is known to have first emerged in Italy in the fourteenth century) and his sevens and zeros.[14]

Back home in England, numerical conventions would take over half a century to catch up. In 1926 Jenkinson commented that the use of Arabic numerals 'at any date before the late fifteenth century may be taken as fairly strong evidence of foreign influence' and that 'in the period after 1500 Arabic figures begin slowly to fight their way into English Archives i.e. into business writings'.[15] The seventy-four surviving accounts in the Views of the Hosts from 1440–4[16] do not contain a single Arabic numeral and neither do the Goldsmiths' Accounts from 1334–1446.[17] Their appearance in the administration of the Mercers is described as 'remarkable as not common at all in this period' and the figures 'are not found with any frequency until the sixteenth century'.[18] So rare is each occurrence, that the editor footnotes each one. In an edition of over 1000 pages, there are only twenty-eight instances with the earliest being in 1397–98.[19]

12 E.g. *Here bygynnyth the weyȝths of iiij^c lxvj pokys wolle* (3a) / *Costes of Florens for 466 pokis wolle of my mayster W. Cantelowe* (11a).

13 In over one hundred dates written in the accounts, there are only eight that do not follow this pattern: two of them (18a, 18c) are of the type *a dì* + [Roman] and six of them (10v, 13e, 14a, 25a, 29j, 31p) are of the type *le* + [Arabic] + *jour.* ME matrix dates in the text always use Roman numerals e.g. *the lettres þat were made at London the xvij and xviij daye of June* (33d).

14 Over a century ago, Hill meticulously compiled a series of tables that are still useful today, comparing the varying forms of the fledging Arabic figures in medieval documents from across Europe: Georges Francis Hill, *The Development of Arabic Numerals in Europe* (Oxford, Clarendon Press, 1911). Balmayn's number fours and sevens (similar to our modern forms) and zeros (without a diagonal line through them) resemble the predominant fifteenth-century Italian forms (pp. 46–49) rather than their English equivalents (pp. 38–41). Professor John Crossley (Monash University), an expert in Historical Mathematics, has confirmed that Balmayn's number forms are 'remarkably modern' (private email correspondence).

15 Jenkinson, 'Arabic and Roman Numerals', 263.

16 Bradley, *Views of the Hosts.*

17 Lisa Jefferson, *Wardens' Accounts and Court Minute Books of the Goldsmiths' Mistery of London, 1334–1446* (Woodbridge, Boydell and Brewer, 2003).

18 Jefferson, *Mercers of London*, p. 11.

19 Subsequently in those for 1398–9, 1399–1400, 1408–9, 1413–14, 1414–15, 1415–16, 1418–19, 1420–1, 1453–4, 1455–6, 1457–8, 1461–2 and 1462–4: Jefferson, *Mercers of London.* As the

Only five of these Arabic numbers are found on their own in the main body of the text (rather than marginalia repeating an existing Roman figure) and only one of these five is before 1455, in a notable example from 1414.[20]

Similarly, other London livery company accounts from the mid-fifteenth century, even those in ME-matrix, show a near total dominance of the traditional Roman numerals, as shown by this example from the Drapers' Masters and Wardens' Accounts in 1439–40:[21]

| | |
|---|---|
| Thys accompt ys made the ix day of Nouembre the xix$^{the}$ yer' of kyng Harry the vj$^{the}$ by John Gedney maist*er* John Wotton John Derby Robert Bertyn & Thom*as* Cook Wardeynes of th*e* craft of draperes for the yer last past ffurst resceyued by the accompt of the olde Wardeynes in the box | xvj$^{li}$ x$^{s}$ |
| Also resceyued of diu*ers* p*er*sonys for fynys y mad for the feyr of seynt mary overey as hit enseweth | |
| Of Richard Thornebery | xx$^{d}$ |
| Of Edmund Miles | iiij$^{d}$ |
| Of Wylli*am* Cornewyk | viij$^{d}$ |
| Of John Hille | iiij$^{d}$ |
| Of Rob*ert* Awnell | iiij$^{d}$ |

Even in the late fifteenth century and into the sixteenth century, widescale Roman numeral use persisted. We do find a few examples of Arabic numerals in the Southampton Stewards' Books, with the earliest appearing in the book of 1457–8. But as Thick notes in her edition, such instances are rare and 'usually only as an addition in the right-hand bottom corner of a page, perhaps a total added at audit' and the new figures were 'introduced only slowly to government accounting. Known as the "vulgar cipher", they were considered improper for official use in spite of their greater flexibility for use in bookkeeping'.[22] In the collection of ME letters and wool accounts belonging to the wealthy Cely family from 1472–88, no Arabic figures are found although 'William Rogers [...] sometimes uses Arabic symbols in auditing their accounts for the Chancery arbiters'.[23] Fifty years later, the ledger (1538–55) of the successful Bristol merchant John Smythe contains a

thirty-year gap over the 1420s to 1450s testifies, Arabic numeral use very much depended on the knowledge of an individual scribe and this was typical of all ME accounts of the period.

[20] Jefferson, *Mercers of London*, p. 270.

[21] Arthur Johnson, *The History of the Worshipful Company of the Drapers of London* (Oxford, Clarendon Press, 1914), p. 333.

[22] Thick, 'Stewards' Books', p. 71.

[23] Alison Hanham, *The Celys and their World. An English Merchant Family of the Fifteenth Century*, 2nd edn (Cambridge, Cambridge University Press, 2002), p. 165.

mixture of Roman and Arabic figures, although interestingly, he always uses the latter when dealing with the *maravedi*, an Iberian coin of Moorish origin.[24] Arabic numerals did not appear on English coins until 1551[25] or on cloth seals, used as an official stamp of quality (see Part 6, below), until the early seventeenth century, in the reign of James I.[26]

Another important point of interest is the appearance of common fractions in the Cantelowe accounts, an innovation which, of course, did not exist in the Roman system.[27] Common (or vulgar) fractions (e.g. ½ or ¾), originally used to distinguish the fractions used in commerce from the sexagesimal ones used in astronomy, and their modern notation (with a horizontal bar) were also pioneered in Europe by Fibonacci.[28] Balmayn clearly uses this system, which had permeated Tuscan accounting by 1400, on six occasions, for example:

> It*em* po*ur* retenc*io*ne de denar*i* 2 de p*ez*. po*ur* fl., lo damno mownta po*ur* toto ¼ de fl. po*ur* C. q*ue* fa fl.63 s.23 d.5 de fl. (11l).
> It*em* le 13 ditto, send by usaunce to Lon*d*o*n* a st. **44 ½** a Lowes Strossy (31e).
> It*em* a d*ì* 11 ditto, send by usaunce to Bruges a gr. **52 ⅓** a Loronxo Banbo (31h).

The English scribe is far ahead of his contemporaries in this regard. Whilst fractions appear in an English treatise on the abacus (the anonymous *Reguncule super Abacum*) as early as ante 1115, we find no further record of them until 1543, in Robert Record's mathematical textbook, *Ground of Artes*. Even then, the author mentions the fraction or 'broken nomber' only very briefly and declares that its study is futile until the reader has grasped other methods of computational practice.[29] Fourteen years later in 1557, however, he does include the addition of fractions in his second treatise (*The Whetstone of Witte*) and they are shown with horizontal lines separating the numerator and the denominator.[30]

[24] Jean Vanes, *The Ledger of John Smythe, 1538–1550: from the Transcript made by John Angus* (London, Bristol Record Society, 1974), p. 19.
[25] Florian Cajori, *A History of Mathematical Notations*, 6th edn (New York, Dover Publications Inc., 1993), p. 50.
[26] Geoff Egan, *Provenanced Leaden Cloth Seals* Ph. D. thesis (University College, University of London, 1987), p. 28.
[27] The mathematical term *fraccioun* was first coined in ME by Chaucer in his scientific treatise *Astrolabe* c. 1400, (MED sub **fraccioun**). He also referred to Arabic numbers: *noumbres of augrim* i.e. 'of algorism'. Chaucer moved in both scholarly and mercantile circles but it would take over another century before such knowledge would be widely disseminated in his home country (Durham, 'Arabic numerals', p. 40).
[28] Boyer, *History of Mathematics*, p. 262; Cajori, *Mathematical Notations*, pp. 269, 310.
[29] Cf. Robert Steele, *The Earliest Arithmetics in English* (London, Early English Text Society, 1922), pp. xiv, 63, 68; Reginald Lane Poole, *The Exchequer in the Twelfth Century*, 2nd edn (London, Routledge, 2013), pp. 48–50. Hanham points out that English wool Staplers in Flanders in the late fifteenth century got round the need to use fractions in their calculations by using special monies of account: the *engelsc* (represented by a small open circle and equal to 1/3 d.) and the *point* (represented by large dot or diamond shape and equal to 1/3 of an *engelsc*) (Hanham, *The Celys*, p. 165).
[30] Cajori, *Mathematical Notations*, p. 164–6.

In other sections of the accounts, Balmayn employs different methods to express the concept of 'a half'. In entry 7a, he writes the traditional Roman numeral with an *s* abbreviation for *semis*. In the lengthy tables of wool weights on pages 3–7, we find an interesting hybrid system: a modern Arabic number followed by a colon divided by a horizontal line to represent a half. The latter symbol is confusingly similar to today's division sign but was common in the Middle Ages.[31]

Overall, Balmayn's extensive adoption of Arabic notation is exceptional for an ME scribe of his day and was a direct result of his working closely with and in the Italian business community. It is important to remember that what we consider now to be simple arithmetic – based on nine digits and a zero – represented 'a part of advanced mathematical education only' in 1450s England and that methods of bookkeeping at the time were based firmly on the centuries' old tradition of an abacus (or counting board).[32] The Cantelowe accounts are of particular importance to the history of arithmetic in England: with their use of both Arabic and Roman notation, they provide a valuable snapshot of an administrative culture in transition prior to the permanent establishment of new mathematical norms c. 1500.

[31] Adriano Cappelli, *Lexicon Abbreviaturarum: Dizionario delle abbreviazioni latine e italiane*, 6th edn (Milano, Ulrico Hoepli, 1979), pp. liv–lv. He also confirms that the modern ½ was not widespread in Europe until the end of the 15th century (pp. 46–7).

[32] Jenkinson, 'Arabic and Roman Numerals', 265. For a discussion of the use of the abacus as opposed to the newer method of writing the numbers directly onto a wax tablet, sand-covered tray or parchment, see Burnett, *Numerals and Arithmetic*, ch. IX, pp. 15–24.

# 6
# Merchant marks

Balmayn is very explicit that each poke of wool in the shipment is numbered and 'marked' with two forms of merchant mark. The first of these marks, which he refers to simply as the *signo contrasigno* ('countersign sign') on several occasions, is clearly designated in the text:

> First for iiij$^{c}$lxvi pochis wolle as folewyth aft*er* þe wey3t et rate of Florens and by of this marke † as for the salle of the wolle (12a).
> ij pok*es* w*ith* signo † *contra*signo and anothir pok*e* þat hadd*e* neyther nombyr nor marke (28b).
> and iij pok*es*, I markyd w*ith* signo *con*tr*a*signo of the marke of all*e* the balys (27f).

The † symbol appears nineteen times throughout the account books: on the front cover (see Fig. 3), in the top left-hand corner of many folios and within the entries themselves.

Although not explicitly stated, this must be the personal merchant mark of William Cantelowe, which is not currently found in English records.[1] The mark does not resemble that used for the Salviati family[2] but it is found in an entry in another account book from the Salviati's Florence office.[3] This records the

[1] The mark is not found in the Mercers' Company archives nor in the definitive work on the topic which catalogues hundreds of examples from 1400–1700 by the field archaelogist, Frank Aldous Girling: *English Merchants' Marks: a field survey of marks made by Merchants and Tradesmen in England between 1400 and 1700* (London, Oxford University Press, 1964). This is not surprising as extant examples represent a tiny handful of the thousands of marks that must have been in use in the Middle Ages: 'Marks in their everyday aspect were essentially ephemeral and few have survived. Some were painted on the canvas covering goods, others branded on the on the heads of casks. [….] Fortunately, a few contemporary representations of bales and wool packs, with the marks shown on them, remain to show the manner in which they were used' (p.18). In a more recent study on merchant marks in the Datini archive, Hayez concurs: 'Tracciate su dei supporti non destinati a una conservazione a lungo termine, tessili e cartacei in particolare, le marche mercantili sono in maggioranza andate perse nella loro materialità originale': Jérôme Hayez, 'Un segno fra altri segni. Forme, significati e usi della marca mercantile verso il 1400', in Elena Cecchi (ed), *Di mio nome e segno. 'Marche' di mercanti nel carteggio Datini (sec. XIV-XV)* (Prato, Istituto di Studi Storici Postali, 2010), pp. ix–xlvi at p. viii.

[2] See Philip Beale, Adrian Almond and Mike Scott Archer, *The Corsini Letters* (Stroud, Amberly, 2011), pp. 135–6.

[3] AS Serie I: 232, carta 131.

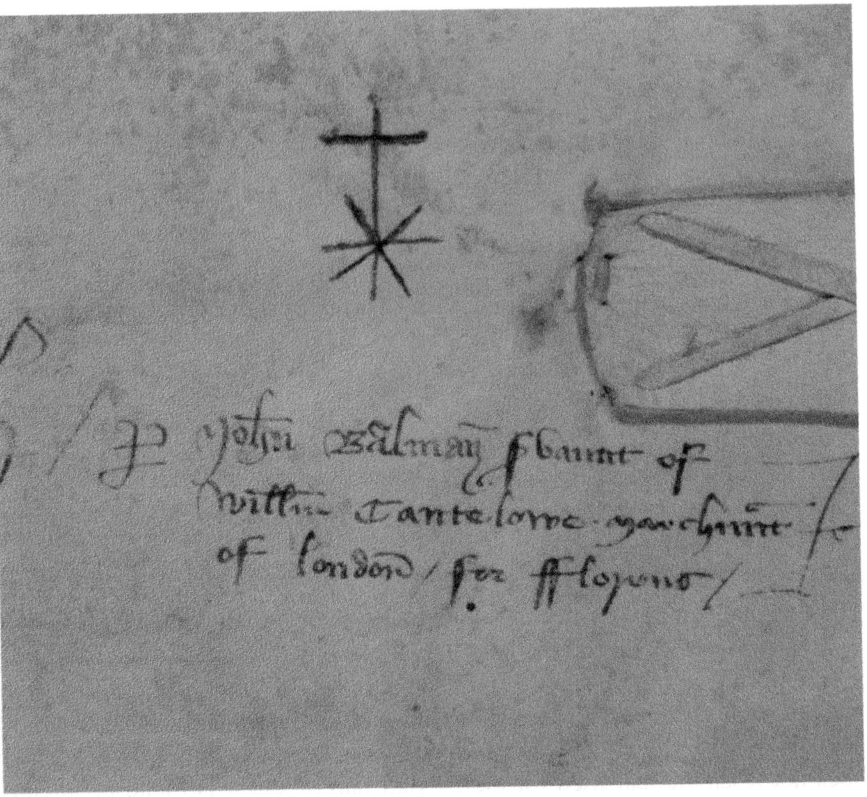

**Fig. 3** Cantelowe's merchant mark: the *signo contrasigno*

same 466 pokes (marked and countermarked) that arrived in Pisa on Antonio Doria's ship:

> Lana dinghilterra che e poiche quatrocento sesanta sei sign † e contrasangniata [sic] di piu contrasangni [sic] che ci mandono da pisa i nostri chebbono [sic] per la naue dantonio doria che di ragione de nostri di Londra per vno conto aparta sign G. [4]

It was common commercial practice in Europe to label woolsacks and other merchandise in this way. This established legal ownership of a particular bale of goods and crucially, made identification of the cargo as quick and easy as possible. When a ship arrived in port, it would frequently contain consignments belonging to numerous merchants who had each divided their goods between

[4] Holmes, 'Anglo-Florentine Trade', 375.

several vessels, given the high risk of piracy or shipwreck.[5] There were also strong religious (or superstitious) connotations with the use of such marks, which were thought to invoke divine protection on a commercial enterprise and the use of the cross shape, as in Cantelowe's case, was near ubiquitous.[6]

The additional twenty-six countermarks listed in the accounts are harder to identify. They contain a wide variety of symbols, including jays, peacocks, sheep, roses, poppies, borage flowers, stars, wreaths, bells and initials. As we have seen, Balmayn goes to great trouble to describe the mark of each lot of wool sold in the buyers' entries (pp. 12–28), as well as carefully summarising them in Latin over pp. 8–9. Table 4 (below) brings together the information we have about Cantelowe's shipment: poke numbers, wool types, Italian buyers and countermark descriptions. The latter is also very useful from a linguistic viewpoint as variations in our scribe's language choice for a particular mark can be easily compared. The shaded sections of the table refer to the Latin matrix summaries of the whole wool consignment near the start of the accounts; we can then 'track' the sale of each numbered, marked poke in the subsequent transactions recorded over the following eleven months. Upon examination of these data, the first key conclusion is that there is no obvious link between the Italian buyer and countermark; most of the companies – such as the Medici, Lachi, Cambini and Aliotto – purchase lots bearing different countermarks.

There is Italian documentary evidence of the practice of the use of the *contrasegna.* We find mentions in thirty-two citations in the digitised corpora of the *Opera del Vocabolario italiano* (OVI) and *Archivio Datini* (AD) but the descriptions are certainly not as detailed as Balmayn's. Overall, they give us little more information as to what this identifying mark was actually identifying. In nearly all cases the *contrasegna* is simply a number or a letter:

> *[...] Quattro torselli contrasegnati di* ***numero XXXIIII, XXXV, XXXVI, XXXVII*** (OVI: Doc. fior., 167.5) (1348–50)
> *Per detto Parasachino vi mandai balle 3 di merce sengnate di nostro sengo e contrasengnate* ***B*** (AD: Milano-Pisa B531/36 507066 296.6) (1395)

However, in the Datini databank there is one example of a lamb and two examples of a small anvil being employed as countermarks:

> *[...] coè balle 3 di nero chontrasegnata N e balle una* ***d'agnelina*** *contrasengnata* (AD: Pisa-Milano B1116/126 6100705 581.8) (1384)
> *150 peze de' fustani bianchi di 2 chandelieri con una* ***anchudinetta*** *per contrasengno* (AD: Milano-Genova B780/28 112591 315.5) (1396)

[5] Girling, *English Merchants' Marks,* p. 10; Beale *et al., Corsini Letters*, p. 19.
[6] Ninety per cent of the marks in the Datini archives, for example, are based on a cross sign of some kind, be it Latin, Greek, St Andrew's or St Anthony's, all embellished in countless ways with bars, loops or triangles (Hayez, 'Un segno fra altri segni,' p. xi).

In another rare example from 1399, Francesco Tornabuoni, of the Datini company, carefully draws a wide range of elaborate marks next to each entry for a consignment of wool bound to Pisa from Southampton. Again, beyond identifying each group of bales, it is not clear what the link is between mark, wool seller and wool buyer.[7]

In the case of the Cantelowe countermarks, we do not know for certain whether they were applied before the shipment left England or upon its arrival in Tuscany, as this is not made explicit in the text. It is possible that our scribe took extra care to record these merchant marks precisely because they were Italian and he (or his master) was unfamiliar with them. However, on balance, it seems much more likely that our writer's detailed record of the countermarks was more for the benefit of his Italian colleagues and that the twenty-seven marks were applied on the sacks in England; indeed Balmayn hints that their use is widespread: *ut moris est depingere lanas de Marchia* (8b).

Local historians in the late nineteenth and early twentieth centuries took a great interest in recording evidence of non-noble, personal marks in late medieval and early modern England. A particularly useful study, cataloguing examples from Cheshire and Lancashire, is provided by John Rylands' paper from 1911.[8] The author notes the wide range of different purposes for which such marks were employed, including signatures to documents (made with a pen or engraved seal);[9] indications of ownership of houses, furniture, farming equipment and livestock; commemoration of owners in church windows or on brasses; certification of craftsmanship on work (i.e. a precursor to the trademark); marking the wares of merchants. He also highlights that these were known as 'merchant marks' as early as the late fourteenth century, citing an extract from the poem *Piers Plowman* which describes monastery windows which 'Shynen with shapen sheldes, To shewen aboute, With merkes of merchants Y-medeled betweene'.[10] He also stresses that many medieval marks were deliberately designed to look heraldic in character and that by the early seventeenth century, regulations were written forbidding their placement on shields, a privilege reserved for coats of arms.[11]

Rylands provides reproductions of eighty-seven such heraldic-type merchant marks from 1280 to the early 1600s, copied from seals, church windows and

[7] A facsimile of the manuscript can be seen in Melis, *Documenti per la storia economica*, p. 327. Some of the marks are stylised crests, others are flowers, stars, initials or small grids.

[8] John Paul Rylands, 'Merchant Marks and Other Mediaeval Personal Marks', *Transactions of the Historic Society of Lancashire and Cheshire*, 62 (1911), 1–34. I am very grateful to Wendy Childs, Emeritus Professor at the University of Leeds, for sending me details of Rylands' paper.

[9] For a recent and extensive overview of all types of British medieval sigillography, see Phillipp Schofield (ed), *Seals and their Context in the Middle Ages* (Oxford, Oxbow, 2014).

[10] Rylands, 'Merchant Marks', 3.

[11] Rylands, 'Merchant Marks', 11.

**Table 4** Summary of wool types, poke numbers, Italian buyers and merchant marks

| Wool type (total in pokes) | Mark type | Poke no.[1] | Description of mark in text | Buyer | Ref. |
|---|---|---|---|---|---|
| **March (35)** | **Handmaiden** | **1–35** | **De numero j ad numerum xxxv: pockes xxxv de lana de la Marche fine, contrasignata de una ancella cum humeris de capite virginis, ut moris est depingere lanas de Marchia** | | **8b** |
| | | 2, 21, 25. | The marke una donzella | Sati | 20e |
| | | 4, 28, 35. | The marke una ancella cum humeris de capite virginis. | Chambini | 23d |
| | | 5, 9, 11, 15, 30. | The marke una ancilla cum humeris de capite virginis | Lamfredini / Guydetti | 23e |
| | | 19, 33. | The marke una donzella | Lachy | 23f |
| | | 3, 7, 13, 17, 20. | The marke una ancilla cum humeris de capite virginis | Bardy | 25a |
| | | 1, 10, 16, 23, 32. | The marke una ancilla cum humeris de capite virginis | Chorbenelli | 25b |
| | | 8, 14, 34. | The marke una donzella | Corbenelli | 25e |
| | | 22, 24, 26. | The marke una donzella | Chambini | 26a |
| | | 27, 31. | The marke una donzella | Bardy | 26b |
| | | 6, 18. | The marke una donzella | Fredericy | 26c |
| | | 12, 29. | The marke una donzella | Lamfredini | 26d |
| **Young March (6)** | **Handmaiden with coral necklace** | **36–41** | De n° xxxvi ad numerum xli: pokes vj de juvene lana de la Marche, contrasignata de una ancella ut supra cum uno pere precius duplice de coralle vermoille | | **8c** |

(*continued*)

**Table 4** (*cont.*)

| **Wool type (total in pokes)** | **Mark type** | **Poke no.**[1] | **Description of mark in text** | **Buyer** | **Ref.** |
|---|---|---|---|---|---|
| | | 36, 37, 39, 40, 41, 38. | w*ith* a maydyn*e* his head w*ith* a peyr of coralle bedis abowte her neke | Barbigia | 28a |
| **Cotswold (314)** | **Hand with bunch of roses with three leaves** | **42–69** | **De nº xlij ad num*erum* lxix: pock*es* xxviij de lana de Cotyswolde fyne co*ntra*signat*a* de una manu cu*m* j manipulo de rosis de tribus foliis** | | **8d** |
| | | 51, 52, 57, 69. | The mark*e* una manu cu*m* uno manipulo de rosis de trib*us* foliis | [G]wyduche | 12d |
| | | 43, 45, 48, 64. | The mark*e* una manu cu*m* uno manip*u*lo de rosis de trib*us* foliis | Rezaliti | 12e |
| | | 44, 46, 53, 56, 63. | The mark*e* de una manu cu*m* uno manipulo de rosis de trib*us* foliis | Ascheto | 13b |
| | | 47, 50, 54, 58, 66, 68. | The mark*e* j una manu cu*m* j manipulo de rosis de trib*us* foliis | Nycholini | 19b |
| | | 42, 49, 55, 59, 60, 61, 62, 65, 67. | The mark*e* una manu cu*m* j manip*u*lo de rosis de trib*us* foliis | Medeci | 22c |
| | **Sheep with crown** | **70–91** | **De nº lxx ad num*erum* lxxxxj: pock*es* xxij de lana de Cotyswold*e* fine co*ntra*signat*a* de uno pecore coronat*o*** | | **8e** |
| | | 76, 77, 80, 91. | The mark*e* uno pecore coronat*o* | Juncta | 12c |
| | | 71, 78, 81, 86, 87 | The marke uno peccore coronat*o* | Contowcho | 14c |
| | | 70, 72, 73, 74, 75, 79, 82, 83, 84, 85, 88, 89, 90. | The marke una peccora coronata | Patsy | 20c |

| | | | | |
|---|---|---|---|---|
| **Sheep with crown and its lamb** | **100–121** | **De nº C ad num*erum* Cxxj: pock*es* xxij de lana de Cotiswolde fine depinct*a* de uno pecore coronat*o* cu*m* suo agnello** | | **8g** |
| | 100, 101, 102, 103, 104, 105, 106, 107, 108, 109, 110, 111, 112, 113, 114, 115, 116, 117, 118, 119, 120, 121. | The mark*e* j$^{a}$ pecora coronata cu*m* suo agnello | Sandro [Barbigia] | 17a |
| **Green double wreath with four flowers** | **131–172** | **De nº Cxxxj ad num*erum* Clxxij: pok*es* xlij de lane fine de Cotyswolde depincta de una chapleta virid*e* duplic*e* cum quatuor floribus** | | **8j** |
| | 131, 136, 139, 141, 142, 145, 146, 152, 153, 156, 160, 161, 162, 171. | The mark*e* una chapleta verid*e* duplic*e* cu*m* quatuor flori*bus*. | Aleotti | 12b |
| | 134, 143, 147, 151, 166, 167, 169, 170. | The mark*e* ys una chapleta virid*e* duplic*e* cu*m* quatuor flori*bus* | Balioni | 15b |
| | 14, 132, 133, 135, 137, 138, 140, 144, 148, 149, 150, 154, 155, 157, 158, 163, 164, 165, 168, 172. | The mark*e* j chapleta v*iri*d*e* duplic*e* cu*m* iiij$^{or}$ flori*bus* | Ginori | 17b |
| **Blue garland with three flowers and red star** | **173 -194** | **De nº Clxxiij ad num*erum* Clxxxxiiij: pok*es* xxij de lana fine de Cotyswold*e* depincte de uno garlando asure videl*ice*t blod*e*[2] de tribus floribus et in medio dict*e* garlande est una stella rubia** | | **8k** |
| | 173, 174, 175, 176, 177, 178, 179, 180, 181, 182, 183, 184, 185, 186, 187, 188, 189, 190, 191, 192, 193, 194. | The mark*e* ys uno garland*o* asure vi*delicet* blod*e* de trib*us* flori*bus* et in medio dict*o* garland*o* est una stella rubia | Galiano | 15c |

*(continued)*

Table 4 (*cont.*)

| Wool type (total in pokes) | Mark type | Poke no.[1] | Description of mark in text | Buyer | Ref. |
|---|---|---|---|---|---|
| | **Peacock** | **195–222** | **De nº Clxxxxv ad num*erum* CCxxij: pok*es* xxviij de lana de Cotyswold*e* fine depincta de uno pavo, a pecok*e*** | | **8l** |
| | | 203, 204, 211, 214. | The mark*e* ys uno pavo | Juncta | 13e |
| | | 213, 216, 220, 222. | The mark*e* ys uno pavo | Borgo | 14a |
| | | 195, 197, 198, 199, 202, 206, 209, 217, 218, 221. | The mark*e* uno pavo | Lanfredini / Guydetti | 16a |
| | | 210. | The mark*e* uno pavo | Chambini | 19d |
| | | 200, 201, 207, 212. | The mark*e* uno pavo | Manetti | 22g |
| | | 196, 205, 208, 215, 219. | The mark*e* uno pavo | Lensy | 23c |
| | **Lamb of God with banner** | **288–345** | **De nº CClxxxviij ad num*erum* iij^c^xlv: pok*e* lviij de lana de Cotiswolde fine depinct*a* de uno agnus Dei cu*m* cruce in vexilla, a baner** | | **8s** |
| | | 294, 303, 326, 339, 341, 344. | The mark*e* ys de uno agnus Dei cu*m* cruce in vexilla | Loteni | 14b |
| | | 289, 290, 292, 296, 298, 316, 327, 328, 340, 342. | The mark*e* ys de uno agnus Dei cu*m* cruce in vexilla | Junctino | 14d |
| | | 299, 318, 333. | The mark*e* ys de uno agnus Dei cu*m* cruce in vexilla | Federisi | 16b |
| | | 291, 302, 317, 320. | The mark*e* ys de uno agnus Dei cu*m* cruce in vexilla | Medeci | 16d |
| | | 304, 313, 321, 338. | The mark*e* ys de uno agnus Dei cu*m* cruce in vexilla | Salustro (de Perosa) | 16e |
| | | 295, 306, 312, 323, 330, 331. | The mark*e* ys de uno agnus Dei cu*m* cruce in vexilla | Fantoni | 17d |
| | | 307, 319. | The mark*e* ys de uno agnus Dei cu*m* cruce in vexilla | Daszo | 18a |

| | | | | |
|---|---|---|---|---|
| | 308, 309, 311, 314, 324, 334, 335, 336, 345, 388. | The mark*e* ys de uno agnus Dei cu*m* cruce in vexilla | Constantino (da Perosa) | 18b |
| | 300, 310, 332, 337. | The mark*e* ys de uno agnus Dei cu*m* cruce in vexilla | Nycholini | 19c |
| | 305, 343. | The mark*e* ys de uno agnus Dei cu*m* cruce in vexilla | Chambini | 19e |
| | 293, 297, 301, 315, 322, 325, 329. | The mark*e* ys de uno agnus Dei cu*m* cruce in vexilla | Stuffa | 24c |
| **Bunch of five poppies labelled with *Laus Deo*** | **352–378** | **De n° iij$^{c}$lij ad num*erum* iij$^{c}$lxxviij: pok*es* xxvij de lana de Cotiswolde fine depinct*a* de uno manipulo de quinq*ue* popies cu*m* una sc*r*iptura que dicit Laus Deo** | | **8u** |
| | 367, 368, 369, 370, 373, 375. | The mark*e* j° mazzo de 5 papavery cu*m* breve q*ue* dixe Laus Deo | Albesi | 16c |
| | 361, 366, 377, 452. | The mark*e* j° manip*u*lo de quinq*ue* popeis cu*m* una sc*r*iptura que dicit Laus Deo | Spineli | 18c |
| | 356, 357, 364, 374. | The mark*e* j° manip*u*lo de quinq*ue* popeis cu*m* j sc*r*iptura que dicit Laus Deo | Fantoni | 18d |
| | 355, 359, 362, 365. | The mark*e* j° manip*u*lo de quinq*ue* popeis cu*m* una sc*r*iptura que dicit Laus Deo | Bewsini | 18e |
| | 354, 360, 371, 376. | The mark*e* j° manip*u*lo de quinq*ue* popeis cu*m* un*a* sc*r*iptura que dicit Laus Deo | Leonardo (d'Arezzo) | 19a |
| | 353, 358, 363. | The mark*e* j° manip*u*lo de quinq*ue* popeis cu*m* j sc*r*iptura que dicit Laus Deo | Resali | 21d |
| | 372. | The mark*e* j° manip*u*lo de quinq*ue* popeis cu*m* una sc*r*iptura que dicit Laus Deo | Medeci | 22e |
| | 378. | The mark*e* j manip*u*lo de quinq*ue* popeis cu*m* j sc*r*iptura que dicit Laus Deo | Medeci | 22f |

(*continued*)

Table 4 (*cont.*)

| Wool type (total in pokes) | Mark type | Poke no.[1] | Description of mark in text | Buyer | Ref. |
|---|---|---|---|---|---|
| | **Jay** | **381–408** | **De n° iij^c^lxxxj ad num*erum* iiij^c^viij: pok*es* xxviij de lana fyn*e* de Cotiswod*e* depinct*a* de uno jaye** | | **8x** |
| | | 382, 383, 386, 387, 388, 391, 393, 394, 396, 397, 406, 408. | The mark*e* una jaye | Corbenelli | 17c |
| | | 384, 392, 405, 407. | The mark*e* una jaye | Tore | 19f |
| | | 381, 385, 389, 390, 395, 398, 399, 400, 401, 402, 403, 404. | The mark*e* una jaye | Baldovini | 21c |
| | **Sun** | **422–450**[3] | **De n° iiij^c^xxij ad num*erum* CCCCl: pok*es* xxix de lana fyn de Cotyswold depinct*a* cu*m* uno sole, ang*lice* a sonne** | | **9c** |
| | | 426, 435, 437, 438, 440. | The mark*e* uno sole | Gwydewchy | 17e |
| | | 429, 430, 434, 434, 439, 441, 442, 446, 447, 448. | The mark*e* una sole | Ginori | 20a |
| | | 436. | The mark*e* una sole | Medeci | 22d |
| | | 422, 423, 424, 425, 427, 428, 433, 436, 443, 444, 445, 453. | The mark*e* uno sole | Stuffa | 24f |
| | **Hand with a bunch of borage with three leaves** | **1- 8**[4] | **De n° j ad num*erum* viij: pok*es* viij de lana de Cotiswolde fine vocat*a* storo depinct*a* de una manu quod tenet un*um* manipulu*m* de borage de trib*us* foliis** | | **9f** |
| | | j, ij, 3, 4, 5, 6, 7, 8. | 8 de borage | Barbigia | 28a |

| | | | | | |
|---|---|---|---|---|---|
| **Young Cotswold (85)** | **Sheep with crown and grass in its mouth** | **92–99**[5] | **De nº lxxxxij ad num*erum* lxxxxix: pok*es* viij de lana juv*ene* de Cotyswolde fyn*e* depinct*a* de uno pecor*e* coronat*o* quod h*ab*et in ore suo modicum de una herba** | | **8f** |
| | | 93, 94, 95, 96, 97, 98, 99. | The mark*e* una peccora coronat*a* quod h*ab*et in ore suo modicu*m* de una erba | Aleoti | 22a |
| | **Sheep with a crown, and its lamb and grass in its mouth** | **122 -130** | **De nº Cxxij ad num*erum* Cxxx: pok*es* ix de lana juv*ene* de Cotyswold*e* fine depincta de uno pecor*e* coronat*o* cu*m* suo agnello et pecus h*ab*et modicum de una herba in ore** | | **8h** |
| | | 122, 123, 128, 129, 130. | The mark*e* una peccora coronat*a* cu*m* suo agnello et pecus h*ab*et modicum de erba in ore | Barbigia | 25c |
| | | 124, 125, 126, 127. | The mark*e* una peccora coronat*a* cu*m* suo agnello et pec*us* h*ab*et modicum de erba in ore | Barbigia | 25d |
| | **Peacock with bell on left foot** | **223–233** | **De nº CCxxiij ad num*erum* CCxxxiij: pok*es* xi de lana fine juv*ene* de Cotyswold*e* depincta de uno pavo cum una campana ad pedem sinistrum** | | **8m** |
| | | 226, 228, 229, 230, 231. | The mark*e* de uno pavo et una campana ad pedem sinistrum | Bartoli | 15a |
| | | 224, 227. | The mark*e* uno pavo cu*m* j campana ad pedem sinistrum | Borgo | 20d |
| | | 223, 225, 232, 233. | The mark*e* uno pavo cu*m* j campana ad pedem sinistrum | Stuffa | 24e |
| | **Two green garlands with a rose** | **234–252** | **De nº CCxxxiiij ad num*erum* CClij: pok*es* xix de lana fine juv*ene* de Cotiswolde depincta de uno garlando virid*i* duplic*i* et in medio dict*i* garland*i* una rosa** | | **8n** |

*(continued)*

**Table 4** (*cont.*)

| **Wool type (total in pokes)** | **Mark type** | **Poke no.**[1] | **Description of mark in text** | **Buyer** | **Ref.** |
|---|---|---|---|---|---|
| | | 241, 246. | The mark*e* uno garland*o* virid*e* duplic*e* et in medio dict*i* garland*i* una rosa | Aleotti | 13c |
| | | 234, 238, 244, 245, 250, 251. | The marke uno garland*o* verid*e* duplic*e* et in medio dict*i* garland*i* una rosa sup*ra* | Aleotti | 13d |
| | | 236, 237, 243, 247, 248, 249. | The mark*e* u*no* garland*o* v*ir*id*e* duplic*e* et in medio dic*ti* garlandi una rosa | Lachy | 23b |
| | | 235, 239, 240, 242, 252. | The mark*e* j garland*o* v*ir*id*e* duplic*e* et in medio dict*i* garland*i* una rosa | Lachy | 24a |
| | **Hand with a straight little finger, holding bunch of roses and three leaves** | **253–264** | **De nº CCliij ad num*erum* CClxiiij: pok*es* xij de lana fine juv*ene* de Cotiswold*e* depinct*a* de una manu cum uno manipulo rosa*rum* de trib*us* foliis et digito auriculare stante recto** | | **8o** |
| | | 259, 261. | The marke ys una manu cu*m* una manipulo rosar*um* de trib*us* foliis et digito ariculare strawte rect*o* | Resalati | 13a |
| | | 253, 254, 255, 256, 257, 258, 260, 262, 263, 264. | The mark*e* jª manu cu*m* manip*u*lo de t*ri*b*us* foliis et digito ariculare stante rect*o* | Sandro [Barbigia] | 20b |
| | **Blue garland with three flowers, red star and 'O'** | **265–273** | **De nº CClxv ad num*erum* CClxxiij: pok*es* ix de lana fyn*e* juv*ene* de Cotiswold*e* depinct*a* de uno garlando asure blod*e* cu*m* t*ri*b*us* florib*us* et in medio garland*o* una stella rubia et in medio stelle iº O** | | **8p** |
| | | 265, 266, 267, 268, 269, 270, 271, 272, 273. | The mark*e* u*no* garland asure blod*e* cu*m* t*ri*b*us* florib*us* et in medio garland*o* una stella rubia et in medio stelle uno O. | Aleoti | 22b |

| | | | | | |
|---|---|---|---|---|---|
| | **Lamb of God without banner** | **346–351** | **De n° iij^c^xlvj ad num*erum* iij^c^lj: pok*es* vj de lane fine juvene de Cotiswolde depinct*a* de uno agnus Dei sine cruce in vexilla** | | **8t** |
| | | 348, 349. | The mark*e* uno agnus Dei sine cruce in vexilla | Spinelli | 20f |
| | | 346, 347, 350, 351. | The mark*e* uno agnus Dei sine cruce in vexilla | Pulesse | 21a |
| | **Bunch of five poppies and 'M'** | **379–380** | **De n° iij^c^lxxix ad num*erum* iij^c^lxxx: pok*es* ij de lana fyn*e* juv*ene* de Cotiswold*e* depinct*a* de uno manipulo de quinq*ue* popies et una M** | | **8w** |
| | | 380 | The mark*e* uno manip*u*lo de quinq*ue* popeis et de uno M | Aschetto | 21b |
| | | 379 | The mark*e* uno manip*u*lo de quinq*ue* popeis et de una M | Resali | 21e |
| | **Jay with grass in its mouth** | **409–410** | **De n° iiij^c^ix ad num*erum* CCCCx: pok*es* ij de lana fine juv*ene* de Cotiswode depinct*a* de una jaye cu*m* erba i*n* ore** | | **8y** |
| | | 409, 410. | The mark*e* una jaye cu*m* erba in ore | Baldoveny | 21f |
| | **Magpie** | **419–421** | **De n° iiij^c^ix ad num*erum* iiij^c^ xxj: pok*es* iij de lana fine juv*ene* de Cotiswold depinct*a* de uno pye** | | **9b** |
| | | 419, 420, 421. | The mark*e* una pye | Lachy | 27a |
| | **No countersign, only Cantelowe's mark: †** | **455–458**[6] | **De n° iiij^c^lv ad num*erum* iiij^c^lviij: pok*es* iiij de lana fine junv*ene* de Cotiswold quilib*et* poch*e* cu*m* duob*us* signis sine *con*trasignis su*n*t de bonitate de le jaye ut sup*ra*** | | **9e** |
| | | 455 | The mark*e* signo *con*trasigno | Lachy | 26e |
| | | 458, 457. | signo † *contra*signo | Barbigia | 28a |
| **Abbey (24)** | **Mitre with cross** | **274–285** | **De n° CClxxiiij ad CClxxxv: pok*es* xij de lana Abbathie *contra*signat*a* cu*m* uno mytro cu*m* cruce sup*ra*** | | **8q** |

(*continued*)

**Table 4** (*cont.*)

| **Wool type (total in pokes)** | **Mark type** | **Poke no.**[1] | **Description of mark in text** | **Buyer** | **Ref.** |
|---|---|---|---|---|---|
| | | 274, 276, 278, 279, 281, 285. | The mark*e* una mitra cu*m* cruce de sup*ra* | Lachy | 21g |
| | | 275, 277, 280, 282, 283, 284. | The mark*e* una mitra cu*m* cruce de sup*ra* | Lachy | 23a |
| | **Crosier** | **411–418** | **De n° CCCCxj ad num*erum* iiij$^{c}$xviij: pok*es* viij de lana Abbathie depinct*a* de uno pastorale, an abbot*s* croyse** | | **9a** |
| | | 411, 412, 413, 414, 415, 416, 417, 418. | The mark*e* a abbot ys crowysse | Lachy | 23g |
| | **Labelled 'storo'** | **451–454**[7] | **De n° CCCClj ad num*erum* iiij$^{c}$liiij: pok*es* iiij de lana Abbathie de illa sorte de pok*es* viij ut sup*ra* depinct*a* de una sc*ri*ptura sup*ra*scri*p*to storo** | | **9d** |
| | | 449, 450, 451, 452, 454. | The mark*e* una sc*ri*ptura sup*ra*scripto storo | Stuffa | 24d |
| **Young Abbey (2)** | **Mitre without cross** | **286–287** | **De n° CClxxxvi ad num*erum* Cclxxxvij: pok*es* ij de lana fine juv*ene* Abbathie depinct*a* de uno mitro sine cruce sup*ra*** | | **8r** |
| | | 286, 287. | The mark*e* una mitra sine cruce | Lachy | 24b |
| ? | ? | ? | the which hathe neyther marke nor nombyr[8] | Barbigia | 28a |
| **Total shipped = 466 pokes** | | **Total sold = 465 pokes** | | | |

1 Careful and methodical as he was, Balmayn still made mistakes in his accounts; there are a few mix-ups with marks and numbers, as we shall see, and the sale of one of the 466 pokes is never recorded.

2 'Dark blue colour': see DMLBS **blodius** / LCC **blod**. In this first instance, Balmayn clarifies *asure* with *videlicet blode* but in following section (pokes no. 265–273), he seems to use *blode* as a qualifier for *asure*. This itself is unusual, as is the fact that in the English record, the only examples of the colour refer to cloth.

3 There are several mistakes here. Pokes no. 450 and 453 seem to have been swapped in the main account as no. 450 is recorded with a *storo* mark (24d) and no. 453 with a sun (24f). No. 449 also appears in entry 24d in the *storo* batch. In addition, there are two pokes (with different weights) recorded as no. 434 in entry 20a and two copies of no. 436 in 22d and 24f. In each case, one of these numbers must have been miswritten. One of these extra pokes must be no. 431 and the other, no.432, neither of which are present in the subsequent account entries.

4 It is unclear why the sacks are numbered 1–458 and then 1–8 instead of 1–466.

5 Poke no. 92 is not recorded later as being sold in the buyers' section (pp. 12–27).

6 Poke no. 456 is not recorded later as being sold in the buyers' section (pp.12–27).

7 As discussed, there are five, not four, pokes marked with the *storo* label in the main account entries (see 24d).

8 This must be one of the missing pokes, either no. 92 or no. 456. The other one remains lost and is absent in the account entries, meaning the final tally of those sold is 465, not 466.

brasses, and including stylised initials, flowers, stars, bells, crowns, arrows and gloves (in the case of a glover). One example from 1584 shows a merchant mark framed by a bale of wool; another (undated) has a more stylised bale of wool and two wool hooks, used to handle the bales.[12] In a few further cases, a merchant's individual mark impales that of the Drapers' Company (three flaming clouds with crowns).[13] This feature is perhaps mirrored in some of the marks Balmayn describes which contain the Maiden's Head, emblem of the Mercers from 1425 onwards.[14]

It seems, therefore, that the woolsacks are countermarked to identify the producers from whom Cantelowe purchased his cargo to sell in Italy. In most cases, it is not clear which wool suppliers they represent, although we can assume that the mitre and crosier, used for the *lana Abbathie* or 'Abbey wool', represent monastic estates.

One puzzling aspect of the countermarks is that they can often be 'paired', with the young wool being a variant of the mark used for the normal wool of that type, as shown in Table 5, below. In most cases, the young wool version has an extra detail such as the peacock's bell or the maiden's necklace, sometimes it is a straight swap e.g. five poppies and *Laus Deo* for Cotswold, five poppies and the initial 'M' for young Cotswold. But this distinction is not clear-cut: the sun, borage and crosier marks have no variants and it is difficult to judge how to categorise the magpie and jay marks, given that the two birds were commonly interchangeable in medieval symbolism.

Even if we hypothesize that each producer of a certain wool type had two marks, one for the older and one for the younger wool, there seems to be no other evidence of such an elaborate double marking system or mention of such symbols in the heyday of medieval contracts for English wool.[15] Another tentative suggestion is that different family members may be countermarking the different kinds of wool supplied. Rylands notes that there was some evidence from the 1400s onwards of 'differenced marks' where which family members would add a figure (such as a crescent) or extra lines to adapt a shared common seal to distinguish themselves from each other.[16]

Overall, it seems plausible that Balmayn records the countermarks as a sort of quality control system, confirming the wool's provenance (and possibly

[12] Rylands, 'Merchant Marks', 27.
[13] Rylands, 'Merchant Marks', 21.
[14] Sutton, *Mercery of London*, p. 181. It is not made explicit in the text if the maiden mark to which Balmayn refers is the Maiden's Head of the Mercers company. As he also refers to the maiden's necklace on two occasions, we can suggest that the mark contains just her head but this is not certain. In English, Balmayn describes this mark as a *maydyne* but in Italian he uses both *donzella* ('young woman, virgin' or 'handmaiden') and *ancella* ('handmaiden').
[15] My thanks to Professor Adrian Bell, co-author of *The English Wool Market c. 1230–1327*, for confirming this.
[16] Rylands, 'Merchant Marks', 8–9.

**Table 5** Marks for 'normal' and 'young' wool types

| **March** | **Young March** |
|---|---|
| Maiden | Maiden + necklace |
| **Cotswold** | **Young Cotswold** |
| Hand + bunch of roses | Hand + straight finger + bunch of roses |
| Sheep + crown | Sheep + crown + grass in its mouth |
| Sheep + crown + lamb | Sheep + crown + lamb + grass in its mouth |
| Lamb of God with banner | Lamb of God without banner |
| Green double wreath + four flowers | Green double wreath + rose |
| Blue garland, 3 flowers + red star | Blue garland, 3 flowers + red star + 'O' |
| Peacock | Peacock + bell |
| 5 poppies + *Laus Deo* | 5 poppies + 'M' |
| Jay | Jay + grass in its mouth |
| X | Magpie |
| Sun | X |
| Bunch of borage | X |
| **Abbey** | **Young Abbey** |
| Mitre with cross | Mitre without cross |
| Crosier | X |
| Labelled 'storo' | X |

type) – this is further hinted at when the author states that a group of sacks with no countermark are of the same quality as those marked with a jay (9e).[17] He obviously considered this guarantee of quality important as he puts so much time and effort into detailing the countermark of each lot of wool sold. One last mystery is his inclusion of colour in these descriptions (blue, green and red). The whole point of the merchant mark was that, as Girling puts it, 'it could be made quickly with a few strokes of a brush'.[18] Are Balmayn's countermarks rare examples of a more time-consuming labelling system where different colours were applied to each woolsack? Or were colours reserved for the written descriptions only, with simpler, monochromatic versions of the marks being painted or stamped onto the

[17] There are potentially some parallels here with the *alnage* system of disposable lead seals used in the cloth industry for quality-control and taxation purposes from the fourteenth to the eighteenth century. Thousands such lead seals have been recovered through archaeological excavation with late medieval specimens consisting of a short strip linking two disks (or 'lobes') onto which symbols could be stamped using a special pair of stamping pliers. See Egan, 'Leaden Cloth Seals'; Walter Endrei and Geoff Egan, 'The Sealing of Cloth in Europe, with Special Reference of the English Evidence', *Textile History*, 13 (1982), 47–75.

[18] Girling, *English Merchants' Marks,* p. 10.

bales? Such questions concerning the marks' application and what (or who) they represent highlight the fact that the historical value of the Cantelowe accounts is far from exhausted. When combined with the opaque list of tare and 'dampness' deductions discussed above, it is obvious that this source still has more to offer experts in the English and Italian wool trade, over twenty-five years after Holmes first unearthed it in the Salviati archives.[19]

[19] Surprisingly, no mention is made of the merchant marks or the tare deductions in 'Anglo-Florentine Trade'.

# 7
# Concluding remarks

The Cantelowe accounts contain a surprising wealth of information for such a short manuscript. In addition to its obvious appeal to historical linguists, it is a valuable source for medieval historians in general, be they interested in the wool market, bills of exchange, merchant marks or the development of Arabic numeral use by English writers. All these points of interest result from the overlap of the English and Italian trading communities in the late Middle Ages, brought to light in unusual detail in this text.

In her still highly regarded monograph *Italian Merchants and Shipping in Southampton 1270–1600*, Ruddock stresses the importance of Italian influence on English business in the fifteenth century:

> [..] the prosperous fifteenth-century English merchant was no fool. The enterprising Englishmen who eventually forced a way into the Mediterranean for their shipping and merchandize, who before the fifteenth century drew to a close, had planted colonies of English factors in those parts [...] had also made themselves familiar with some of the techniques of Italian businessmen and were already employing some of the techniques in their own affairs [....] Translations of business manuals, reaching them from French or Flemish publications in the Low Countries, no doubt added a great deal to their knowledge of the finer points of book-keeping and accountancy in the sixteenth century, but it was by the practical experience in the previous century that the English merchants laid the foundations of their knowledge of the Italian methods of business. They acquired their knowledge not from books but from Italians living in their own community, buying and selling from them, acting as their factors overseas, sometimes entering their households and marrying into their families and in Southampton, if not elsewhere, holding municipal offices and exercising a very real influence on the lives of their English neighbours.[1]

Balmayn's records of his work in Tuscany offer a tangible example of precisely this kind of knowledge transfer. He does not use double-entry bookkeeping but the document still represents 'proof of contact': we can see how one author, immersed in Italian for professional reasons, learned the terms of the trade on

[1] Ruddock, *Italian Merchants*, pp. 199, 205.

the job and then how specific lexis (and indeed numeral use) filtered back into his own native writing. As stressed in the introduction, current evidence of such direct language contact between English and Italian dialects that predates the sixteenth century is extremely rare. The Cantelowe accounts provide a glimpse of English merchant practice in 1450, a practice that has just shifted from AF into ME and one that was increasingly eager to embrace the methods of the undisputed leaders in European commerce.

Judging Balmayn's writing is a delicate area. From the 1990s onwards, there has been a backlash against the ideological stance that mixed-language medieval records must be the result of scribal ignorance or eccentricity. It is an ideology

> [...] that values uniformity and purity above all things. If texts are 'dirty', then they have to be cleansed. Variation is ignored and dismissed again and again in the tradition because it is viewed as random or accidental, or a result of ignorance and incompetence on the part of the scribes Yet it is arrogant to believe that a modern editor can know Middle English better than a medieval scribe did.[2]

But the Cantelowe accounts represent a new kind of medieval multilingual source from England, given that Italian was not part of England's longstanding scribal heritage. No research has been done into 'second language' Italian written by ME speakers, indeed non-native writing is an area which has barely been touched. As we have seen, it is impossible to tell if we are dealing with a new mixed code as, unlike standard trilingual English business texts, we have nothing to compare to this scribe's language use.

We can only resolve to judge Balmayn's language on its own terms and ask if it fulfilled the function of its text type. The answer, I believe, is yes, and in wide lexical detail. It is true that there are minor slips in article use and gender but in the majority of cases, the writer employs clear business Italian. His anglicized spelling and English hand may alarm the Italian medievalist (and no-one is suggesting that Balmayn is a poet to rival Boccaccio) but within the parameters of his profession, he seems more than competent. This, of course, should come as no surprise: one would wonder why he would be sent to Italy to oversee a valuable sale if he could not acquit himself well in the language. As Bradley says of London merchant society, 'It was a literate, numerate and intensely skilled practical world, and its entire purpose was to cross national boundaries'.[3]

[2] Jim Milroy, 'The ideology of a standard language', in Laura Wright (ed), *The Development of Standard English, 1300–1800: Theories, Descriptions, Conflicts* (Cambridge, Cambridge University Press, 2006), pp. 11–28 at p. 21. For related arguments, see also Laura Wright, 'The Records of Hanseatic Merchants: Ignorant, Sleepy or Degenerate?', *Multilingua,* 16 (1997), 339–50; William Rothwell, 'Ignorant Scribe and Learned Editor: Patterns of Textual Error in Editions of Anglo-French Texts', Anglo-Norman On-Line Hub, April 2004, http://www.anglo-norman.net/articlesA/scribe.xml.
[3] Bradley, 'Saluti da Londra', p. 103.

Fascinating questions remain concerning his professional education and whether he had been to Italy before. We know nothing about Balmayn's background or experience, but we do know that German merchants went to Italy specifically to receive training in the latest techniques:

> From the fourteenth century on, merchants from the north travelled to Italy, particularly to Venice, to learn the *Arte dela mercandanta* of the Italians. Sons of German businessmen flocked to Venice to study the *Welsche Praktik*, the foreign practices of business, commercial arithmetic and currency exchange. After acquiring these skills, they returned home with such terms as *disagio*, discount, *credito*, credit, *valuta*, value, *netto*, at a net price etc.[4]

Evidence from c. 1493–1500 also exists of at least one draper's son from London being sent to Pisa, specifically to be schooled in Italian and accounting, while a Florentine immigrant to Southampton, Cristoforo Ambruogi, took in and taught local youths 'the practices of merchanting'.[5] Bradley emphasizes that the 'Italian citizens of London [...] provided an important link between the English and Italian communities by educating the next generation of young Englishmen in their trade': the Worshipful Company of Grocers included a Lucchese, Vivian Roger, as a founding member, and he took on four English apprentices into his staff in 1348.[6] Similarly, the same company was partly run in 1428 by Italians who also trained English apprentices and a 'select band of Italian entrepreneurs' continued to be sponsored there throughout the fifteenth century.[7]

Balmayn's clearly English handwriting implies that he was not formally trained to write in Italy but learnt the language as an adult. The same is true of his spelling, which suggests he was learning 'on the ground' with Tuscan colleagues, and, at times, producing his best approximation of vocabulary. From the accounts, we know that Balmayn discussed business with Jacob[8] and it seems very likely that he worked with Francesco and Giovanni Salviati of the Pisa branch and with their father, Alamanno, from the head office in Florence too.[9] It

[4] Frank Swetz, *Capitalisation and Arithmetic: the New Math of the 15th Century* (La Salle IL, Open Court, 1987), p. 10. This commercial and linguistic exchange worked both ways: a German-Italian (or rather Bavarian-Venetian) phrasebook and grammar manual specifically for merchants was produced in 1424 by Giorgo di Norimberga who also gave lessons to Venetians wishing to improve their German (Francesco Guidi Bruscoli, 'I mercanti italiani e le lingue straniere' in Isa Lori Sanfilippo and Giuliano Pinto (eds), *Comunicare nel Medioevo: La conoscenza e l'uso delle lingue nei secoli XII-XV* (Roma, Instituto Storico Italiano per il Medio Evo, 2015), pp. 105–31 at pp. 112, 119).

[5] Ruddock, *Italian Merchants*, pp. 202–3.

[6] Bradley, 'Saluti da Londra', p. 111.

[7] Bradley, *Views of the Hosts*, p. xxi; cf. Nightingale, *Grocers' Company*, p. 182, p. 185.

[8] See the letter he wrote to Cantelowe from Italy in which he passes on Jacob's advice about further wool shipments (p. 33).

[9] As we have seen above, we also know that Balmayn interacted with the Salviati firm in London and that he appears several times in the London Salviati accounts, doing business on behalf of Cantelowe, prior to his departure for Tuscany.

is fascinating to imagine their conversations and how they communicated with each other.[10]

The intended readership of these accounts also raises questions. As Wright points out: 'Finance justifies the existence of a business, and it is therefore crucial that the written record of accounts is accessible and comprehensible to the auditor.'[11] Unless our scribe was very bad at his job, then logic dictates that he was not producing some garbled, eccentric jargon but an entirely legitimate written code. We have to assume that his master, William Cantelowe, knew enough Italian to understand these documents. If these records were meant solely for Italian eyes, why include ME sections and vice versa? Or was Jacob Salviati also able to read English? Given his professional experience in London, this would seem entirely reasonable.[12] A mixed-language text such as this gives us an exciting glimpse into its readers as well as its writer.[13]

It is also worth reiterating that this flow of lexis was by no means one-directional. The Salviati's own London book contains numerous Anglo-French and Middle English borrowings, providing evidence of contact between their own native Florentine and the local languages of business.[14] Without a doubt, the Tuscan, Venetian and Genoese communities in England relied heavily on close trading and social networks with their fellow aliens.[15] However, business would have been impossible without some level of mutual trust and interaction between Italian and English merchants, even if tensions did flare up in times of economic hardship (cf. n. 70, above).

In conclusion, the Cantelowe accounts offer invaluable proof of language contact through mercantile channels. Whilst it is intriguing to consider that Balmayn's text may be the sole survivor of a more widespread practice in Anglo-Italian business, his language use still represents an idiolect and the written idiosyncrasies

[10] Written sources, of course, do not offer a complete picture of an individual's oral skills, but scholars increasingly accept that medieval texts do offer us a 'window on to multilingual speech of the period' (Ingham, 'Medieval Bilingualism', p. 319). The evidence provided by Balmayn's writing together with the practicalities of the work he was paid to do in Tuscany allow us to assume that he could also speak the local language reasonably well.

[11] Wright, 'Code-Intermediate Phenomena', 472.

[12] Metalinguistic comment regarding Italian merchants' competence in England is also extremely rare. One surviving example is a letter confirming the necessity of good English for promotion in the Medici London bank in 1446 (Guidi Bruscoli, 'Mercanti italiani', p. 116).

[13] Cf. Herbert Schendl and Laura Wright (eds), *Code-Switching in Early English* (Berlin, De Gruyter, 2011), p. 20.

[14] Cf. Tiddeman, 'Early Anglo-Italian Contact'; Tiddeman, 'Lexical Exchange with Italian'. Intriguingly, some AF / ME lexemes were borrowed by the Italian writer even though there was a widely used Tuscan equivalent (e.g. *brocchore* < *broker* instead of *sensale*), a fact which hints at their linguistic immersion.

[15] Bradley, 'Saluti da Londra'; Guidi Bruscoli and Lutkin, 'Italian Communities'; Lambert, 'Nostri fratelli da Londra'.

of one man. Nevertheless, all language contact and borrowing occurs not between two great abstract entities – such as 'Middle English' and 'Italian' – but is rather the product of hundreds of thousands of interactions between one individual and another. In this way, this rare document is surely representative of countless commercial encounters that occurred daily between English and Italian merchants between the thirteenth and fifteenth centuries.

# Editor's notes

The key characteristic of the Cantelowe material is that it is mixed-language and so it is not immediately evident which editorial method should be used. We find extended Middle English entries together with shorter Italian and Latin-matrix segments, all interspersed with a few but persistent elements of Anglo-French. The rules and regulations of edition (especially of non-literary sources) still form an area of controversy that varies from country to country and from field to field. Despite attempts by philologists across Europe over the decades, we are still far from creating a universal editing system for administrative and commercial material. As the guide to edition of *sources documentaires* by the École Nationale des Chartes notes, 'À échelle international, leur confrontation est chose récente, leur harmonisation forcée semble hors d'atteinte.'[1]

To take just two examples, the abbreviations in the Cantelowe accounts would nearly always be expanded by an Italian linguist in round brackets whereas an Anglo-Normanist would generally use italics. A continental French specialist may also use italics or, more traditionally, expand abbreviations without any typological signal. An Anglicist may use silent expansion, brackets or capital letters or typographically reproduce the abbreviation. As regards layout and punctuation, the most common approach now amongst historical linguists in the UK and France is to impose modern punctuation and adapt the text's layout for ease of interpretation. In Italy, however, the transcription is presented in dense blocks, line by line as it is in the original, with the scribe's oblique lines (/) replicated between short sections of the text.

An Italian-style edition has been ruled out here as (despite their invaluable Italian content), the accounts were written by an Englishman and their transcription here is designed primarily to be read by Anglophone academics. Modern UK historians, economists and Anglicists favour a diplomatic transcription method for AF, ME and Latin documents but this has not been fully embraced in the field of Anglo-Norman studies.[2] Even so, since the late nineteenth century, there has been

[1] Olivier Guyotjeannin, *Conseils pour l'édition des textes médiévaux, Vol II: actes et documents d'archives* (Paris: Comité des travaux historiques et scientifiques, Librarie Droz, 2001), p. 9. The guide also stresses that the discipline of non-literary edition has been even slower than its literary counterpart to look beyond entrenched traditions and embrace international discussion, if not consensus (p. 11).

[2] David Trotter (ed), *Manuel de la philologie de l'édition* (Berlin, De Gruyter, 2015), p. 6. See also the following from 'Trop fidèle pour être belle: l'édition historique en anglo-normand', an unpublished

a strong British tradition of 'minimal editorial intervention and maximum faithfulness to the manuscript'[3] continuing to this day. In its most extreme form, this has led to the development of 'record type' where *graphies* are printed exactly as they are in the original document using a special type face. Such a style of edition - which attempts, as far as possible, to be an imitative copy of the manuscript - has notably been used by Laura Wright.[4] A principal advantage is that it allows abbreviations in the trilingual, non-literary texts examined to be equally expandable as BML, AF or ME. From this perspective, the transcription of extracts of these sources is very successful: it effectively demonstrates to the reader the translingual nature of these graphical shortcuts, and the specialised commercial code they create.

However, whilst Wright's methods are ideal for transcribing short segments of text and following them with commentary, this editing style is less appropriate for an extended transcription of thirty-five folios. Within the scope of this publication, my aims are to focus on readability and the use of Italian mercantile lexis by the scribe. To this end, the Cantelowe accounts have been edited in semi-diplomatic style, mainly adhering to the principles outlined by the École Nationale des Chartes.[5] These rules have been adapted as far as possible for this mixed-language text but overall, they allow us to produce a transcription which is widely accessible to an academic audience. In those cases where the expansion of an abbreviation is problematic, alternative interpretations are discussed in a footnote to the lexeme e.g. the town 'Port- Pisan-' could be read as either the ME / AF 'Port*e* Pisan*e*' or Italian 'Port*o* Pisan*o*'; the weight deduction 'tar-' could be ME /AF tar*e* or Italian tar*a*. The expansion of the abbreviation *p*° as pour throughout the

article by David Trotter from 2015: 'Au niveau le plus simple, elle modernise certains éléments (majuscules et ponctuation); elle en laisse d'autres intacts (séparation des mots, absence d'accents, *u* / *v* comme dans les manuscrits) et elle en masque d'autres encore (abréviations résolues sans indication typographique). Au niveau linguistique, certaines décisions (notamment concernant la coupure des mots et les accents) sont problématiques car elles semblent impliquer qu'une présentation médiévale (à l'aide d'un système graphique différent du nôtre) trahit une réalité linguistique qui, elle, est différente aussi - ce qui n'est nullement le cas [...]. Il ne s'agit donc pas d'une amélioration par rapport à la méthodologie des romanistes, ni du point de vue de la lisibilité (même si c'est un critère moins important), ni au niveau de cohérence, ni de point de vue strictement linguistique, ni en ce qui concerne une juste appréciation de la tradition graphique et ce qu'elle représente.'

[3] Julia Marvin (ed), *The Oldest Anglo-Norman Prose Brut Chronicle* (London, Boydell and Brewer, 2006), p. 67.

[4] See, for example, Laura Wright, *Sources of London English: Medieval Thames Vocabulary* (Oxford, Clarendon Press, 1996) and Laura Wright, 'On variation and change in London medieval mixed-language business documents', in Merja Stenroos, Martti Mäkinen and Inge Særheim (eds), Language Contact and Development around the North Sea, (Amsterdam, John Benjamins, 2012), pp. 99–115.

[5] This is also the authoritative guide in the modern Anglo-Norman field and the one used by the ANTS and the AND editorial team with whom I worked as a PhD student and a Post-Doctoral Research Assistant; cf. Heather Pagan and Geert De Wilde. 'L'édition de texte et l'Anglo-Norman Dictionary' in Stephen Dörr and Yan Greub (eds), *Quelle philologie pour quelle lexicographie? Actes de la section 17 du XXVIIème Congrès International de Linguistique et de Philologie Romanes*, (Heidelberg: Universitätsverlag Winter, 2016), pp. 107–16.

accounts was a difficult editorial decision to make as *per* would have made much more sense in the Italian-matrix sections and it is probable that Balmayn perceived the abbreviation as shorthand for both *per / pour*. In this instance, simply using the 'language-neutral' p̄ would have been a valid option. However, as the writer clearly uses the standardised forms of 'p' for the abbreviations *pour*, *per*, *pro-* and *par-*, it was decided to expand them as such in the transcription.

## Key points

*Letters and accents:*

- Modern capitalisation is used throughout.
- The scribe's use of both *þ* (thorn) and *th* and ȝ (yogh) and *g* is replicated exactly.
- *The letters u / v* are distinguished as per modern spelling (*usance* not *vsance*), as are *j / i* (*jour* not *iour*).
- The AF definite article is accented (*lé*) before plural nouns e.g. *lé sackes, lé costes*. Similarly, the AF past participle *preste* is written as *presté*.
- Accents have been added to the final letters of the following Italian words: *arsinà, dì, più, suprapiù*.
- Abbreviations are expanded as italics with the exception of some units of weight and currency (see below).

*Punctuation and layout:*

- The scribe's widespread use of oblique lines (/), oblique lines with median dots (·/) and single median dots (·) is not replicated and is replaced by systematic, modern punctuation.
- Square brackets are placed around a word or figure that is missing from the original text.
- Word spaces are removed or inserted according to modern usage, e.g. *there fore* becomes *therefore* and *dalloro* becomes *da lloro*.
- Line divisions are not reproduced but paragraph divisions normally are. Where appropriate, a single long paragraph is sub-divided into separate sentences, especially in the list of tare deducted from each lot of wool (pages numbered 12–28 of the transcription).
- For the purpose of reference, the folios (which are numbered non-consecutively in the extant material) have been given page numbers and each paragraph / item in the accounts is allocated a letter of the alphabet. This allows specific citations to be identified as 13b, 18a, 26e etc.

*Numbers and symbols:*

- The vast majority of numbers in the original Cantelowe MS are (exceptionally) in Arabic figures and do not need to be modernised. Rarer Roman numerals have been retained in the transcription to highlight Balmayn's use of both systems. The use of a 'graphical j' in figures (e.g. *viij pokes* / *j poke*) has been maintained.
- The use of the symbol ÷ to mean 'a half' is retained in the pages numbered 3–7 of the transcription, contrasting with the scribe's use of modern fractions elsewhere in the accounts.
- The transcription reproduces the author's convention of (nearly always) putting a dash to signify zero after a unit of currency (e.g. fl. 12 s.5 d.–).

*Units of currency and weights:*

- The '£' symbol is used for a pound (English sterling or Italian *lira*) in currency and 'lb' for a pound in weight, even though they are both represented by the same 'l' symbol in the original MS.
- In the case of other currencies and units of weight (see Tables 6 and 7, below), the following advice has been followed:
  Les abréviations des noms des monnaies, des poids et mesures sont très variables et parfois, d'interprétation délicate. Il y aura intérêt à utiliser des abréviations normalisées, explicitées en introduction, et aussi sévères que le permet leur compréhension immédiate. Il convient d'adopter un système homogène d'abréviations par suspension (point), qui allège en outre la lecture des documents riches en données chiffrées .[6]

**Table 6** Abbreviations used for units of currency

| Manuscript | Edition | Coin type | Notes |
|---|---|---|---|
| l 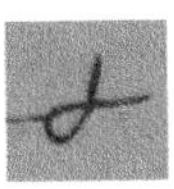 | £ | pound / lira | The abbreviation is never expanded. It refers to the English pound or represents the Italian silver *lira,* used as a money of account.[1] |
| ffl  | fl. | fiorini / florins[2] | Also written in full as *florino, florini, florinys, floryne* and *floryny.* This is replicated in the transcript. |

[6] Guyotjeannin, *Conseils pour l'édition,* p. 138.

**Table 6** (*cont.*)

| Manuscript | Edition | Coin type | Notes |
|---|---|---|---|
| st-  | st. | English sterling | The abbreviation is never expanded in full in the MS and appears in both ME and mixed-language segments. On one occasion, the scribe writes *sterl-* but it is unclear whether he meant ME *sterling* or the Italianised version *sterlini* (or indeed, both) when using this and the shorter abbreviation. |
| s  | s. | soldi / shillings | Used in the text with pounds (English and Italian) and florins, all of which were divided into 20 shillings / *soldi* or 240 *denari* / pence. The expanded form *denari* occurs occasionally in the text but 's.' always remains abbreviated. |
| d  | d. | denari / pence | |
| g°  | gr. | Venetian grossi[3] | Also written in full occasionally as *grossy*, which is replicated in the transcript. |
| doc-  | doc. | Venetian docati / ducati[4] | This never appears in expanded form in the original MS. |
| pezoly / p-   | *pez.* | Florentine piccioli or Venetian pizoli[5] | *Pezoly* is either based on Florentine *piccioli* or Venetian *pizoli*. The first two times Balmayn writes *pezoly* in full, before switching to a dotted p with a suspension mark. As the full form is unusual, I have used p*ez*. to replicate Balmayn's abbreviation. |

[1] This means that the *lira* did not exist as a coin at the time but represented on paper the equivalent of 240 *denari* which had been coined from one pound in weight of silver cf. Goldthwaite, *Economy of Renaissance Florence*, p. 609.

[2] The florin was a gold coin (bearing a lily symbol) and first minted in Florence in 1252. Nearly all the prices recorded are *a oro*, referring to a gold florin divided into 20 *soldi* or 240 *denari*. When Balmayn records a price *a florini* (12b), he is referring to a Florentine money of account, not represented by a real coin and equivalent to twenty twenty-ninths of a florin (De Roover, *Rise and Decline*, p. 33).

[3] A Venetian silver coin, first minted in 1202 (cf. Introduction, Part 4.viii). It was also known as a *matapane* (from the Arabic coin name *mautabān*) or, confusingly, in some early records, a *ducato*: see VTO sub **grosso / matapane** and Stahl, *Zecca*, pp. 16–27.

[4] Gold Venetian ducats (later known as *zecchini*) were introduced in 1284. See Stahl, *Zecca*, pp. 28–40.

[5] *Piccioli* or *pizoli* were small, low-value coins of a copper-silver mix (cf. Introduction, Part 4.viii). When Balmayn gives a price as so many *soldi de pezoly* (as he does in entries 11c, d, g, i and n), it is to underline that he refers to a *soldo* that is one twentieth of a *lira* (or pound) and not a *soldo* that is one twentieth of a florin: cf. Goldthwaite, *Economy of Renaissance Florence*, p. 610.

**Table 7** Abbreviations used for units of weight

| Manuscript | Edition | Unit of weight for wool | Notes |
|---|---|---|---|
| l  | lb | pound / *libra* | The abbreviation for *libra* is never expanded in the text and always appears as 'l'. |
| unc-  | unc*e* | ounce | |
| sack- 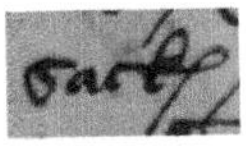 | sack*es* | sack (364 lb) | There are two clearly separate abbreviations which are expanded according to their ME / Italian forms. The word also appears once in full as ME *sackys*. |
| sach-  | sach*i* | | |
| pok-  | pok*e* / pok*es* pock*es* | poke (182 lb) | As above. ME *poke*, *pokys*, *pochis* and It. *poche* are also attested in full in the text. |
| pock –  | | | |
| poch-  | poch*e* | | |
| clo-  | clo*ves* | clove (7lb) | This never appears in expanded form in the original MS. |
| le C-  | le C. | *centum* i.e. hundredweight. | This never appears in expanded form in the original MS. |
| t-  | tar*a* / tare *tara* / *tare* | (varying) amount of weight deducted from the gross for packaging etc. | *Tare* is represented by *tar-* / *t-* . *Tara* is hence never clearly written but I have expanded the abbreviation in the Italian-matrix sections with this singular form where is made grammatical sense to do so. |
| tar-  | | | |

**Table 7** (*cont.*)

| Manuscript | Edition | Unit of weight for wool | Notes |
|---|---|---|---|
| $n^t$<br><br>netta<br>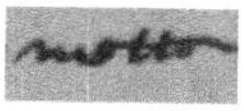 | *net* | amount of weight remaining after deductions for tare | *Netta* is written out in full six times in Italian-matrix sections. Usually Balmayn writes an abbreviated form ($n^t$) which I expand in the transcription as *net*. The same abbreviation appears once in a ME-matrix section and I have chosen to write this as: "And so reste clere n*et*" (7a). |

*Personal names*

- Personal names are spelt exactly as they are in original MS. Balmayn refers to forty-four separate Italian wool buyers in the accounts, some of whom are mentioned in several separate entries over transcription pages 12–28. He also lists the Italian companies or individuals who are involved in the series of bills of exchange to send payment to London, detailed over transcription pages 29–31.
- Table 8 below lists wool buyers next to their corresponding Italian name in the Salviati's Florentine accounts from 1448–52 (AS Serie I: 232), as transcribed by Holmes. In nearly all cases, it is clear to which Italian company Balmayn is referring, despite Holmes' inference that his 'English adaptation' is difficult to comprehend.[7] However, in two instances (see no. 5 and no. 16 below), part of the name written by the English scribe seems to be completely different to the Italian version.
- In Table 9 below, the names of payers and payees are compared to their Italian equivalents as they appear scattered in other banking transactions throughout the Salviati's London accounts from 1448–51 (AS Serie I: 336), as transcribed by Cavalloro. Once again, it is usually perfectly obvious to whom Balmayn is referring. However, eleven individuals that he mentions do not seem to have entries in the Salviati book examined.[8]

[7] Holmes, 'Anglo-Florentine Trade', 374.

[8] These are *Lucha Chapponi* (29b), *Lowes Pigo* (or *Pige*) (29g), *[?] Mirabelly* (29o), *Benet de Fransisco de Strossy* (30b), *Antonio de Branocha* (30c), *Johan del Pulesse* (30j), *Jorge Luke* (30k), *Jacopo Pissamano* (31h), *Pero Bassato* (31i) and *Johan de Matheo Gryty* (31t). *Pero de Galiano* (30a) is not in the Salviati London records but appears in their Florentine ones (see no. 12 in Table 8).

**Table 8** Wool buyer names in the Cantelowe accounts compared to the Salviati Florence accounts

| | **AS Serie I: 339. Cantelowe accounts**[1] | **AS Serie I: 232. Account book of Salviati Florence office, 1448–52**[2] | **Wool buyers' entries in Cantelowe accounts** |
|---|---|---|---|
| 1 | Fraunces de Christoforo Aleotti | Francesco di Christoforo Aliotto | 12b, 13c, 13d, 22a, 22b |
| 2 | Juncta Ibindo de Williamo Juncta | Giunta e Bindo di Guglielmo di Giunta | 12c, 13e |
| 3 | Pero et Johanne Gwydewchy | Pietro a Giovanni Guiducci | 12d, 17e |
| 4 | Ubertino de Gerardo Rezaliti | Ubertino di Gherardo Risaliti | 12e, 13a |
| 5 | Johanne de Phelippo de Ascheto | Giovane de Filippo Ghiacutto | 13b, 21b |
| 6 | Jelyano de Johne dai Borgo | Giuliano di Giovanni dal Borgo | 14a, 20d |
| 7 | Apardo de Nicolo de Lorenxo Loteni | Pardo di Nicholaio di Lorenzo Lottini | 14b |
| 8 | Piero Matheo de Contowcho | Piero Matteo di Contucco | 14c |
| 9 | Antonio de Guydo de Junctino | Antonio di Guido di Giuntino | 14d |
| 10 | Genoby de Leonardo Bartoli | Zanobi di Leonardo Bartoli | 15a |
| 11 | Leonardo de Angelo de Balioni | Leonardo d'Agnolo del Baglione | 15b |
| 12 | Pero de Galiano | Piero de Gagliano | 15c |
| 13 | Jachobo d'Orsino Lanfredini et Francesco Guydotti | Jacopo d'Orsino Lanfredini & Francesco Guidetti & Co. | 16a, 23e, 26d |
| 14 | Dominicho de Jachobo Federisi | Domenico di Jacopo di Federighi | 16b |
| 15 | Pagino de Johne de Albesi | Pangino di Giovanni di Gentile degli Albizzi | 16c |
| 16 | Bernardo d'Auremo de Medeci | Bernardo d'Antonio de' Medici | 16d |

**Table 8** (*cont.*)

| | AS Serie I: 339. Cantelowe accounts[1] | AS Serie I: 232. Account book of Salviati Florence office, 1448–52[2] | Wool buyers' entries in Cantelowe accounts |
|---|---|---|---|
| 17 | Johanne et Williamo de Mysser Salustro de Perosa | Giovanni & Guglielmo di Messer Saluestro de Perugia | 16e |
| 18 | Nycholas de Johne de Sandro | Niccolo di Giovanni di Sandro Barbigia | 17a, 25c, 28a |
| 19 | Attimo de Johne Ginori | Attimo di Giovanni de' Ginori | 17b |
| 20 | Larenxo de Paris Corbenelli | Lorenzo di Parigi Corbinelli | 17c, 25b, 25e |
| 21 | Francisco de Simoni de Nozo Fantoni | Francesco di Simone Fantoni | 17d, 18d |
| 22 | Danyelle de Nofry Daszo | Daniello di Nofri Dazzi | 18a |
| 23 | Brancho Costantino da Perosa | Brancha di Costantino da Perguia | 18b |
| 24 | Laurens de Rinieri Spineli | Lorenzo di Rinieri Spinelli | 18c, 20f |
| 25 | Francesco et Thomaxo Bewsini | Francesco di Tommaso Busini | 18e |
| 26 | Donato de Messer Leonardo d'Arezzo | Donato di Messer Leonardo d'Arezzo | 19a |
| 27 | Bernardo Lappe da Zuane[3] Nycholini | Bernardo di Lapo Niccolini | 19b, 19c |
| 28 | Antonio de Chambino Chambini | Antonio di Cambino Cambini | 19d, 19e, 23d, 26a |
| 29 | Leonardo et Dominicho del Tore | Leonardo et Domenico di Torre | 19f |
| 30 | Gino de Zuane Ginori | Gino di Giovanni Ginori | 20a |
| 31 | Antonio de Zuane de Sandro | Antonio di Giovanni Barbigia | 20b |
| 32 | Pero et Jacobo de Patsy | Pietro e Jacopo de' Pazzi | 20c |

(*continued*)

**Table 8** (*cont.*)

| | AS Serie I: 339. Cantelowe accounts[1] | AS Serie I: 232. Account book of Salviati Florence office, 1448–52[2] | Wool buyers' entries in Cantelowe accounts |
|---|---|---|---|
| 33 | Simone d'Amercho Sati | Simone d'Amerigo Zati | 20e |
| 34 | Zuane de Jacabo del Pulesse | Giovanni di Jacopo del Pugliese | 21a |
| 35 | Pero de Soldo de Antonio Baldovini | Piero di Soldo e Antonio Baldovini. | 21c, 21f |
| 36 | Thomaso de Ubertino Resali | Tommaso d'Ubertino Risaliti | 21d, 21e |
| 37 | Matheo de Nycholao Lachy | Matteo di Nicolaio Lachi | 21g, 23a, 23b, 23f, 23g, 24a, 24b, 26e, 27a |
| 38 | Pero de Cosimo de Medeci | Piero di Cosimo de' Medici | 22c, 22d, 22e, 22f |
| 39 | Bernardo de Genotzo Manetti | Bernardo di Giannozzo Manetti | 22g |
| 40 | Antonio Lensy | Antonio Lanzi | 23c |
| 41 | Andrea de Loteryncho de la Stuffa | Andrea di Loteringo della Stuffa | 24c, 24d, 24e, 24f |
| 42 | Laurenxo de Larione de Bardy | Lorenzo di Larione de' Bardi | 25a, 26b |
| 43 | Simone de Zuane de Sandro Barbigia | Simone di Giovanni di Sandri Barbigia | 25d |
| 44 | Jachobo Federicy | Pagolo di Jacopo Federighi | 26c |

1 My transcription.
2 Holmes, 'Anglo-Florentine Trade', 374–5.
3 Note that *Zuane* is a common Venetian variant of *Giovanni*.

**Table 9** Payer and payee names in the Cantelowe accounts compared to the Salviati London accounts

| | **AS Serie I: 339. Cantelowe accounts**[1] | **AS Serie I: 336. Account book of Salviati London office, 1448–51**[2] | **Bill of exchange entries in Cantelowe accounts** |
|---|---|---|---|
| 1 | Johan Russelay et Vanni Francisco de Strossy | Giovanni Rucellai e Giovan Francesco Strozzi | 29a–p, 30a–g, 30i, 31b |
| 2 | Antonio de la Luna | Antonio della Luna | 29b, 31p, 31q |
| 3 | Johan Portenary | Giovanni Portinari | 29c, 29m |
| 4 | Cosmo de Medici | Coximo de' Medici | 29d, 29e, 30d |
| 5 | Antonio Partini | Antonio Partini | 29h, 31e, 31f, 31v |
| 6 | Pero [et herede] de Partino Partini | Piero Partino Partini | 29h |
| 7 | Michaelle Rondenelly | Michele Rondinelli | 29k |
| 8 | Phelyppe Inggorani | Filippo Inghirrami | 29l |
| 9 | Jacob de Benzy | Iacopo Benzi | 29o |
| 10 | Lowes Thechyatzy / Lowes Techiassy | Luigi Teghiaci | 30g, 31o |
| 11 | Pero de Medici and Jerozzo de Pili | Piero Medici e Gerezzo Pilli | 30j, 30l, 30m |
| 12 | Alysandyr Beremey | Alessando Borromei | 30k |
| 13 | Antonio Beremay | Antonio Borromei | 30k, 31r |
| 14 | Johan and Pero Francischo de Medici | Giovanni e Piero Medici | 30m |
| 15 | Umfrido Justyane | Onfre Iustiniani | 31c |
| 16 | Pancras Justyane | Pancrato Iustiniani | 31c |
| 17 | Sebestyane et Jerolimis Bawdwere | Sebastiano e Girolamo Badueri | 31d |
| 18 | Vittore Capelle and his brotherys | Vittor Capello e fratelli | 31d |
| 19 | Lowes Strossy | Ludovico Strozzi | 31e, 31f, 31k, 31p, 31t |
| 20 | Filice de Fagniano | Felice da Fagnano | 31g |

(*continued*)

**Table 9** (*cont.*)

| | **AS Serie I: 339. Cantelowe accounts**[1] | **AS Serie I: 336. Account book of Salviati London office, 1448–51**[2] | **Bill of exchange entries in Cantelowe accounts** |
|---|---|---|---|
| 21 | Lorenxo Banbo | Lorenzo Bembo | 31h |
| 22 | Damiano Ruffini | Damiano Ruffini | 31i |
| 23 | Antonio de Rabatta et Bernard Cambi | Antonio da Rabatta e Bernardo Cambi | 31j, 31o |
| 24 | Vinceguerra Justynyane | Vinceguerra Iustiniani | 31j |
| 25 | Leonardo Cattano | Leonardo Cattano | 31m |
| 26 | […] Lomelini[3] | (?) Lomellino[4] | 31n |
| 27 | Francischo Jerolimo […] nynysy | Francesco e Girolamo Guinigi | 31s |
| 28 | Johan Beremay | Giovanni Borromei | 31s |

1 My transcription.
2 Cavalloro, 'Jacopo di Alamanno Salviati', pp. 87–163.
3 Balmayn gives no forename(s) in this entry.
4 There are no fewer than eight individuals with the surname *Lomellino* in the Salviati London book: *Andalo* [sic], *Carlo*, *Cristofano*, *Filippo*, *Francesco*, *Girolamo*, *Ludovico* and *Napoleone*.

# The Cantelowe Accounts, 1450–1451

## (Archivio Salviati, Serie I: 339)

**Cover:**

†

M[l] cccc[o] lj

P*er* Joh*an* Balmay*ne*, s*er*vaunt of Will*ia*m Cantelowe,

marchau*n*t of London, for Florens.

**[Weights of the wool sacks]**

**Page 2 [1r.]**

Ih*esus* 1451 Maria

fl.1

**a)** M*emorand*u*m* that this boke ys for the rekenyng of resceyvyng of my mayst*er* Wyll*ia*m Cantelowe ys wolle and othyr march*a*untyse[1] send fro London and fro Hampton*e* to Pyse and Florens, the yere of oure Lorde God a*nno* m[ll] iiij[c] l and for the ret*or*ne agayn*e* of the seyd woll*e*, made by Jacob Salviatis and by me, Joh*an* Balmay*n*, s*er*vaunt of the seyd Will*iam* Cantelowe.

**b)** And for the which*e* woll*e* and more þ*a*t schall*e* com*e* by the g*ra*ce of God, I, the seyd Joh*an* Balmay*n*, was send fro London by my seyd mayst*er* to Florens the xiij daye of Maye, the yere of our Lord*e* God a*nno* m[ll] iiij[c] lj and I, the seyd s*er*vaunt, cam*e* to Florens the xxiiij[e] daye of Jun*e* next folewyng, the whych*e* was missom*er* daye and Corpus daye C*hristi*[2] etc.[3]

[1] *and othyr marchauntyse*: scribal insertion, superscript with an arrow symbol.
[2] *xpi*: standard medieval abbreviation for *Christi* (cf. Cappelli, *Lexicon Abbreviaturarum,* p. xxii).
[3] This opening paragraph is transcribed as follows in Holmes ('Anglo-Florentine Trade', 372). I include it here to highlight the differences in editorial styles and occasional different readings: *Memorandum that this boke ys ffor the rekenyng of resceyvyng of my mayster Wylliam Cantelowe ys wolle and othyr marchauntyse send fro London and fro hampton to pyse and fflorens the yere of oure lorde god a M*[l] *iiij* [c]*l and for the returne agayne of the seyd wolle made by Jacob Saluiatis and by me Johane Balmayn seruaunte of the seyd William Cantelowe. And ffor the which wolle and more that schall come by the grace of god I the seyd Johan Balmayn was send fro London by my seyd mayster to fflorens the xiij daye of maye the yere of oure lord god a M*[l] *iiij*[c] *Cj* [sic] *and I the syd servaunt came to fFlorens the xxiiij daye of June next ffolowyng the which was missomer daye and corpus daye Christi etc.*

**Page 3 [2r.]**

1450

fl.2

**a)** M*emorandum* *þat* by the gr*a*ce of God here bygynnyth the ~~wh~~ weyȝth*s* of iiij$^{C}$lxvj pokys wolle aftyr the rate of þ*e* weyȝth*s* of Engeland*e*, schippyd in a caryk of Jene at Southeh*a*mpton*e* *anno* m$^{ll}$ iiij$^{c}$ l in the name of Joh*an* de Albycys,[4] for to be delyv*er*ed by the gr*a*ce of God at Pyse to Frawnsis et Joh*an* Salviat*is*, or to suche as schall*e* be ther in theyr name. And þ*e* patrone ys name ys Antoni de Aurea[5] de Jenua.

**b)** The whyche pokys be undyr thys marke above †.

| | | **Pokes** | **Cloves** | | | **Pokes** | **Cloves**[6] |
|---|---|---|---|---|---|---|---|
| N° | 164 | 1 | 5 | N° | 138 | 1 | 3 ÷ |
| | 63 | 1 | 2 | | 132 | 1 | 3 ÷ |
| | 152 | 1 | 2 | | 166 | 1 | 2 |
| | 157 | 1 | 4 | | 162 | 1 | 3 |
| | 153 | 1 | 3 | | 61 | 1 | 3 ÷ |
| | 59 | 1 | 3 ÷[7] | | 143 | 1 | 3 |
| | 171 | 1 | 1 | | 68 | 1 | 2 ÷ |
| | 163 | 1 | 2 ÷ | | 67 | 1 | 3 |
| | 151 | 1 | 4 ÷ | | 56 | 1 | 2 ÷ |
| | 49 | 1 | 2 | | 60 | 1 | 3 |
| **Pokes** 10 | **Sacks** | 5 ÷ | 3 ÷ | **Pokes** 10 | **Sacks** | 5 ÷ | 3 ÷ |
| | 137 | 1 | 5 | | 158 | 1 | 3 ÷ |
| | 57 | 1 | 3 | | 53 | 1 | 2 ÷ |
| | 148 | 1 | 4 ÷ | | 45 | 1 | 4 ÷ |

4 = Giovanni degli Albizzi, Jacob Salviati's partner at the London office.

5 = Antonia Doria of Genoa.

6 Over five folios, Balmayn meticulously catalogues the precise weight of each numbered poke of wool, presumably in the random order in which they were unloaded from the ship at Livorno. These figures are not mentioned by Holmes and I have added the units of measurement 'pokes', 'cloves' and 'sacks' (in bold) to the lists to make them immediately understandable. One English sack weighed 364lb (*avoirdupois*) and with a clove equalling 7lb; so, there were fifty-two cloves to the sack. A poke was officially half a sack, i.e. 182lb although this could vary in practice. As noted in the Introduction, all the pokes in the Cantelowe accounts weighed over 200lb before deductions for tare. Our 466 pokes are grouped into forty-five lots of ten and two of eight. Their weight is recorded in pokes (always '1') and cloves and then tallied up at the the bottom of each sub-section in sacks and cloves.

7 In these lists of figures Balmayn uses a colon divided by a horizontal line to represent ½ (confusingly similar to today's division sign, but a common medieval practice, see Cappelli, *Lexicon Abbreviaturarum*, pp. liv-v). However, he does also use modern fractions several times later on in the accounts (cf. Introduction, Part 5).

| | | | | | | | |
|---|---|---|---|---|---|---|---|
| | 48 | 1 | 3 | | 142 | 1 | 5 |
| | 42 | 1 | 4 | | 195 | 1 | 2 |
| | 69 | 1 | 3 ÷ | | 210 | 1 | 4 |
| | 161 | 1 | 4 | | 260 | 1 | 5 |
| | 64 | 1 | 3 | | 159 | 1 | 1 ÷ |
| | 136 | 1 | 4 | | 243 | 1 | 4 |
| | 167 | 1 | 5 ÷ | | 188 | 1 | 5 |
| **Pokes** 10 | **Sacks** | 5 ÷ | 13 ÷ | **Pokes** 10 | **Sacks** | 5 ÷ | 11 |
| | 46 | 1 | 4 ÷ | | 175 | 1 | 2 |
| | 131 | 1 | 3 ÷ | | 150 | 1 | 4 ÷ |
| | 139 | 1 | 3 ÷ | | 219 | 1 | 5 |
| | 47 | 1 | 4 ÷ | | 133 | 1 | 2 |
| | 52 | 1 | 5 ÷ | | 196 | 1 | 3 |
| | 43 | 1 | 2 ÷ | | 146 | 1 | 6 ÷ |
| | 160 | 1 | 2 ÷ | | 208 | 1 | 3 ÷ |
| | 54 | 1 | 4 ÷ | | 170 | 1 | 2 |
| | 156 | 1 | 4 | | 256 | 1 | 4 |
| | 55 | 1 | 3 ÷ | | 154 | 1 | 4 ÷ |
| **Pokes** 10 | **Sacks** | 5 ÷ | 12 ÷ | **Pokes** 10 | **Sacks** | 5 ÷ | 11 |
| | 147 | 1 | 5 | | 236 | 1 | 4 ÷ |
| | 149 | 1 | 4 ÷ | | 174 | 1 | 2 ÷ |
| | 51 | 1 | 2 | | 251 | 1 | 5 ÷ |
| | 165 | 1 | 4 | | 267 | 1 | 4 ÷ |
| | 44 | 1 | 4 ÷ | | 194 | 1 | 4 ÷ |
| | 58 | 1 | 3 | | 201 | 1 | 4 |
| | 141 | 1 | 4 | | 271 | 1 | 4 ÷ |
| | 66 | 1 | 3 ÷ | | 254 | 1 | 4 |
| | 50 | 1 | 4 ÷ | | 269 | 1 | 5 |
| | 62 | 1 | 3 | | 207 | 1 | 3 |
| **Pokes** 10 | **Sacks** | 5 ÷ | 12 | **Pokes** 10 | **Sacks** | 5 ÷ | 16 |

**Page 4 [2v.]**

†

| | | **Pokes** | **Cloves** | | | **Pokes** | **Cloves** |
|---|---|---|---|---|---|---|---|
| N° | 182 | 1 | 4 | N° | 186 | 1 | 3 |

| | | | |
|---|---|---|---|
| | 173 | 1 | 2 ÷ |
| | 192 | 1 | 3 ÷ |
| | 191 | 1 | 3 |
| | 262 | 1 | 4 |
| | 180 | 1 | 3 ÷ |
| | 240 | 1 | 5 ÷ |
| | 189 | 1 | 4 |
| | 190 | 1 | 3 |
| | 198 | 1 | 4 |
| **Pokes** 10 | **Sacks** | 5 ÷ | 11 |
| | 199 | 1 | 4 ÷ |
| | 257 | 1 | 3 ÷ |
| | 183 | 1 | 4 |
| | 248 | 1 | 2 |
| | 212 | 1 | 3 ÷ |
| | 193 | 1 | 3 |
| | 225 | 1 | 4 |
| | 223 | 1 | 3 ÷ |
| | 224 | 1 | 4 |
| | 268 | 1 | 3 |
| **Pokes** 10 | **Sacks** | 5 ÷ | 9 |
| | 244 | 1 | 3 ÷ |
| | 258 | 1 | 3 |
| | 135 | 1 | 4 |
| | 265 | 1 | 3 ÷ |
| | 155 | 1 | 2 ÷ |
| | 206 | 1 | 3 |
| | 242 | 1 | 3 ÷ |
| | 243 | 1 | 4 |
| | 231 | 1 | 3 ÷ |
| | 134 | 1 | 3 ÷ |
| **Pokes** 10 | **Sacks** | 5 ÷ | 8 |
| | 261 | 1 | 3 |
| | 160 | 1 | 3 ÷ |
| | 177 | 1 | 5 |

| | | | |
|---|---|---|---|
| | 178 | 1 | 4 ÷ |
| | 217 | 1 | 4 |
| | 213 | 1 | 3 ÷ |
| | 232 | 1 | 3 |
| | 214 | 1 | 4 |
| | 218 | 1 | 4 |
| | 176 | 1 | 6 ÷ |
| | 200 | 1 | 4 |
| | 202 | 1 | 2 |
| **Pokes** 10 | **Sacks** | 5 ÷ | 12 ÷ |
| | 209 | 1 | 4 |
| | 203 | 1 | 3 |
| | 220 | 1 | 4 ÷ |
| | 181 | 1 | 3 ÷ |
| | 266 | 1 | 3 ÷ |
| | 184 | 1 | 5 ÷ |
| | 216 | 1 | 4 |
| | 227 | 1 | 5 |
| | 211 | 1 | 2 |
| | 262 | 1 | 4 ÷ |
| **Pokes** 10 | **Sacks** | 5 ÷ | 13 ÷ |
| | 204 | 1 | 2 ÷ |
| | 241 | 1 | 6 |
| | 169 | 1 | 6 |
| | 250 | 1 | 5 |
| | 255 | 1 | 4 ÷ |
| | 252 | 1 | 5 ÷ |
| | 273 | 1 | 1 ÷ |
| | 238 | 1 | 6 |
| | 168 | 1 | 3 ÷ |
| | 239 | 1 | 4 ÷ |
| **Pokes** 10 | **Sacks** | 5 ÷ | 19 |
| | 30 | 1 | 4 |
| | 295 | 1 | 1 ÷ |
| | 291 | 1 | 3 |

| | | | | | | | |
|---|---|---|---|---|---|---|---|
| | 246 | 1 | 5 | | 288 | 1 | 5 |
| | 205 | 1 | 2 | | 290 | 1 | 3 |
| | 233 | 1 | 2 ÷ | | 297 | 1 | 4 ÷ |
| | 215 | 1 | 3 ÷ | | 310 | 1 | 2 ÷ |
| | 249 | 1 | 4 | | 312 | 1 | 4 |
| | 226 | 1 | 5 | | 294 | 1 | 4 |
| | 185 | 1 | 2 ÷ | | 293 | 1 | 2 ÷ |
| **Pokes** 10 | **Sacks** | 5 ÷ | 10 | **Pokes** 10 | **Sacks** | 5 ÷ | 8 |
| | 172 | 1 | 5 | | 289 | 1 | 3 |
| | 272 | 1 | 4 ÷ | | 324 | 1 | 2 |
| | 247 | 1 | 4 | | 292 | 1 | 5 |
| | 221 | 1 | 4 ÷ | | 313 | 1 | 3 |
| | 197 | 1 | 2 | | 332 | 1 | 1 |
| | 177 | 1 | 3 ÷ | | 315 | 1 | 4 ÷ |
| | 229 | 1 | 2 | | 308 | 1 | 5 |
| | 228 | 1 | 2 ÷ | | 322 | 1 | 3 ÷ |
| | 230 | 1 | 4 | | 328 | 1 | 4 |
| | 179 | 1 | 4 | | 319 | 1 | 4 ÷ |
| **Pokes** 10 | **Sacks** | 5 ÷ | 10 | **Pokes** 10 | **Sacks** | 5 ÷ | 9 ÷ |

## Page 5 [3r.]

†

fl.3

| | | **Pokes** | **Cloves** | | | **Pokes** | **Cloves** |
|---|---|---|---|---|---|---|---|
| Nº | 317 | 1 | 4 | Nº | 296 | 1 | 3 |
| | 329 | 1 | 5 | | 308 | 1 | 2 |
| | 331 | 1 | 2 | | 298 | 1 | 3 |
| | 326 | 1 | 3 | | 323 | 1 | 3 |
| | 87 | 1 | 2 | | 97 | 1 | 5 ÷ |
| | 320 | 1 | 3 | | 111 | 1 | 4 ÷ |
| | 321 | 1 | 3 ÷ | | 120 | 1 | 2 |
| | 117 | 1 | 4 ÷ | | 77 | 1 | 3 ÷ |
| | 325 | 1 | 4 ÷ | | 96 | 1 | 4 ÷ |
| | 318 | 1 | 4 | | 127 | 1 | 4 ÷ |
| **Pokes** 10 | **Sacks** | 5 ÷ | 9 ÷ | **Pokes** 10 | **Sacks** | 5 ÷ | 9 ÷ |

| | | | |
|---|---|---|---|
| | 309 | 1 | 4 ÷ |
| | 305 | 1 | 5 ÷ |
| | 316 | 1 | 3 |
| | 304 | 1 | 3 ÷ |
| | 300 | 1 | 3 |
| | 314 | 1 | 4 ÷ |
| | 327 | 1 | 3 ÷ |
| | 303 | 1 | 4 |
| | 80 | 1 | 2 ÷ |
| | 76 | 1 | 3 |
| **Pokes** 10 | **Sacks** | 5 ÷ | 11 |

| | | | |
|---|---|---|---|
| | 81 | 1 | 2 ÷ |
| | 70 | 1 | 3 ÷ |
| | 330 | 1 | 3 |
| | 301 | 1 | 3 ÷ |
| | 299 | 1 | 3 ÷ |
| | 114 | 1 | 4 |
| | 104 | 1 | 3 |
| | 112 | 1 | 2 ÷ |
| | 74 | 1 | 4 ÷ |
| | 98 | 1 | 2 ÷ |
| **Pokes** 10 | **Sacks** | 5 ÷ | 6 ÷ |

| | | | |
|---|---|---|---|
| | 123 | 1 | 5 |
| | 115 | 1 | 3 |
| | 302 | 1 | 4 ÷ |
| | 93 | 1 | 4 |
| | 100 | 1 | 4 ÷ |
| | 79 | 1 | 4 |
| | 116 | 1 | 3 |
| | 124 | 1 | 3 ÷ |
| | 206 | 1 | 4 |
| | 109 | 1 | 5 |
| **Pokes** 10 | **Sacks** | 5 ÷ | 14 ÷ |

| | | | |
|---|---|---|---|
| | 122 | 1 | 4 ÷ |
| | 113 | 1 | 3 ÷ |
| | 129 | 1 | 3 ÷ |
| | 101 | 1 | 3 ÷ |
| | 103 | 1 | 3 |
| | 91 | 1 | 2 |
| | 82 | 1 | 3 ÷ |
| | 119 | 1 | 3 ÷ |
| | 105 | 1 | 3 |
| | 75 | 1 | 4 ÷ |
| **Pokes** 10 | **Sacks** | 5 ÷ | 8 ÷ |

| | | | |
|---|---|---|---|
| | 118 | 1 | 3 ÷ |
| | 71 | 1 | 2 |
| | 92 | 1 | 4 ÷ |
| | 89 | 1 | 3 |
| | 126 | 1 | 6 ÷ |
| | 83 | 1 | 3 |
| | 95 | 1 | 5 |
| | 125 | 1 | 5 |
| | 102 | 1 | 2 ÷ |
| | 108 | 1 | 4 ÷ |
| **Pokes** 10 | **Sacks** | 5 ÷ | 13 ÷ |

| | | | |
|---|---|---|---|
| | 121 | 1 | 4 |
| | 110 | 1 | 3 |
| | 94 | 1 | 2 ÷ |
| | 128 | 1 | 4 |
| | 130 | 1 | 5 ÷ |
| | 72 | 1 | 3 ÷ |
| | 237 | 1 | 4 ÷ |
| | 245 | 1 | 5 |
| | 259 | 1 | 3 |
| | 253 | 1 | 7 |
| **Pokes** 10 | **Sacks** | 5 ÷ | 16 |

| | | | | | | | |
|---|---|---|---|---|---|---|---|
| | 90 | 1 | 2 ÷ | | 235 | 1 | 4 ÷ |
| | 84 | 1 | 3 ÷ | | 234 | 1 | 4 ÷ |
| | 65 | 1 | 4 ÷ | | 145 | 1 | 4 |
| | 73 | 1 | 2 | | 270 | 1 | 5 |
| | 88 | 1 | 3 ÷ | | 222 | 1 | 3 ÷ |
| | 86 | 1 | 4 | | 264 | 1 | 4 |
| | 107 | 1 | 4 ÷ | | 285 | 1 | 4 ÷ |
| | 85 | 1 | 3 ÷ | | 287 | 1 | 4 ÷ |
| | 311 | 1 | 3 | | 280 | 1 | 4 ÷ |
| | 99 | 1 | 5 | | 274 | 1 | 5 |
| **Pokes** 10 | **Sacks** | 5 ÷ | 10 | **Pokes** 10 | **Sacks** | 5 ÷ | 18 |

## Page 6 [3v.]

†

| | | Pokes | Cloves | | | Pokes | Cloves |
|---|---|---|---|---|---|---|---|
| N° | 278 | 1 | 4 | N° | 429 | 1 | 2 ÷ |
| | 277 | 1 | 5 | | 442 | 1 | 1 ÷ |
| | 281 | 1 | 4 | | 446 | 1 | 1 |
| | 276 | 1 | 5 | | 419 | 1 | 1 |
| | 275 | 1 | 5 | | 438 | 1 | 0 |
| | 284 | 1 | 4 ÷ | | 440 | 1 | 0 |
| | 279 | 1 | 5 | | 427 | 1 | 2 ÷ |
| | 282 | 1 | 5 ÷ | | 439 | 1 | 0 |
| | 283 | 1 | 6 | | 431 | 1 | 2 |
| | 286 | 1 | 4 | | 443 | 1 | 0 |
| **Pokes** 10 | **Sacks** | 5 ÷ | 22 ÷ | **Pokes** 10 | **Sacks** | 5 | 10 ÷ |
| | 333 | 1 | 2 ÷ | | 445 | 1 | 0 ÷ |
| | 336 | 1 | 3 | | 441 | 1 | 0 |
| | 78 | 1 | 0 ÷ | | 430 | 1 | 3 ÷ |
| | 342 | 1 | 3 | | 434 | 1 | 1 ÷ |
| | 341 | 1 | 3 ÷ | | 435 | 1 | 2 |
| | 338 | 1 | 3 | | 423 | 1 | 1 ÷ |
| | 339 | 1 | 4 | | 444 | 1 | 1 ÷ |
| | 340 | 1 | 4 ÷ | | 447 | 1 | 1 ÷ |

| | | | |
|---|---|---|---|
| | 357 | 1 | 4 |
| | 348 | 1 | 5 |
| **Pokes** 10 | **Sacks** | 5 ÷ | 7 |
| | 337 | 1 | 3 ÷ |
| | 352 | 1 | 3 ÷ |
| | 355 | 1 | 2 |
| | 363 | 1 | 3 ÷ |
| | 366 | 1 | 2 |
| | 353 | 1 | 4 |
| | 365 | 1 | 2 ÷ |
| | 364 | 1 | 4 ÷ |
| | 343 | 1 | 2 |
| | 347 | 1 | 3 ÷ |
| **Pokes** 10 | **Sacks** | 5 ÷ | 5 |
| | 360 | 1 | 3 ÷ |
| | 354 | 1 | 4 ÷ |
| | 349 | 1 | 4 |
| | 344 | 1 | 2 |
| | 356 | 1 | 4 |
| | 361 | 1 | 2 |
| | 362 | 1 | 4 ÷ |
| | 334 | 1 | 2 ÷ |
| | 358 | 1 | 5 |
| | 359 | 1 | 1 |
| **Pokes** 10 | **Sacks** | 5 ÷ | 7 |
| | 351 | 1 | 3 |
| | 13 | 1 | 2 ÷ |
| | 19 | 1 | 5 ÷ |
| | 27 | 1 | 4 |
| | 18 | 1 | 3 |
| | 40 | 1 | 4 ÷ |
| | 15 | 1 | 4 |
| | 9 | 1 | 3 |
| | 38 | 1 | 4 ÷ |

| | | | |
|---|---|---|---|
| | 432 | 1 | 2 ÷ |
| | 425 | 1 | 2 ÷ |
| **Pokes** 10 | **Sacks** | 5 | 17 |
| | 422 | 1 | 2 ÷ |
| | 433 | 1 | 1 ÷ |
| | 436 | 1 | 1 ÷ |
| | 428 | 1 | 2 |
| | 437 | 1 | 0 |
| | 448 | 1 | 0 |
| | 431 | 1 | 1 ÷ |
| | 449 | 1 | 2 |
| | 452 | 1 | 0 |
| | 424 | 1 | 3 |
| **Pokes** 10 | **Sacks** | 5 | 14 |
| | 458 | 1 | 4 |
| | 450 | 1 | 0 |
| | 455 | 1 | 1 ÷ |
| | 451 | 1 | 0 ÷ |
| | 453 | 1 | 2 |
| | 454 | 1 | 1 |
| | 456 | 1 | 0 ÷ |
| | 403 | 1 | 2 ÷ |
| | 401 | 1 | 4 ÷ |
| | 369 | 1 | 4 |
| **Pokes** 10 | **Sacks** | 5 | 20 ÷ |
| | 400 | 1 | 7 ÷ |
| | 376 | 1 | 4 |
| | 404 | 1 | 3 |
| | 406 | 1 | 2 ÷ |
| | 390 | 1 | 3 |
| | 389 | 1 | 3 ÷ |
| | 409 | 1 | 3 ÷ |
| | 392 | 1 | 6 ÷ |
| | 398 | 1 | 4 |

| | | | | | | | |
|---|---|---|---|---|---|---|---|
| | 29 | 1 | 2 | | 399 | 1 | 4 |
| **Pokes** 10 | **Sacks** | 5 ÷ | 10 | **Pokes** 10 | **Sacks** | 5 ÷ | 16 |

**Page 7 [4r.]**

†

fl.4

| | | Pokes | Cloves | | | Pokes | Cloves |
|---|---|---|---|---|---|---|---|
| N° | 335 | 1 | 3 | N° | 368 | 1 | 0 |
| | 345 | 1 | 5 | | 414 | 1 | 3 |
| | 388 | 1 | 3 | | 413 | 1 | 2 ÷ |
| | 350 | 1 | 3 ÷ | | 420 | 1 | 5 ÷ |
| | 402 | 1 | 4 | | 419 | 1 | 4 ÷ |
| | 346 | 1 | 3 | | 421 | 1 | 4 ÷ |
| | 384 | 1 | 6 ÷ | | 25 | 1 | 3 ÷ |
| | 386 | 1 | 4 | | 33 | 1 | 4 |
| | 395 | 1 | 2 ÷ | | 31 | 1 | 4 ÷ |
| | 410 | 1 | 4 | | 26 | 1 | 2 |
| **Pokes** 10 | **Sacks** | 5 ÷ | 12 ÷ | **Pokes** 10 | **Sacks** | 5 ÷ | 8 |
| | 385 | 1 | 3 | | 23 | 1 | 3 |
| | 397 | 1 | 4 | | 34 | 1 | 3 |
| | 382 | 1 | 6 ÷ | | 20 | 1 | 5 ÷ |
| | 381 | 1 | 4 ÷ | | 39 | 1 | 4 ÷ |
| | 393 | 1 | 4 ÷ | | 35 | 1 | 4 ÷ |
| | 396 | 1 | 6 | | 10 | 1 | 4 |
| | 394 | 1 | 5 ÷ | | 5 | 1 | 3 |
| | 387 | 1 | 4 | | 28 | 1 | 3 |
| | 391 | 1 | 2 | | 22 | 1 | 4 |
| | 383 | 1 | 4 ÷ | | 11 | 1 | 2 ÷ |
| **Pokes** 10 | **Sacks** | 5 ÷ | 18 ÷ | **Pokes** 10 | **Sacks** | 5 ÷ | 11 |
| | 417 | 1 | 2 ÷ | | 21 | 1 | 3 ÷ |
| | 418 | 1 | 0 | | 12 | 1 | 3 ÷ |
| | 405 | 1 | 4 | | 3 | 1 | 4 |
| | 379 | 1 | 7 ÷ | | 4 | 1 | 3 |
| | 415 | 1 | 4 | | 2 | 1 | 5 |

| | | | |
|---|---|---|---|
| | 407 | 1 | 2 |
| | 370 | 1 | 3 |
| | 412 | 1 | 4 |
| | 408 | 1 | 6 |
| | 367 | 1 | 3 |
| **Pokes** 10 | **Sacks** | 5 ÷ | 10 |

| | | | |
|---|---|---|---|
| | 37 | 1 | 5 ÷ |
| | 24 | 1 | 4 |
| | 9 | 1 | 4 |
| | 17 | 1 | 2 ÷ |
| | 8 | 1 | 2 ÷ |
| **Pokes** 10 | **Sacks** | 5 ÷ | 11 ÷ |

| | | | |
|---|---|---|---|
| | 377 | 1 | 4 ÷ |
| | 373 | 1 | 5 |
| | 378 | 1 | 5 |
| | 380 | 1 | 3 ÷ |
| | 416 | 1 | 4 |
| | 374 | 1 | 6 ÷ |
| | 375 | 1 | 5 |
| | 371 | 1 | 1 ÷ |
| | 372 | 1 | 4 |
| | 411 | 1 | 0 ÷ |
| **Pokes** 10 | **Sacks** | 5 ÷ | 13 ÷ |

| | | | |
|---|---|---|---|
| | 14 | 1 | 3 ÷ |
| | 7 | 1 | 3 |
| | 41 | 1 | 3 ÷ |
| | 1 | 1 | 4 |
| | 30 | 1 | 3 |
| | 16 | 1 | 4 |
| | 36 | 1 | 5 |
| | 32 | 1 | 3 |
| **Pokes** 8 | **Sacks** | 4 ÷ | 3 |

| | | | |
|---|---|---|---|
| | 6 | 1 | 3 |
| | 8 | 1 | 1 ÷ |
| | 5 | 1 | 2 ÷ |
| | 2 | 1 | 2 ÷ |
| | 7 | 1 | 4 |
| | 3 | 1 | 3 ÷ |
| | 9 | 1 | 4 ÷ |
| | 4 | 1 | 2 |
| **Pokes** 8 | **Sacks** | 4 | 23 ÷ |

**a)** S*umma* tot*a*le in pok*es*: CCCC$^{mo}$ lxvj$^{o}$.

The whych*e* makyth in sackys CC° lxiiij° s*emis*[8] and v clo*ves semis*, of the whych*e* ys rebatyd for the tare of ev*ery* pok*e*, j clo*ve semis*. Þ*e* whych*e summa* ys xiij *sackys*[9] et xxiij clo*ves*. And so reste clere ne*t*: cc° lj *sackys* clo*ves* viij *semis*.[10]

**Page 8 [4v.]**

†

1450

**a)** Factura lana*rum* pock*es* cccclxvj signat*a*, num*er*at*a* et depinct*a*, p*ro*ut inferius contine*tur*,[11] carigat*a* in carraca unde est patronus Antonio de Aurea de Janua, no*mine* Johan*nis* de Albic*is* consignand*o* in portu de Pis*e*, Francisco et Johan*ni* et sociis vel aliis qui fuer*ant* pro ip*s*is.

**b)** De num*ero* j ad num*erum* xxxv: pock*es* xxxv de lana de la March*e* fine, co*ntra*signat*a* de una ancella *cum* hum*er*is de capite virginis, ut moris est depingere lanas de Marchia: pok*es* xxxv.

**c)** De n° xxxvi ad num*erum* xli: pok*es* vj de juvene[12] lana de la March*e*, co*ntra*signat*a* de una ancella ut supra *cum* uno pere preci*us* duplic*e* de corall*e* vermoill*e*:[13]pok*es* vi.

**d)** De n° xlij ad num*erum* lxix: pock*es* xxviij de lana de Cotyswolde fyne, co*ntra*signat*a* de una manu cu*m* j manipulo de rosis de tribus foliis: pock*es* xxviij.

**e)** De n° lxx ad num*erum* lxxxxj: pock*es* xxij de lana de Cotyswold*e* fine, co*ntra*signat*a* de uno pecore coronat*o*: pok*es* xxij.

**f)** De n° lxxxxij ad num*erum* lxxxxix: pok*es* viij de lana juv*ene* de Cotyswolde fyn*e*, depinct*a* de uno pecore coronat*o* quod h*ab*et in ore suo modicum de una herba: pok*es* viij.

**g)** De n° C ad num*erum* Cxxj: pock*es* xxij de lana de Cotiswolde fine, depinct*a* de uno pecore coronat*o* cu*m* suo agnello: pok*es* xxij facto.

**h)** De n° Cxxij ad num*erum* Cxxx: pok*es* ix de lana juv*ene* de Cotyswold*e* fine, depincta de uno pecore coronat*o* cu*m* suo agnello et pecus h*ab*et modicu*m* de una herba in ore: pok*es* ix.

[8] Balmayn uses an 'S' abbrevation four times in this sentence, meaning *semis* or a half (Cappelli, *Lexicon Abbreviaturarum*, pp. liv-v).
[9] Here the scribe writes simply 'ss' but presumably, he means *sackys* / *sackes* as written on the line above.
[10] The 466 pokes equate therefore to 264½ sacks and 5 ½ cloves. Tare is calculated at 1½ clove per poke, making a total weight to be deducted of 13 sacks 23 cloves. This leaves a net weight of 251 sacks 8½ cloves.
[11] 'Exactly as enclosed below'.
[12] This is the first attestation of this word, written clearly in full as *juvene*. It is usually abbreviated as *juv-* from then on. In this text, it is Italian / Latin *juvene* but probably not AF *jun* as Holmes ('Anglo-Florentine Trade', 373) writes it.
[13] = 'bright red / vermilion coral'. Compare Balmayn's corresponding description of the same mark in ME later on in the document, the following year: *with a maydyne his head with a peyr of coralle bedis abowte her neke* (28b). *Vermoille* is an unusual spelling variant but there is clearly an *o* in the original MS. See AND1 sub **vermeil**.

**i)** Lane vermoile: Nota q*uo*d in pok*es* in num*er*o lxx sunt lane rubie. Et in num*er*o Cxxx[e] su*n*t lane vocat*e* flese woll*e* que ponderant cl*o*v*es* vij de lane fine de Cotyswold*e* de rac*io*ne yong*e*.

**j)** De n° Cxxxj ad num*erum* Clxxij: pok*es* xlij de lane fine de Cotyswolde, depincta de una chapleta[14] virid*e* duplic*e* cum quatuor floribus. Et in n° Cxxxj su*n*t lane rubie. Et in n° Cxxij sunt lane rubie: pok*es* xlij facto.

**k)** De n° Clxxiij ad num*erum* Clxxxxiiij: pok*es* xxij de lana fine de Cotyswold*e*, depincte de uno garlando asure, videl*ice*t blod*e*, de tribus floribus et in medio dict*e* garlande est una stella rubia: pok*es* xxij facto

**l)** De n° Clxxxxv ad num*erum* CCxxij: pok*es* xxviij de lana de Cotyswold*e* fine, depincta de uno pavo, a pecoke:[15] pok*es* xxviij.

**m)** De n° CCxxiij ad num*erum* CCxxxiij: pok*es* xi de lana fine juv*ene* de Cotyswold*e*, depincta de uno pavo cum una campana ad pedem sinistrum: pok*es* xi.

**n)** De n° CCxxxiiij ad num*erum* CClij: pok*es* xix de lana fine juv*ene* de Cotiswolde, depincta de uno garlando virid*i* duplic*i* et in medio dict*i* garland*i*, una rosa: pok*es* xix.

**o)** De n° CCliij ad num*erum* CClxiiij: pok*es* xij de lana fine juv*ene* de Cotiswold*e*, depinct*a* de una manu cum uno manipulo rosa*rum* de trib*us* foliis et digito auriculare stante recto: pok*es* xij.

**p)** De n° CClxv ad num*erum* CClxxiij: pok*es* ix de lana fyn*e* juv*ene* de Cotiswold*e*, depinct*a* de uno garlando asure blod*e* cu*m* t*ri*b*us* florib*us* et in medio garland*o*, una stella rubia, et in medio stelle, i° O: pok*es* ix.

**q)** De n° CClxxiiij ad CClxxxv: pok*es* xij de lana Abbathie, c*o*nt*ra*signat*a* cu*m* uno mytro cu*m* cruce sup*ra*: pok*es* xij.

**r)** De n° CClxxxvi ad num*erum* CClxxxvij: pok*es* ij de lana fine juv*ene* Abbathie, depinct*a* de uno mitro sine cruce sup*ra*: pok*es* ij.

**s)** De n° CClxxxviij ad num*erum* iij[c]xlv: pok*es* lviij de lana de Cotiswolde fine, depinct*a* de uno agn*us* Dei cu*m* cruce in vexilla, a baner:[16] pok*es* lviij.

**t)** De n° iij[c]xlvj ad num*erum* iij[c]lj: pok*es* vj de lane fine juvene de Cotiswolde, depinct*a* de uno agnus Dei sine cruce in vexilla: pok*es* vj.

**u)** De n° iij[c]lij ad num*erum* iij[c]lxxviij: pok*es* xxvij de lana de Cotiswolde fine, depinct*a* de uno manipulo de quinq*ue* popies[17] cu*m* una sc*ri*ptura que dicit Laus Deo: pok*es* xxvij.

**v)** Lane vermoile et nota in n° iij[c]lxxvij sunt lane rubie et in n° iij[c]lxxviij sunt medie lane rubie.

[14] This is either < It. *cappelletto* or a Latinised / Italinised verion of AF *chapelet*. In heraldic terms, a chaplet was either a wreath or crown of flowers. See TLIO sub **cappelletto** / AND sub **chapelet** / OED2 sub **chaplet**.

[15] *a pecoke*: scribal insertion above *pavo* and one of four examples in this section of an English gloss.

[16] *a baner*: scribal insertion above *vexilla*.

[17] Here (and in entry 8w) ME *popies* ('poppies') is clearly written in full in the middle of the Latin-Italian matrix. Compare with same mark description in entry 16c: *The marke j° mazzo de 5 papavery cum breve que dixe Laus Deo.*

**w)** De n° iij^c^lxxix ad num*erum* iij^c^lxxx: pok*es* ij de lana fyn*e* juv*ene* de Cotiswold*e*, depinct*a* de uno manipulo de quinq*ue* popies et una M: pok*es* ij facte

**x)** De n° iij^c^lxxxj ad num*erum* iiij^c^viij: pok*es* xxviij de lana fyn*e* de Cotiswod*e*, depinct*a* de uno jaye: pok*es* xxviij.

**y)** De n° iiij^c^ix ad num*erum* CCCCx: pok*es* ij de lana fine juv*ene* de Cotiswode depinct*a* de una jaye cu*m* erba i*n* ore: pok*es* ij.

**Page 9 [5r.]**

†

fl.5

**a)** De n° CCCCxj ad num*erum* iiij^c^xviij: pok*es* viij de lana Abbathie, depinct*a* de uno pastorale, an abbot*s* croyse: pok*es* viij facto.

**b)** De n° iiij^c^ix ad num*erum* iiij^c^ xxj: pok*es* iij de lana fine juv*ene* de Cotiswold, depinct*a* de uno pye: pok*es* iij.

**c)** De n° iiij^c^xxij ad num*erum* CCCCl: pok*es* xxix de lana fyn de Cotyswold, depinct*a* cu*m* uno sole, ang*li*ce a sonne:[18] pok*es* xxix.

**d)** De n° CCCClj ad num*erum* iiij^c^liiij: pok*es* iiij de lana Abbathie de illa sorte de pok*es* viij ut sup*ra*, depinct*a* de una sc*ri*ptura sup*ra*scri*p*to storo: pok*es* iiij.

**e)** De n° iiij^c^lv ad num*erum* iiij^c^lviij: pok*es* iiij de lana fine juv*ene* de Cotiswold, quilib*et* poche cu*m* duob*us* signis sine *con*trasignis su*n*t de bonitate de le jaye ut sup*ra*:[19] pok*es* iiij.

**f)** De no j ad num*erum* viij:[20] pok*es* viij de lana de Cotiswolde fine, vocat*a* storo, depinct*a* de una manu quod tenet un*um* manipulu*m* de borage de trib*us* foliis:[21] pok*es* viij.

Sum*ma* to*ta*le pok*es*: CCCClxvj

**g)** De quib*us* sunt poche xxxv de le March*e* fine: poch*e* xxxv
Poche vj de juvene lana de le Marche: pock*es* vj
Poche xxiiij de Abbathie fine: pock*es* xxiiij[22]
Poche ij de lana juv*ene* de Abbathia fine: pock*es* ij
Poche CCCxiiij de lana de Cotiswold*e* fine: pock*es* CCCxiiij
Poche lxxxv de juv*ene* Cotiswold*e* fine: pock*es* lxxxv

**h)** Lane de le Marche constant hic quarte p*ar*ti plus q*u*am fine lane de Cotiswold*e*. Et juv*ene* lane de Costiswolde su*n*t peiori quarta p*ar*te q*u*am lane fine de Cotiswold*e*. Hoc vobis dico ad hoc ut h*ab*eatis attendere ad vendic*ion*em. Et ut intelligatis ut vos gubernare habeatis.

[18] *a sonne*: scribal insertion, preceded by the Latin marker, *ang(lice)*.
[19] This lot of pokes has not been marked with a countermark like the others and only bears Cantelowe's mark: †. Balmayn points out that the wool is the same quality (*bonitate*) as the wool marked with a jay.
[20] Balmayn reaches 358 and then counts the last eight pokes as 1 to 8 again. These are the 8 pokes under the borage mark sold on 11th October 1451 in 28a, after he has tallied up the 448 others on 6th October 1451.
[21] This is not marked specifically as *storo* (unlike the wool in 9d) but has a mark of borage.
[22] This figure is given incorrectly as twenty-three pokes in Holmes, 'Anglo-Florentine Trade', 373.

## [Expenses incurred at Pisa and Florence]

### Page 10 [f.41r.]

| | | |
|---|---|---|
| | Cost*es* | fl.41 |
| **a)** | M*emorandum* that this ben*e* the cost*es* þat ben*e* don*e* upon a poke of wolle and upon othyr march*a*untyse, as for the cost*es* firste[23] fro þe Port*e* Pysan*e* to Lyvorne and to Pysse and so at Florens, as folewyth: | We paye nothyng*e* and ther we sette nothyng*e*. |
| **b)** | Firste, for the costys of iiij$^{c}$ lxvi pok*es* woll*e* of my mayst*er*, Wyll*ia*m Cantelowe, comyd to the Port*e* Pysane in the caryke of Antonio de Aurea, patron*e* et march*a*unt of Jene, send fro H*a*mptone to Pyse by Joh*an* de Albycys et *compagni*a, march*a*unt of Florens, to Fraunces et Joh*an* Salviati et *compagni*a in Pisa and they for to send hit to Florens to Jacob Salviati et *compagni*a: | |
| **c)** | The whych*e* was ondyr this marke † the whych*e* iiij$^{c}$ lxvi pok*es* ben*e* at the begynnyng of this boke wretyn. Thys ys the rekenyng of the seyd iiij$^{c}$ lxvi pok*es* woll*e* resceyved by the schippe of Antoni de Aurea send by oure felyschip[24] of London to us and to you. | |
| **d)** | Fyrst for the frey3th and for the custome of Jene: | |
| **e)** | It*em* for the p*ro*vysyon*e* of the oste of Lyvorne and for the unlading fro the schippe s.10 po*ur* pok*e*: | Sum*ma* £233 fl. 54. 4. 4. |
| **f)** | It*em* s.1 po*ur* poke for the ry3th of the schipe house þat ys for to saye the arsinà of Lyvorn*e*: | Sum*ma* £23 s.6 d.0[25] fl. 5. 8. 4. |
| **g)** | It*em* for caryage fro Lyvorne to Pyse s.10 po*ur* pok*e*: | Sum*ma* £233 fl. 54. 4. 4. |
| **h)** | It*em* for onladyng owte of the carte into the custom*e* house of Pise and for the weyng*e* and beryng*e* hom*e* s.2 po*ur* pok*e*: | Sum*ma* £46 s.12 fl. 10. 16. 8. |
| **i)** | It*em* for the custom*e* of Pyse for a cxvij st*one* iiij$^{xx}$xvj lb wey3th a s. 25 le C., sum*ma* £1466 s.4 d.0, and for the custom*e* of the ry3th of þe ospytall*e* callyd Chare[26] £3 and for the custom*e* of the xij p*a*rte of the þe grete sum*ma* aboveseyd £122 s.8 d.8 and for the p*ar*cell*e* wretyng*e* to þe clerkys, £2: | Sum*ma* £1593 s.9 d.0 fl. 382. 15. 7. |
| **j)** | It*em* for to have hit owte of Pyse, s.1 po*ur* pok*e* at the gate: | Sum*ma* £23 s. 6 fl. 5.10.9. |

[23] *firste:* scribal insertion above the main line.

[24] This must refer to the Mercers' Company; see OED3 sub **fellowship**, 'A guild or other incorporated body of practitioners of a trade or craft (att. 1415).

[25] On this folio only we have some rare examples of Balmayn using an Arabic zero (rather than a dash) in a price to mean 'nothing' i.e. *d. 0* not *d.* -.

[26] This word is not clearly transcribable but presumably Balmayn is referring to the Ospedale di Santa Chiara, the largest hospital in medieval Pisa. Like other ecclesiastical institutions, it probably extracted income from the city by claiming a percentage of the custom levied on wool. I would like to express my thanks to Professor John Henderson (Birkbeck, University of London) for his advice on this matter.

| | | |
|---|---|---|
| k) | It*em* for the passage at S*anct*a Gondda,[27] s.1 d.10 po*ur* poke: | Sum*ma* £42 s.14 d.4 fl. 10. 3. 4 |
| l) | It*em* for the avery of the galley or schippe the whych*e* ys to saye þ*at* eve*ry* march*a*unt shall bere his pa*r*te aft*er* the rate of his march*a*untyse for all mann*er* of cost*es* don*e* upon þe galleys or schippe for cause of ennemyis to the savacon*dyd* of the godys: | Nothynge payd |
| m) | It*em* for the ryȝth of the Offycyall*e* of þ*e* See þe whych*e* was juge bytwex us and þ*e* patron*e* for dive*rse* harneys[28] of the woll*e*: | fl. 1. |
| n) | It*em* to the man þ*at* sawe the harneys of the woll*e*: | fl. 1. 2. 1. |
| o) | It*em* for the porto*urs* for pylyng*e* up of þ*e* seyd wolle et for our*e* pylyng: | fl. 5. |
| p) | It*em* for the mendyng*e* of the pockys wher*e*as they were ibroke | fl. 1.17. 6. |
| q) | It*em* for div*erse* cost*es* done to þe Offysyall*e* of the See and for to have the plee wretyne for to send hit to London: | fl. 2. |
| r) | It*em* for ladyng*e* upon*e* a botte iiij^xx^ xlj[29] pok*es* and for the weyng*e* et beryng*e*, s. 2 po*ur* poke: | S*um*ma £9 s.12 d.0 fl. 2. 4. 9 |
| s) | It*em* for house hyre where the wolle stodde and for ostelage: | fl. 4. |
| t) | It*em* for the cost*es* of Jacob Salviati for to ryde to Pyse for þe seyd woll*e*: | fl. 1. |
| u) | It*em* for our*e* p*ro*vesyon*e* the viij pa*r*te of a floryn*e* po*ur* le poke: | fl. 58.5. |
| v) | Sum*ma* de lé cost*es* de Pise:[30] | fl. 599 s. 12 d.8 a or*o* |
| w) | P*er* Fraunces et Joh*an* Salviati[31] in Pisa et *compagni*a. Directe to Alaman Salviati in Ferens[32], le 16[33] *jour* de nove*mbre* 1450. | |

[27] This is the Camoldese abbey of Santa Gonda (also known as Santa Gioconda) located in the river Arno valley in the commune of San Miniato. Its position mid-way between Pisa and Florence meant that it was ideally placed to collect custom taxes on goods passing through.(Emanuele Repetti, *Dizionario Geografico, Fisico e Storico della Toscana*, Volume 1 (Firenze, A. Tofani, 1883), pp. 182–3, pp. 464–6). I am most grateful to Dr Angelo Nicolini for his help in identifying this placename and sharing this reference with me.

[28] It is not clear what Balmayn means by the *harneys of the wolle*. He could be referring to the harness attached to carts to move the wool at the dockside or, more generally, to some kind of equipment or gear involved in the wool's storage on board ship or its transportation; cf. AND2 sub **harneis**, MED sub **harneis**, OED2 sub **harness**.

[29] *iiij*^xx^ = 80 or literally 'quatre-vingt'; hence it appears that 121 (eighty plus forty-one) pokes were loaded onto a boat in this instance.

[30] *de Pise*: scribal insertion, superscript.

[31] These are Jacopo's brothers, Francesco and Giovanni, who controlled family operations in Pisa at the time.

[32] This is Jacopo's father and the company head, Alamanno Salviati.

[33] The first of only six examples in the text where an Arabic (rather than a Roman) numeral precedes AF *jour* in the entry's date (cf. Part 5 in the Introduction). The other five examples are found at 13e, 14a, 25a, 29j and 31p.

**Page 11 [41v.]**

†

| | | |
|---|---|---|
| **a)** | Cost*es* of Florens for 466 pok*is* woll*e* of my mayst*er* W. Cantelowe ys of þe [marke] | |
| **b)** | Firste for the costes of Pyse the whych*e* was send to us for to paye and there*fore* we sette hit in oure rekenyng a fl.: | fl.599 s.18. d.5[34] |
| **c)** | It*em* for cariours the which*e* be callyd victura for the bryngyng*e* fro Pise to Florens the foreseyd 466 pok*es* woll*e*, weyng lb.123000[35] a s.18 le C. de pezoly[36] q*ue* fa £1107. The valewe ys s.85 po*ur* Florino: | fl.260 s.13 d.8 |
| **d)** | It*em* for the custom*e* of Florens for the seyd 466 pok*es*, weyng lb 123067 a fl. uno, s.16 de pezoly le C. q*ue* fa fl.1230. Et po*ur* le s.16 q*ue* fa £987 s.4 d.3 de p*ez.*[37], de le valeuta de £ a s.73 d.4 po*ur* fl., q*ue* fa fl.269, £- s.17 d.7 de p*ez.* S*um*ma in toto fl.1499, £- s.17 d.7 de p*ez.* Et po*ur* duodesimo, þe whych*e* ys uno p*ar*te de xij p*ar*te de le maiore. S*um*ma ut sup*ra* q*ue* fa fl.124, £4 s.- d.8 de p*ez.* Et po*ur* la p*ar*tita to the clerkys, £2. S*um*ma to*ta*le fl. 1623 [….] po*ur* solid*i*, £6 s.18 d.3 de p*ez.*, valeuta de grossy:[38] | fl.1624 s.18 d.4 |
| **e)** | It*em* po*ur* la deminuc*ione* del *con*tento de pok*es* 466 po*ur* lb.123067 a s.1 d.8 a or*o* le C. q*ue* fa fl.102 s.11 d.2 a or*o*: | fl.102 s.16 d.2 |
| **f)** | It*em* pour averia po*ur* *con*sely de mare[39] po*ur* le dyd 466 pok*es* po*ur* lb.123067. Estimate a fl.20 le C. de la lana q*ue* fa fl. 24614. The whych*e* payth*e* halffe a fl. po*ur* C. fl. q*ue* fa fl.123 s.1 d.5 a or*o* q*ue* fa fl.: | fl.123 s.2 d. 2 |
| **g)** | It*em* po*ur* pisare a comperatory et po*ur* portare a lor*o* ỉ botega s.3 d.4. de p*ez.* po*ur* pok*e* q*ue* fa pok*es* 448 come appare p*er* vendute q*ue* fa £74 s.13 d.4 de p*ez.* u*no*, fl.: | fl. 17 s.16. d.6 |
| **h)** | It*em* po*ur* sensaria de le dyd 448 pok*es* a s.15 po*ur* poke come appare p*er* vendute q*ue* fa £336 s.- d.-, valeno: | fl.79 s.1 d.9 |
| **i)** | It*em* po*ur* taratura q*ue* fa le[40] tare de le lana s.2 d.6 de p*ez.* po*ur* poke q*ue* fa pok*es* 448 come appare p*er* vendute q*ue* [fa] £56 de p*ez.*, valeno: | fl.13 s.5 d.2 |

[34] It is unclear why this figure is not identical to the sum of the *costes of Pyse* on the previous folio.

[35] Balmayn gives the total weight of the 466 pokes as 123000lb here but then writes the slightly higher figure of 123067lb in the following three entries (11d, 11e, 11f).

[36] This makes no sense and Balmayn must surely have meant to write *weyng lb.123000 a s.18 de pezoly le C.* as he does in the entry below at 11d. Stating that a price is in so many *soldi de pezoly* (i.e. *soldi di piccioli*) underlines the fact it is in Italian *lire* and not in florins.

[37] Balmayn abbreviates *pezoly* from this point onwards, using a dotted *p* with suspension mark.

[38] = Venetian *grossi*, abbreviated elsewhere as *gr.*

[39] = *Consoli del mare,* Florentine magistrates who were specialised in maritime law, one of many offices with judiciary powers in the city state (TLIO sub **console**). Earlier in the accounts, Balmayn refers elsewhere to an *Offycyalle of þe See* (10m / 10q). Cf. Michael Mallet, 'The Sea Consuls of Florence in thFifteenth Century', *Papers of the British School at Rome*, 27 (1959), 156–169.

[40] I am assuming that this is the Italian feminine plural, *le*, and not the AF plural, *lé*.

j) It*em* po*ur* farle styvare et restivare più volte quando sono mostro a chomperatore. Et po*ur* spago po*ur* *con*sare le dyd pok*es* non se mitte nulla, q*ue* seribbino più di [due][41] fl.: fl.- d.-

k) It*em* po*ur* magasino de le dyd lane: fl. 15 s. - d. -

l) It*em* po*ur* retenc*ion*e de denar*i* 2 de p*ez.* po*ur* fl. lo damno mownta po*ur* toto ¼[42] de fl. po*ur* C. q*ue* fa fl.63 s.23 d.5 de fl.: fl. 63 s. 23 d.6

m) It*em* po*ur* nostra *pro*visione de fl.100, uno fl. po*ur* noi q*ue* fa fl.255 s.7 d.- a fl.: fl. 255 s.7 d.-

n) A it*em* for weyng*e* in the custom*e* house of Florens and for the beryng*e* to the magasyn*e*, s.2 de p*ez.* po*ur* pok*e* que *fa* £46 s.12 de p*ez.*, valeno: fl. 10 s. 28 d. -

S*um*ma to*ta*le: fl. 3165 s.5 d.8

o) P*er* Alaman*o* Salviati in Ferens, a d*ì* 28 septemb*re* 1451

## [Sale of lots of wool to Italian buyers]

**Page 12 [65r.]**

Ih*esus*

fl.65

a) M*emorandum* that this ys the ret*ur*ne fro Florens to London of my mayst*er* Will*ia*m Cantelowys wollys and other mauch*a*untyse made by me John Balmay*n* s*er*vaunt of the seyd Will*ia*m. First for iiij$^{c}$lxvi pochis wolle[43] as folewyth aft*er* þe weyȝt et rate of Florens and by of this marke † as for the salle of the wolle.

b) First, solde to Fraunces de C*hrist*foro Aleotti et *com*panio*u*ns, clothemakers, doit le xiij jo*ur* de novembr*e* 1450 po*ur* xiiij pok*es* woll*e* q*ue* poi*se* cu*m* tare.

| | | | | | |
|---|---|---|---|---|---|
| N° | 156 | lb 260 | N° | 161 | lb 265 |
| | 152 | lb 250 | | 136 | lb 260 |
| | 153 | lb 261 | | 160 | lb 260 |
| | 162 | lb 256 | | 139 | lb 263 |
| | 146 | lb 245 | | 171 | lb 240 |
| | 142 | lb 266 | | 145 | lb 269 |
| 14 | 131 | lb 260 | | 141 | lb 270 |

[41] The word is difficult to read clearly.
[42] This is the first modern fraction to appear in the accounts.
[43] *wolle*: scribal insertion above the line.

S*um*ma de po*ise* cu*m* tare de 14 pok*es*:[44] iij m$^{ll}$ vi$^{c}$ xxv lb
Tare po*ur* uso et maca3oni et sup*r*apiù de sack*es* de canevas: lb.16 po*ur* le pok*e*
Et po*ur* fradisch*o*: lb 2
Et po*ur* sup*ra*più de pezo de le pok*es*: lb 5
S*um*ma de tar*e*: lb 231 unc*e* 6
Rest*e* net lb 3393 unc*e* 6, a florini 25 po*ur* le C.
S*um*ma: viij$^{c}$ xlviij florins and vij s. of gold*e* q*ue* fa fl. 848 s.10, a payer argent *con*tent

The mark*e* una chapleta verid*e* duplic*e* cu*m* quatuor florib*us*.

**c)** Juncta Ibindo de Will*ia*mo Juncta et *compagni*a, lanaiuoli, doit le xxiij jo*ur* de novembr*e* po*ur* iiij pok*es* q*ue* po*ise* cu*m* t*are*:

| | | | | | |
|---|---|---|---|---|---|
| N° | 80 | lb 256 | N° | 77 | lb 262 |
| 4 | 76 | lb 262 | | 91 | lb 251 |

S*um*ma de po*ise* cu*m* t*are* de 4 pok*is*: lb 1032
Tar*e* po*ur* uso et maca3oni et sup*ra*più de sack*es* et sup*ra*più de pezo et po*ur* umido: lb.18 po*ur* pok*e* q*ue* fa lb.72
Reste n*e*t lb 960, a fl. 24 le C.
S*um*ma: fl. 230 s. 8 a or*o*,
S*um*ma: fl. 230 s. 11 d.7, argent *con*tent

The mark*e* uno pecore coronat*o*.

**d)** A Petro et Joh*a*n Wyduche et *compagni*a, lanaiuoli, doit a d*ì* 20 janev*er* po*ur* iiij pok*es* q*ue* po*ise* cu*m* tar*e*:

| | | | | | |
|---|---|---|---|---|---|
| N° | 51 | lb 248 | N° | 69 | lb 266 |
| 4 | 57 | lb 264 | | 52 | lb 284 |

S*um*ma de po*ise* cu*m* t*are*: lb 1062
T*ara* po*ur* uso: lb 11 po*ur* poke
Et po*ur* maca3oni: lb 16
Et po*ur* umido et fradyscho: lb 8
Et po*ur* lé sack*es*: lb 5

[44] *pokes*: scribal insertion above the line.

Et po*ur* sup*ra*più de pezo: lb 3
S*um*ma de tare: lb 76
Rest*e* net lb 986, a fl. 24 le C.
S*um*ma: fl. 236 s. 12 a or*o*
S*um*ma: fl. 236 s. 17 d. 4, argent *con*tent

The mark*e* una manu cu*m* uno manipulo de rosis de trib*us* foliis.

**e)** Obertino de Gerardo Rezaliti et *compagni*a, doit a d*ì* 25 janev*er* po*ur* iiij pok*es* q*ue* po*ise* cu*m* t*are*:

| | | | | | |
|---|---|---|---|---|---|
| N° | 64 | lb 258 | N° | 45 | lb 271 |
| 4 | 48 | lb 261 | | 43 | lb 258 |

S*um*ma de po*ise* cu*m* t*are*: lb 1048
T*are* po*ur* uso et macaȝoni et sup*ra*più de sack*es* et sup*ra*più de pezo et umido: lb 18 po*ur* poke
S*um*ma: lb 72
Rest*e* net lb 976, a fl. 24 le C.
S*um*ma: fl. 234 s. 4 a or*o*
S*um*ma: fl. 234 s. 5 d. 9, argent *con*tent

The mark*e* una manu cu*m* uno manip*u*lo de rosis de trib*us* foliis.
Pok*es* 26 S*um*ma pok*es* 26

**Page 13 [65v.]**

† Yhesus

**a)** Obertino de Gerardo Resaliti et *compagni*a, doit a d*ì* 25 janev*er* po*ur* ij pok*es* lane q*ue* po*ise* cu*m* t*are*:

| | | |
|---|---|---|
| N° | 261 | lb 261 |
| 2 | 259 | lb 265 |

S*um*ma de po*ise* cu*m* t*are*: lb 526
Tar*a* po*ur* uso: lb 11 po*ur* pok*e*
Et po*ur* umido: lb 1 po*ur* pok*e*
Et po*ur* sup*ra*più de sack*es*: lb 4
S*um*ma: lb 28
Reste net lb 498, a fl. 18 le C.
S*um*ma: fl. 89 s. 12 a or*o*
S*um*ma: Fl 89 s. 17 d. 4, arg*ent* *con*tent

The marke ys una manu cu*m* una manip*u*lo rosar*um* de trib*us* foliis et degito ariculare strawte[45] rect*o*

**b)** Joh*an* de Phelippo de Ascheto, doit le xxv jo*ur* de Janev*er* po*ur* v pok*es* lane q*ue* poi*se* cu*m* t*are*:

| | | | | | |
|---|---|---|---|---|---|
| N° | 53 | lb 255 | N° | 63 | lb 261 |
| 5 | 56 | lb 256 | | 46 | lb 273 |
| | | | | 44 | lb 266 |

S*umm*a de poi*se* cu*m* t*are*: lb 1311
T*are* po*ur* uso et macaȝoni et sup*ra*più de sack*es* et d sup*ra*più e pezo et po*ur* umido: lb 18 po*ur* pok*e*
S*umm*a: lb 90
Reste n*e*t lb 1221, a fl. 24 le C.
Summa: fl. 293 s. - d. -, argent *con*tent

The mark*e* de una manu cu*m* uno manipulo de rosis de trib*us* foliis.

**c)** Fraunces Cr*isto*foro Aleotti et *compagni*a, lanaiuoli, doit le iiij jo*ur* de fev*er*elle po*ur* ij pok*es* lane q*ue* poi*se* cu*m* tar*e*:

| | | |
|---|---|---|
| N° | 241 | lb 283 |
| 2 | 246 | lb 276 |

S*umm*a de poi*se* cu*m* t*are*: lb 559
Tar*a* po*ur* uso: lb 11 po*ur* pok*e*
Et po*ur* lé sack*es*: lb 3
Et po*ur* sup*ra*più de pezo: lb 3
S*umm*a: lb 28
Reste n*e*t lb 531, a fl. 18 s. 15 a or*o* le C.
S*umm*a: fl. 99 s. 11 a or*o*
S*umm*a: fl. 99 s. 15 d. 11, argent *con*tent

The mark*e* uno garland*o* virid*e* duplic*e* et in medio dict*i* garland*i* una rosa.

[45] Balmayn has clearly written *strawte* ('straight'?) here and not *stante* as in entry 20b.

**d)** It*em* le dyd Fraunces Chr*isto*foro Aleotti, doit le dyd jo*ur* po*ur* vj pok*es* q*ue* po*ise* cu*m* t*are*:

| | | | | | |
|---|---|---|---|---|---|
| N° | 250 | lb 280 | N° | 234 | lb 274 |
| 6 | 244 | lb 270 | | 245 | lb 279 |
| | 238 | lb 288 | | 251 | lb 282 |

S*um*ma de po*ise* cu*m* t*are*: lb 1673
T*ara* po*ur* uso: lb ii po*ur* pok*e*.
Et po*ur* lé sack*es*: lb 7
Et po*ur* sup*ra*più de pezo: lb 7
S*um*ma: lb 80
Rest*e* net lb 1593, a fl. 18 st 15 a or*o* le C.
S*um*ma: fl. 298 s. 14 a oro
S*um*ma: fl. 298 s. 20 d. 3, argent *con*tent

The marke uno garland*o* verid*e* duplic*e* et in medio dict*i* garland*i* una rosa sup*ra*.

**e)** Juncta Ibendo de Will*ia*mo Juncta, doit le 5 jo*ur* de fev*er*ell*e* po*ur* iiij pok*es* lane q*ue* po*ise* cu*m* t*are*:

| | | | | | |
|---|---|---|---|---|---|
| N° | 204 | lb 257 | N° | 203 | lb 262 |
| 4 | 214 | lb 268 | | 211 | lb 254 |

S*um*ma de po*ise* cu*m* t*are*: lb 1041
T*ara* po*ur* uso: lb 11 po*ur* pok*e*
Et po*ur* macaʒoni: lb 19 unc*e* 4
Et po*ur* lé sack*es*: lb 3 unc*e* 6
Et po*ur* umido: lb 4
Et po*ur* fradischo: lb 1 unc*e* 9
S*um*ma: lb 74
Rest*e* net lb 967, a fl. 24 le C.
S*um*ma: fl. 232 s. 1 a or*o*
S*um*ma: fl. 232 s. 1 d. 5, argent *con*tent

The mark*e* ys uno pavo.

S*um*ma pok*es* 19
S*um*ma fl. 1022. 18 a or*o*

**Page 14 [66r.]**

fl. 66

Ih*esus*

**a)** Jelyan*o* de Joh*a*n dai Borgo, doit le 5 jo*ur* de fev*er*ell*e* po*ur* iiij pok*es* lane q*ue* po*ise* cu*m* tare:

| | | | | | |
|---|---|---|---|---|---|
| N° | 213 | lb 262 | N° | 216 | lb 267 |
| 4 | 222 | lb 265 | | 220 | lb 278 |

S*um*ma de po*ise* cu*m* *tare*: lb 1072
T*ara* po*ur* uso: lb 11 po*ur* pok*e* q*ue* fa lb 44
Et po*ur* maca ʒoni: lb 18 unc*e* 6
Et po*ur* sack*es*: lb 7 unc*e* 6
Et po*ur* fradisch*o*: lb 10
Et po*ur* umido: lb 6
Et po*ur* sup*ra*più de pezo: lb 3
S*um*ma: lb 89
Reste ne*t* lb 983, a fl. 24 le C.
S*um*ma: fl. 235 s. 18 a or*o*
S*um*ma: fl. 235 s. 26, argent *con*tent

The mark*e* ys uno pavo.

**b)** Apardo de Nicolo de Lorenxo Loteni, doit le viiij jo*ur* fev*er*ell*e* po*ur* vj pok*es* lane q*ue* po*ise* cu*m* *tare*:

| | | | | | |
|---|---|---|---|---|---|
| N° | 341 | lb 269 | N° | 294 | lb 267 |
| 6 | 339 | lb 270 | | 326 | lb 261 |
| | 344 | lb 254 | | 303 | lb 269 |

S*um*ma de poise cu*m* *tare*: lb 1590
T*ara* po*ur* uso: lb 11 po*ur* poke
Et po*ur* macaʒoni: lb 25
Et po*ur* sup*ra*più de sack*es*: lb 9÷
Et po*ur* sup*ra*più de pezo: lb 4
Et po*ur* umido: lb 6
S*um*ma: lb 110 unc*e* 6
Reste ne*t* lb 1479 unc*e* 6, a fl. 24 le C.
S*um*ma: fl. 335 s. 1 a or*o*
S*um*ma: fl. 255 s. 1 d. 5, argent *con*tent

The mark*e* una agn*us* Dei cu*m* cruce in vexilla.

**c)** Pero Matheo de Contowcho, doit le viij jo*ur* de fev*er*ell*e* po*ur* v pok*es* lane q*ue* pois*e* cu*m* t*are*:

| | | | | | |
|---|---|---|---|---|---|
| N° | 87 | lb 253 | N° | 81 | lb 253 |
| 5 | 78 | lb 254 | | 86 | lb 266 |
| | | | | 71 | lb 251 |

S*um*ma de pois*e* cu*m* t*are*: lb 1277
T*are* po*ur* uso et macaȝoni et sup*ra*più de sack*es* et sup*ra*più de pezo et po*ur* umido: lb 18 po*ur* pok*e*
S*um*ma: lb 90
Reste n*e*t lb 1187 a fl. 24 le C.
S*um*ma: Fl 284 s. 17 a or*o*
S*um*ma: Fl 284 s. 24 d. 7, argent *con*tent

The mark*e* uno peccore coronat*o*.

**d)** Antonio de Guydo de Junctino et *compagni*a, lanaiuoli, doit le xiij jo*ur* de fev*er*ell*e* po*ur* x pok*es* lane q*ue* pois*e* cu*m* t*are*:

| | | | | | |
|---|---|---|---|---|---|
| N° | 328 | lb 269 | N° | 327 | lb 262 |
| | 316 | lb 265 | | 296 | lb 261 |
| | 298 | lb 263 | | 340 | lb 273 |
| | 342 | lb 264 | | 290 | lb 264 |
| 10 | 289 | lb 258 | | 292 | lb 276 |

S*um*ma de pois*e* cu*m* t*are*: lb 2655
T*ara* po*ur* uso: lb 11 po*ur* pok*e*
Et po*ur* macaȝoni: lb 63 unc*e* 4
Et po*ur* sup*ra*più de sack*es*: lb 17 unc*e* 6
Et po*ur* sup*ra*più de pezo: lb 10
S*um*ma: lb 208
Reste n*e*t lb 2447, a fl. 24 le C.
S*um*ma: fl. 587 s. 5 a or*o*
S*um*ma: fl. 587 s. 7 d. 9, argent *con*tent

The mark*e* ys de uno Agn*us* Dei cu*m* cruce in vexilla.

S*um*ma pok*es* 25
S*um*ma fl. 1463. 1 a or*o*

**Page 15 [66v.]**

† Ihe*sus*

**a)** Genoby de Leonardo Bartoli et *compagni*a, doit a d*ì* 13 feve*r*ell*e* pou*r* v pock*es* lane q*ue* po*ise* cu*m* *tare*:

| | | | | | |
|---|---|---|---|---|---|
| N° | 229 | lb 249 | N° | 231 | lb 267 |
| 5 | 230 | lb 266 | | 228 | lb 265 |
| | | | | 226 | lb 282 |

S*um*ma de po*ise* cu*m* *tare*: lb 1329
T*ara* pou*r* uso: lb 11 pou*r* pok*e*
Et pou*r* lok*es*: lb 2
Et pou*r* sup*ra*più de sack*es*: lb 4
Et pou*r* fradisch*o*: lb 1
Et pou*r* umido: lb 5
Et pou*r* sup*ra*più de pezo: lb 4
S*um*ma: lb 71
Reste n*e*t lb 1258, a fl. 18 le C.
S*um*ma: fl. 226 s. 8 a or*o*
S*um*ma: fl. 226 s. 11 d.7, argent *con*tent

The mark*e* de uno pavo et una campana ad pedem sinistrum.

**b)** Leonardo de Angelo de Balioni et *compagni*a, doit le xiij jou*r* de feve*r*ell*e* pou*r* viij pok*es* lane q*ue* po*ise* *cum* *tare*:

| | | | | | |
|---|---|---|---|---|---|
| N° | 143 | lb 258 | N° | 170 | lb 247 |
| | 147 | lb 272 | | 151 | lb 277 |
| | 134 | lb 261 | | 169 | lb 285 |
| 8 | 166 | lb 250 | | 167 | lb 278 |

S*um*ma de po*ise* cu*m* *tare*: lb 2128
T*ara* pour uso: lb 11 pou*r* pok*e*
Et pou*r* macaȝoni: lb 34 unc*e* 4
Et pou*r* sup*ra*più de sack*es*: lb 8 unc*e* 6
Et pou*r* fradyscho: lb 6
Et pou*r* umido: lb 8
Et pou*r* sup*ra*più de pezo: lb 6 unc*e* 2
S*um*ma: lb 151
Reste n*e*t lb 1977, a fl. 24 le C.

S*umm*a: fl. 474 s. 10 a or*o*
S*umm*a: fl. 474 s. 14 d. 6, argent *con*tent

The mark*e* ys una chapleta virid*e* duplic*e* cu*m* quatuor florib*us*.

**c)** Pero de Galiano et *compagni*a, doit le xiij jo*ur* de fev*er*ell*e* po*ur* xxij pok*es* lane q*ue* po*is*e cu*m* t*ar*e:

| | | | | | |
|---|---|---|---|---|---|
| N° | 187 | lb 266 | N° | 186 | lb 264 |
| | 184 | lb 284 | | 190 | lb 260 |
| | 193 | lb 261 | | 185 | lb 256 |
| | 194 | lb 270 | | 174 | lb 256 |
| | 177 | lb 274 | | 182 | lb 275 |
| | 179 | lb 265 | | 180 | lb 256 |
| | 176 | lb 283 | | 191 | lb 250 |
| | 181 | lb 272 | | 189 | lb 268 |
| 22 | 188 | lb 276 | | 183 | lb 272 |
| | 175 | lb 254 | | 178 | lb 278 |
| | 192 | lb 262 | | 173 | lb 253 |

S*umm*a de po*is*e cu*m* t*ar*e: lb 5855
Tar*e* po*ur* uso et macaȝoni et sup*ra*più de sack*es* et sup*ra*più de pezo et po*ur* umido: lb 20 po*ur* pok*e*
Et più po*ur* fradyscho: lb 10
S*umm*a: lb 450
Reste n*e*t lb 5405, a fl. 24 le C.
S*umm*a: fl. 1297 s. 4 a or*o*
S*umm*a: fl. 1297 s. 5 d. 9, argent *con*tent

The mark*e* ys uno garland*o* asure vi*delicet* blod*e* de trib*us* florib*us* et in medio dict*o* garland*o* est una stella rubia.

S*umm*a pok*es* 35
S*umm*a fl. 1998. 2

**Page 16 [67r.]**

†

fl.67

**a)** Jachobo d'Orsino Lanfredini et Francesco Guydotti et *compagni*a, doit a d*ì* 13 februar*e* po*ur* x pok*es* lane q*ue* po*is*e cu*m* t*ar*e:

| | | | | | |
|---|---|---|---|---|---|
| N° | 202 | lb 255 | N° | 198 | lb 266 |
| | 218 | lb 265 | | 197 | lb 252 |
| | 199 | lb 275 | | 195 | lb 248 |
| | 217 | lb 272 | | 221 | lb 273 |
| 10 | 209 | lb 270 | | 206 | lb 264 |

S*umma* de po*ise* *cum* *tare*: lb 2640
T*are* po*ur* uso et macaʒoni et sup*ra*più de sack*es* et sup*ra*più de pezo et po*ur* umido: lb 19 po*ur* pok*e*
Summa: lb 190
Reste n*e*t lb 2450, a fl. 24 le C. q*ue* fa fl. 558 s. - d. -
S*umma*: fl. 588, argent *con*tent

The mark*e* uno pavo.

**b)** Dominicho de Jachobo Federisi et *compagni*a, doit a d*ì* 11 march*e* 1450[46] po*ur* iij pok*es* lane q*ue* po*ise* cu*m* *tare*:

| | | |
|---|---|---|
| N° | 333 | lb 257 |
| 3 | 299 | lb 266 |
| | 318 | lb 266 |

S*umma* de po*ise* *cum* *tare*: lb 789
T*ara* po*ur* uso: lb 11 po*ur* poke, lb 33
Et po*ur* macaʒoni: lb 14 unc*e* 6
Et po*ur* sup*ra*più de sach*i*:[47] lb 7 unc*e* 6
Et po*ur* sup*ra*più de pezo: lb 2
Et po*ur* fradysch*o*: lb 8
Et po*ur* umido: lb 3
S*umma*: lb 68
Reste n*e*t lb 721, a fl. 24 le C. q*ue* fa fl. 173 s. - d. -
S*umma*: fl. 173 s. - d. -, argent *con*tent

The mark*e* uno agn*us* Dei cu*m* cruce in vexilla.

**c)** Pagino de Joh*anne* de Albesi et *compagni*a, doit a d*ì* ditto po*ur* vj pok*es* lane q*ue* po*ise* cu*m* *tare*:

[46] 11 March 1451 in modern calendar usage.
[47] At this point in the entries, Balmayn switches from ME *sackes* to Italian *sachi*.

| | | | | | |
|---|---|---|---|---|---|
| Nº | 367 | lb 263 | Nº | 368 | lb 236 |
| 6 | 369 | lb 269 | | 375 | lb 281 |
| | 370 | lb 262 | | 373 | lb 285 |

S*um*ma de po*ise* cu*m* *tare*: lb 1596
T*are* po*ur* uso et maca3oni et sup*ra*più de sach*i* et sup*ra*più de pezo et po*ur* umido: lb 18 unc*e* 6 po*ur* pok*e*
S*um*ma de tar*e*: lb 111
Reste n*e*t lb 1485, a fl. 24 le C. q*ue* fa fl. 356. 8. 9
S*um*ma: fl. 356 s. 11 d. 7, argent *con*tent

The mark*e* jº mazzo de 5 papavery cu*m* breve q*ue* dixe Laus Deo.

**d)** Bernardo d'Auremo de Medeci et *compagni*a, doit a d*ì* 15 ditto po*ur* iiij pok*es* lane q*ue* po*ise* cu*m* *tare*:

| | | |
|---|---|---|
| Nº | 320 | lb 262 |
| | 291 | lb 260 |
| | 317 | lb 271 |
| 4 | 302 | lb 271 |

S*um*ma de po*ise* cu*m* *tare*: lb 1064
T*ara* po*ur* uso lb 11 po*ur* pok*e*: lb 44
Et po*ur* maca3oni: lb 23
Et po*ur* sup*ra*più de sach*i*: lb 8
Et po*ur* sup*ra*più de pezo: lb 3
Et po*ur* umido: lb 4
Et più lb 4 d'achordo
Summa de tar*e*: lb 86
Reste n*e*t lb 978, a fl. 24 le C. q*ue* fa fl. 234. 14 a or*o*
S*um*ma: fl. 234 s. 20 d. 3, argent *con*tent

The mark*e* uno agn*us* Dei cu*m* cruce in vexilla.

**e)** Joh*anne* et Will*ia*mo de M*y*ss*er*[48] Salustro de Perosa et *compagni*a, doit a d*ì* ditto po*ur* iiij pok*es* lane q*ue* po*ise* cu*m* *tare*:

[48] The abbreviation *mys-* or *mes-*, as it appears elsewhere in the text, represents *mysser* or *messer* ('Mister'), from the Italian *messere* cf. OVI sub **messere**. Note that this borrowing is not currently attested in an English-matrix sentence until 1566: see OED3 sub **Messer**.

| | | |
|---|---|---|
| N° | 304 | lb 266 |
| | 313 | lb 265 |
| | 321 | lb 265 |
| 4 | 338 | lb 261 |

S*um*ma de po*ise* c*um* t*are*: lb 1057
T*ara* po*ur* uso, lb 11 po*ur* pok*e*: lb 44
Et po*ur* macaʒoni: lb 14 unce 6
Et po*ur* sup*ra*più de sach*i*: lb 6 unce 6
Et po*ur* sup*ra*più de pezo: lb 3
Et po*ur* umido: lb 4
Et più lb 4 d'achordo
S*um*ma de tar*e*: lb 76
Reste n*e*t lb 981, a fl. 24 le C. monta fl. 235 s. 8 a or*o*
S*um*ma: fl. 235 s. 11 d. 7, argent *con*tent

The mark*e* uno agn*us* Dei cu*m* cruce in vexilla.

Pok*es* 27

**Page 17 [67v.]**

†

**a)** Nycholas de Joh*anne* de Sandro *et com*pagni*a*, lanaiuoli, doit a d*ì* 15 de march*e* 1450[49]
po*ur* xxij pok*es* lane q*ue* po*ise* cu*m* t*are*:

| | | | | | |
|---|---|---|---|---|---|
| N° | 106 | lb 266 | N° | 109 | lb 277 |
| | 117 | lb 275 | | 118 | lb 267 |
| | 121 | lb 267 | | 119 | lb 262 |
| | 114 | lb 266 | | 105 | lb 255 |
| | 104 | lb 254 | | 116 | lb 258 |
| | 107 | lb 271 | | 111 | lb 271 |
| | 100 | lb 267 | | 113 | lb 264 |
| | 120 | lb 254 | | 103 | lb 255 |
| | 112 | lb 256 | | 110 | lb 264 |
| | 101 | lb 262 | | 102 | lb 257 |
| 22 | 115 | lb 262 | | 108 | lb 270 |

[49] 15 March 1451 in modern calendar usage.

S*um*ma de po*ise* cu*m* *tare* lb 5800
T*are* po*ur* uso et macaʒoni et sup*ra*più de sach*i* et po*ur* sup*ra*più de pezo et po*ur* umido et più po*ur* fradisch*o* lb 34 q*ue* fa lb 20 po*ur* pok*e*
S*um*ma de tare: lb 440
Rest*a* netta lb 5360, a fl. 23 le C. que fa fl. 1232 lb 16 a or*o*
Summa: fl. 1232 s. 23 d. 2, arge*nt* *con*te*nt*

The mark*e* j[a] pecora coronata cu*m* suo agnello.

**b)** Attimo de Joh*anne* Ginori et *compagni*a, lanaiuoli, doit a d*ì* ditto po*ur* xx pok*es* lane q*ue* po*ise* cu*m* *tare*:

| | | | | | |
|---|---|---|---|---|---|
| N° | 149 | lb 267 | N° | 165 | lb 268 |
| | 155 | lb 250 | | 148 | lb 272 |
| | 150 | lb 269 | | 133 | lb 254 |
| | 137 | lb 270 | | 168 | lb 267 |
| | 163 | lb 253 | | 172 | lb 271 |
| | 154 | lb 268 | | 158 | lb 259 |
| | 157 | lb 264 | | 135 | lb 267 |
| | 132 | lb 261 | | 14 | lb 295 |
| | 138 | lb 262 | | 140 | lb 252 |
| 20 | 164 | lb 275 | | 144 | lb 265 |

S*um*ma de po*ise* cu*m* *tare*: lb 5309
T*are* po*ur* uso et macaʒoni et sup*ra*più de sach*i* et sup*ra*più de pezo et po*ur* umido: lb 17 po*ur* poke
S*um*ma de tare: lb 340.
Reste n*e*t lb 4969, a fl. 24 le C. q*ue* fa fl. 1192 s. 11 a or*o*
S*um*ma: fl. 1192 s.15 d. 11, argent *con*tent

The mark*e* j[a] chapleta v*iri*d*e* duplic*e* cu*m* iiij[or] flori*bus*.

**c)** Larenxo de Paris Corbenelli et *compagnia*, doit a d*ì* ditto po*ur* xij pok*es* lane q*ue* po*ise* cu*m* *tare*:

| | | | | | |
|---|---|---|---|---|---|
| N° | 382 | lb 292 | N° | 397 | lb 273 |
| | 408 | lb 294 | | 394 | lb 288 |
| | 388 | lb 263 | | 391 | lb 255 |
| | 396 | lb 293 | | 386 | lb 274 |
| | 406 | lb 264 | | 383 | lb 277 |
| 12 | 387 | lb 277 | | 393 | lb 276 |

*Summa* de po*ise* cu*m* t*are*: lb 3326
T*are* pou*r* uso lb 11 pou*r* pok*e*: lb 132
T*are* pou*r* macaȝoni et sup*ra*più de sach*i* et sup*ra*più de pezo et pou*r* umido: lb 8 pou*r* pok*e* q*ue* fa lb 96
S*um*ma de tar*e*: lb 228
Reste n*e*t lb 3098, a fl. 24 le C q*ue* fa fl. 743 s. 10 a or*o*
S*um*ma: fl. 743 s. 14 d. 6, argent *con*tent

The mark*e* una jaye.

**d)** Francisco de Simoni de Nozo Fantoni et *compagni*a, doit le xvj jo*ur* de march*e* 1450[50] po*ur* xj pok*es* lane que po*ise* c*um* t*are*:

| | | | | | |
|---|---|---|---|---|---|
| Nº | 295 | lb 253 | Nº | 330 | lb 257 |
| 6 | 331 | lb 254 | | 306 | lb 270 |
| | 312 | lb 270 | | 323 | lb 263 |

S*um*ma de po*ise* cu*m* t*are*: lb 1567
T*ara* pou*r* uso: lb 11 pou*r* poke, lb 66
Et pou*r* macaȝoni: lb 17 unc*e* 6
Et sup*ra*più de sach*i*: lb 12 unc*e* 6
Et sup*ra*più de pezo: lb 3
Et pou*r* fradisch*o*: lb 4
Et pou*r* umido: lb 6
S*um*ma de tar*e*: lb 109
Reste n*e*t lb 1458, a fl. 24 le C. q*ue* fa fl. 349 s. 18 a or*o*
S*um*ma: fl. 349 s. 26 d. j, argent *con*tent

The mark*e* jº agn*us* Dei cum cruce in vexilla.

**e)** Pero et Joh*anne* Gwydewchy et *compagni*a, doit a d*ì* ditto pou*r* v pok*es* lane q*ue* po*ise* c*um* t*are*:

| | | |
|---|---|---|
| Nº | 437 | lb 233 |
| | 435 | lb 263 |
| | 338 | lb 223 |
| | 440 | lb 246 |
| 5 | 426 | lb 250 |

[50] 16 March 1451 in modern calendar usage.

S*um*ma de po*ise* cu*m* *tare*: lb 1215
T*ara* pou*r* uso: lb 11 pou*r* pok*e* *que* fa lb 55
Et pour macaʒoni: lb 18 unc*e* 6
Et po*ur* sup*ra*più de sach*i*: lb 2 unc*e* 6
Et po*ur* sup*ra*più de pezo: lb 0 unce 6
Et po*ur* umido: lb 5
S*um*ma de tar*e*: lb 81 unc*e* 6
Reste n*e*t lb 1133 unc*e* 6, a fl. 24 le C. q*ue* fa fl. 272
S*um*ma: fl. 272 s. 0 d. -,[51] argent *con*tent

The mark*e* uno sole.

Pok*es* 65

**Page 18 [68r.]**

†

fl. 68

**a)** Danyell*e* de Nofry Daszo et *compagni*a, doit a d*ì* xviij de march*e* 1450[52] po*ur* ij pok*es* lane que po*ise* *cum* *tare*:

| | | |
|---|---|---|
| N° | 307 | lb 251 |
| 2 | 319 | lb 275 |

S*um*ma de po*ise* cu*m* *tare*: lb 526
T*are* pou*r* uso et macaʒoni et sup*ra*più de sach*i* et de pezo et po*ur* umido: lb 19 unc*e* 6 pou*r* poke
S*um*ma de tar*e*: lb 39
Rest*a* netta: lb 487, a fl. 24 le C. q*ue* fa fl. 116 s. 17 a or*o*
S*um*ma: fl. 116 s. 24 d.7, argent *con*tent

The mark*e* uno agn*us* Dei cum cruce in vexilla.

**b)** Brancho Costantino da Perosa et *compagni*a, doit a d*ì* ditto po*ur* x pok*es* lane q*ue* poi*se* *cum* *tare*:

| | | | | | |
|---|---|---|---|---|---|
| N° | 336 | lb 260 | N° | 324 | lb 250 |
| | 311 | lb 260 | | 314 | lb 274 |
| | 308 | lb 280 | | 345 | lb 281 |

[51] The scribe uses both a zero and dash in this price.
[52] 18 March 1451 in modern calendar usage. This is also one of just two examples where the author uses a Roman (rather than an Arabic) numeral after the Italian word *dì* in the date entry (cf. Introduction, Part 5). The second example is just below on the same folio at 18c.

| | | | | |
|---|---|---|---|---|
| | 334 | lb 256 | 388 | lb 276 |
| 10 | 309 | lb 279 | 335 | lb 257 |

S*um*ma de po*ise* cu*m* *tare*: lb 2673
T*ara* pou*r* uso: lb 11 pou*r* sach*i* q*ue* fa lb 110
Et pou*r* macaʒoni: lb 30
Et pou*r* sup*ra*più de sack*es*: lb 20 unc*e* 6
Et pou*r* sup*ra*più de pezo: lb 7 unc*e* 6
Et pou*r* umido: lb 10
Et pou*r* fradysch*o*: lb 4
S*um*ma: lb 182
Reste net lb 2491, a fl. 24 le C. monta fl. 597 s. 16 a or*o*
S*um*ma: fl. 597 s. 23 d. 2, argent c*on*tent

The mark*e* uno agn*us* Dei cum cruce in vexilla.

**c)** Laurens de Rinieri Spineli et *compagni*a, doit a d*ì* iij de ap*re*ll*e* 1451 pou*r* iiij pok*es* lane q*ue* po*ise* cu*m* *tare*:

| | | |
|---|---|---|
| N° | 361 | lb 257 |
| | 377 | lb 278 |
| | 366 | lb 256 |
| 4 | 352 | lb 267 |

S*um*ma de po*ise* cu*m* *tare*: lb 1058
T*are* pou*r* uso: lb 11 pou*r* pok*e* q*ue* fa lb 44
Et pou*r* macaʒoni: lb 17
Et più lb 10 in le pok*e* de n° 377 for hit was not sewyng*e*
Et pou*r* sup*ra*più de sach*i*: lb 5
Et pou*r* sup*ra*più de pezo: lb 3
Et pou*r* umido: lb 4
S*um*ma: lb 83
Reste net lb 975, a fl. 24 le C. q*ue* fa fl. 234 s. - d. -
S*um*ma fl. 234 s. - d. -, argent *con*tent

The mark*e* j° manip*u*lo de quinq*ue* popeis cu*m* una sc*ri*ptura que dicit Laus Deo.

**d)** Francisco de Simon*e* de Nozzo Fantoni et *compagni*a, doit a d*ì* ditto pou*r* iiij pok*es* lane q*ue* po*ise* cu*m* *tare*:

| | | |
|---|---|---|
| N° | 374 | lb 290 |
| | 357 | lb 271 |
| | 364 | lb 274 |
| 4 | 356 | lb 271 |

S*um*ma de po*ise* cu*m* t*are*: lb 1106
T*are* pou*r* uso: lb 11 po*ur* pok*e*, lb 44
Et po*ur* macaʒoni: lb 17
Et pou*r* sup*ra*più de sach*i*: lb 7
Et po*ur* sup*ra*più de pezo: lb 5
Et po*ur* umido: lb 4
Et più lb 2 d'achordo
S*um*ma de tar*e*: lb 79
Reste n*e*t lb 1027, a fl. 24 le C. q*ue* fa fl. 246 s. 9 a or*o*
S*um*ma: fl. 246 s.13 d. -, argent *con*tent

The mark*e* j° manip*u*lo de quinq*ue* popeis cu*m* j sc*ri*ptura que dicit Laus Deo.

**e)** Francisco et Thomaxo Bewsini et *compagni*a, doit a jo*ur* xij de ap*relle* 1451 po*ur* iiij pok*es* lane q*ue* po*ise* cu*m* t*are*:

| | | |
|---|---|---|
| N° | 365 | lb 262 |
| | 362 | lb 279 |
| | 355 | lb 254 |
| 4 | 359 | lb 248 |

S*um*ma de po*ise* cu*m* t*are*: lb 1043
T*are* pou*r* uso: lb 11 po*ur* pok*e*, lb 44
Et po*ur* macaʒoni: lb 10
Et po*ur* sup*ra*più de sach*i*: lb 6 unc*e* 6
Et po*ur* sup*ra*più de pezo: lb 2
Et po*ur* umido: lb 4
S*um*ma de tar*e*: lb 66 unc*e* 6
Rest*a* netta lb 976 unce 6, a fl. 24 le C. q*ue* fa fl. 234 s. 7 a or*o*
Summa: fl. 234 s. 10 d. […],[53] argent *con*tent

The mark*e* uno manip*u*lo de quinq*ue* popeis cu*m* una sc*ri*ptura que dicit Laus Deo
Pok*es* 24

[53] The scribe has scribbled out this figure.

**Page 19 [68v.]**

**a)** A Donato de M*esser* Leonard*o* d'Arezzo et *compagni*a, doit le xij jo*ur* de aprell*e* 1451 po*ur* iiij pok*es* lane q*ue* po*ise* cu*m* t*are*:

| | | |
|---|---|---|
| N° | 376 | lb 272 |
| | 371 | lb 251 |
| | 354 | lb 278 |
| 4 | 360 | lb 266 |

S*um*ma de po*ise* cu*m* t*are*: lb 1067
T*are* pou*r* uso: lb 11 po*ur* poke, lb 44
Et po*ur* maca3oni: lb 15 unc*e* 6
Et po*ur* sup*ra*più de sach*i*: lb 4 unc*e* 6
Et po*ur* sup*ra*più de pezo: lb 3
Et po*ur* umido: lb 4
S*um*ma de t*are*: lb 71
Reste ne*t* lb 996, a fl.24 le C. q*ue* fa fl. 239 s. - d. -
S*um*ma: fl. 239 s. - d. - argent *con*tent

The mark*e* j° manip*u*lo de quinq*ue* popeis cu*m* un*a* sc*ri*ptura que dicit Laus Deo.

**b)** Bernardo Lappe da Zuane Nycholini et *compagni*a doit le dyd jo*ur* pou*r* vj pok*es* lane q*ue* po*ise* cu*m* t*are*:

| | | |
|---|---|---|
| N° | 47 | lb 275 |
| | 66 | lb 263 |
| | 54 | lb 264 |
| | 58 | lb 258 |
| 6 | 50 | lb 274 |
| | 68 | lb 259 |

S*um*ma de po*ise* cu*m* t*are*: lb 1593
T*are* pou*r* uso et po*ur* maca3oni et sup*ra*più de sach*i* et sup*ra*più de pezo et po*ur* umido: lb 18 po*ur* pok*e*
S*um*ma: lb 108
Reste ne*t* lb 1485, a fl. 24 le C. q*ue* fa fl. 356 s.8 a or*o*
S*um*ma: fl. 356 s.11 d.7, argent *con*tent

The mark*e* j<sup>a</sup> manu cu*m* j° manip*u*lo de rosis de trib*us* foliis.

**c)** It*em* le dyd Bernardo, doit le dyd jo*ur* pou*r* iiij pok*es* lane q*ue* po*ise* cu*m* t*are*:

| | | |
|---|---|---|
| N° | 310 | lb 255 |
| | 332 | lb 242 |
| | 300 | lb 252 |
| 4 | 337 | lb 263 |

S*um*ma de po*ise* cu*m* *tare*: lb 1012
T*are* *pour* uso: lb 11 po*ur* pok*e*, lb 44
Et po*ur* macaʒoni: lb 15 unc*e* 6
Et po*ur* sup*ra*più de sach*i*: lb 4 unc*e* 6
Et po*ur* sup*ra*più de pezo: lb j
Et po*ur* fradisch*o*: lb 4
Et po*ur* umido: lb 4
S*um*ma de tare: lb 73
Reste n*e*t lb 939, a fl. 24 le C. q*ue* fa fl. 225 s. 7 a or*o*
S*um*ma: fl. 225 s. 10 d. -, argent *con*tent

The mark*e* uno agn*us* Dei cum cruce in vexilla.

**d)** Antonio de Chambino Chambini et *compagni*a, doit le dyd jo*ur* po*ur* j pok*e* lane q*ue* po*ise* cu*m* *tare*:

| | | |
|---|---|---|
| N° | 210 | lb 269 |
| j | | |

T*are* po*ur* uso et macaʒoni et sup*ra*più de sach*i* et po*ur* umido: lb 19
Et più lb 2 po*ur* fradisch*o*
S*um*ma de tar*e*: lb 21
Reste n*e*t lb 248 a fl. 24 le C. q*ue* fa fl. 59 s.10 a or*o*
S*um*ma: fl. 59 s.14 d. 6, argent *con*tent

The mark*e* uno pavo.

**e)** It*em* le dyd Antonio, doit le dyd jo*ur* po*ur* ij pok*es* lane q*ue* po*ise* cu*m* *tare*:

| | | |
|---|---|---|
| N° | 343 | lb 255 |
| 2 | 305 | lb 283 |

S*um*ma de po*ise* cu*m* *tare*: lb 538
T*are* po*ur* uso et macaʒoni et sup*ra*più de sach*i* et sup*ra*più de pezo et po*ur* umido: lb 19 po*ur* poke
S*um*ma de tar*e*: lb 38

Reste n*e*t lb 500, a fl. 24 le C. q*ue* fa fl. 120 s. - d. -
S*um*ma: fl. 120 s. - d. -, argent *con*tent

The mark*e* uno agn*us* Dei cum cruce in vexilla.

**f)** Leonardo et Dominicho del Tore et *compagni*a, doit le dyd jo*ur* po*ur* iiij pok*es* lane q*ue* po*ise* cu*m* t*are*:

| | | |
|---|---|---|
| N° | 384 | lb 290 |
| | 407 | lb 252 |
| | 405 | lb 267 |
| 4 | 392 | lb 297 |

S*um*ma de po*ise* cu*m* t*are*: lb 1106
T*are* po*ur* uso et macaȝoni et sup*ra*più de sach*i* et sup*ra*più de pezo et po*ur* umido lb 18 unc*e* 6 po*ur* pok*e*
S*um*ma: lb 74
Rest*a* netta lb 1032, a fl. 28 le C. q*ue* fa fl. 288 s. 19 a or*o*
S*um*ma: fl. 288 s. 27 d. 6, a payer a un anne[54]

The mark*e* una jaye.

Pok*es* 21

**Page 20 [69r.]**

fl. 69

**a)** A Gino de Zuane Ginori et *compagni*a, lanaiuoli, doit le xij jo*ur* de ap*relle* 1451 po*ur* x pok*es* lane q*ue* po*ise* cu*m* t*are*:

| | | | | | |
|---|---|---|---|---|---|
| N° | 448 | lb 249 | N° | 446 | lb 249 |
| | 447 | lb 254 | | 430 | lb 272 |
| | 429 | lb 261 | | 434 | lb 256 |
| | 439 | lb 242 | | 441 | lb 239 |
| 10 | 442 | lb 257 | | 434[55] | lb 266 |

S*um*ma de po*ise* cu*m* t*are*: lb 2545
T*are* po*ur* uso et macaȝoni et sup*ra*più de sach*i* et sup*ra*più de pezo et po*ur* umido: lb 18 po*ur* poke

[54] This is the only example of this AF expression in the accounts, presumably meaning that the buyer will pay for the wool within the year.
[55] Poke no. 434 is repeated twice in same entry but with different weights.

S*um*ma de tar*e*: lb 180
Rest*e* n*e*t lb 2365, a fl. 24 le C. q*ue* fa fl. 567 s.12 a or*o*
S*um*ma: fl. 567 s.17 d.4, argent *con*tent

The mark*e* una sole.

**b)** Antonio de Zuane de Sandro et *compagni*a, doit le dyd jo*ur* po*ur* x pok*es* lane q*ue* po*ise* c*um* t*are*:

| | | | | | |
|---|---|---|---|---|---|
| N° | 264 | lb 270 | N° | 257 | lb 266 |
| | 253 | lb 294 | | 262 | lb 279 |
| | 260 | lb 276 | | 258 | lb 265 |
| | 256 | lb 274 | | 255 | lb 277 |
| 10 | 263 | lb 266 | | 254 | lb 263 |

S*um*ma de po*ise* cu*m* t*are*: lb 2730
T*ara* po*ur* uso: lb 11 po*ur* pok*e*, lb 110
Et po*ur* sup*ra*più de sach*i*: lb 16
Et po*ur* sup*ra*più de pezo: lb 10
Et più lb 5 d'achordo
S*um*ma: lb 141
Rest*e* n*e*t lb 2589, a fl. 18 le C. q*ue* fa fl. 466 s. - d. -
S*um*ma: fl. 466 s. - d. -, argent *con*tent

The mark*e* j<sup>a</sup> manu cu*m* u*no* manip*ulo* de t*ribus* foliis[56] et digito ariculare stante rect*o*.

**c)** Pero et Jacobo de Patsy et *compagni*a, lanaiuoli, doit le xxiiij jo*ur* de ap*relle* po*ur* xiij pok*es* lane q*ue* po*ise* cu*m* t*are*:

| | | | | | |
|---|---|---|---|---|---|
| N° | 75 | lb 269 | N° | 82 | lb 263 |
| | 84 | lb 268 | | 70 | lb 265 |
| | 88 | lb 268 | | 90 | lb 259 |
| | 85 | lb 259 | | 74 | lb 265 |
| | 73 | lb 249 | | 72 | lb 260 |
| | 79 | lb 262 | | 83 | lb 258 |
| 13 | 89 | lb 257 | | | |

[56] The scribe has missed out the word *rosis* here.

S*um*ma de po*ise* cu*m* t*are*: lb 3402
T*are* po*ur* uso et maca3oni et sup*ra*più de sach*i* et sup*ra*più de pezo et po*ur* umido: lb 18 po*ur* pok*e*, s*um*ma lb 234
Et più po*ur* fradisch*o*: lb 15
S*um*ma de tar*e*: lb 249
Rest*e* net lb 3153, a fl. 24 le C. q*ue* fa fl. 756 s. 14 a or*o*
S*um*ma: fl. 756 s. 20 d. 3, arge*nt* *con*tent

The mark*e* una peccora coronata.

**d)** Angelo de Zuane dai Borgo et *compagni*a, doit le v jo*ur* de magio[57] 1451 po*ur* ij pok*es* lane q*ue* po*ise* cu*m* t*are*:

| | | |
|---|---|---|
| Nº | 224 | lb 269 |
| 2 | 227 | lb 270 |

S*um*ma de po*ise* cu*m* t*are*: lb 539
T*ara* po*ur* uso: lb 11 po*ur* pok*e*, lb 22
Et po*ur* sup*ra*più de sach*i*: lb 2 unc*e* 6
Et po*ur* sup*ra*più de pezo: lb 1 unc*e* 6
Et po*ur* umido: lb 3
S*um*ma de tar*e*: lb 29
Rest*a* netta: lb 510, a fl. 18 le C. q*ue* fa fl. 91 s.16 a or*o*
S*um*ma: fl. 91 s.23 d.2, argent *con*tent

The mark*e* uno pavo cu*m* j campana ad pedem sinistrum.

**e)** Simone d'Amercho Sati et *compagni*a, doit le xiij jo*ur* de maye 1451 po*ur* iij pok*es* lane q*ue* poise cu*m* t*are*:

| | | |
|---|---|---|
| Nº | 21 | lb 270 |
| | 2 | lb 281 |
| 3 | 25 | lb 269 |

S*um*ma de poise cu*m* t*are*: lb 820
Tar*e* po*ur* uso: lb 11 po*ur* pok*e* que fa lb 33
Et po*ur* maca3oni: lb 9 unc*e* 6
Et po*ur* sup*ra*più de sach*i*: lb 2 unc*e* 6
Et po*ur* intingim*ento*: lb 2

[57] A rare example of a 'hybrid' date: AF *jour* + It. *magio* (cf. Introduction, Part 5).

Et po*ur* umido: lb 3
Et po*ur* sup*ra*più de pezo: lb 3
Et più d'acordo: lb 6
S*um*ma de tar*e*: lb 59
Rest*e* net lb 761, a fl. 26 s. 10 a or*o*[58] le C. q*ue* fa fl. 201 s.13 a or*o*
S*um*ma: fl. 201 s.18 d.10, argent *con*tent

The mark*e* una donzella.

**f)** Lorenxo de Rynery Spinelli et *compagni*a, lanaiuoli, doit le dyd jo*ur* po*ur* ij pok*es* lane q*ue* po*ise* cu*m* *tare*:

| | | |
|---|---|---|
| N° | 349 | lb 276 |
| 2 | 348 | lb 281 |

S*um*ma de po*ise* cu*m* *tare*: lb 557
T*ara* po*ur* uso: lb 11 po*ur* pok*e*, lb 22
Et po*ur* sup*ra*più de sach*i*: lb 4 unc*e* 6
Et po*ur* sup*ra*più de pezo: lb 2 unc*e* 2
Et po*ur* umido: lb 2
S*um*ma de tar*e*: lb 31
Rest*e* net lb 526, a fl. 18 le C. q*ue* fa fl. 94 s. 13 a or*o*
S*um*ma: fl. 94 s. 18 d. 10, argent *con*tent

The mark*e* uno agn*us* Dei sine cruce in vexilla.

Pok*es* 40

**Page 21 [69v.]**

**a)** Zuane de Jacabo del Pulesse et *compagni*a, doit le xii jo*ur* de maye 1451 po*ur* iiij pok*es* lane q*ue* po*ise* cu*m* *tare*:

| | | |
|---|---|---|
| N° | 351 | lb 257 |
| | 347 | lb 268 |
| | 350 | lb 265 |
| 4 | 346 | lb 265 |

S*um*ma de po*ise* cu*m* *tare*: lb 1055
T*ara* po*ur* uso: lb 11 po*ur* pok*e*, lb 44
Et po*ur* sup*ra*più de sach*i*: lb 6 unc*e* 6

[58] The scribe repeats *a oro* here.

Et po*ur* sup*ra*più de pezo: lb 2 unc*e* 6
Et po*ur* umido: lb 4
S*um*ma de tar*e*: lb 57
Rest*e* net lb 998, a fl. 18 le C. q*ue* fa fl. 179 s.12 a or*o*
S*um*ma: fl. 179 s.17 d.4, argent *con*tent

The mark*e* uno agn*us* Dei sine cruce in vexilla.

**b)** Zuane de Phelippo de Aschetto et *compagni*a, doit le dyd jo*ur* po*ur* j pok*e* lane que po*ise* cu*m* t*are*:

| | | |
|---|---|---|
| N° | 380 | lb 269 |
| j | | |

T*ara* po*ur* uso: lb 11
Et po*ur* sup*ra*più de sach*i*: lb 1 unc*e* 6
Et po*ur* sup*ra*più de pezo: unc*e* 6
Et po*ur* umido: lb 1
S*um*ma de tar*e*: lb 14
Rest*e* net lb 255, a fl. 18 le C. q*ue* fa fl. 45[59]18 a or*o*
S*um*ma: fl. 45 s. 26 d. -, argent *con*tent

The mark*e* uno manip*u*lo de quinq*ue* popeis et de uno M.

**c)** A Pero de Soldo de Antonio Baldovini et *compagni*a, doit le xxij jo*ur* de maye po*ur* xij pok*es* lane q*ue* po*ise* cu*m* t*are*:

| | | | | | |
|---|---|---|---|---|---|
| N° | 390 | lb 263 | N° | 395 | lb 259 |
| | 389 | lb 266 | | 402 | lb 273 |
| | 381 | lb 280 | | 401 | lb 287 |
| | 400 | lb 308 | | 385 | lb 267 |
| | 404 | lb 267 | | 399 | lb 280 |
| 12 | 398 | lb 274 | | 403 | lb 263 |

S*um*ma de po*ise* cu*m* t*are*: lb 3287
T*are* po*ur* uso et macaȝoni et sup*ra*più de sachi et sup*ra*più de pezo et po*ur* umido: lb 18 unc*e* 6 po*ur* poke
Et po*ur* fradisch*o*: lb j
S*um*ma de tar*e*: lb 223
Rest*e* net lb 3064, a fl. 24 le C. q*ue* fa fl. 735 s.7 a or*o*
S*um*ma: fl. 735 s.10 d. -, argent *con*tent

[59] The scribe has omitted to put s. in front of 18.

The mark*e* una jaye

**d)** Thom*as* de Ubertino Resali et *compagni*a, doit le v jo*ur* de jun*e* 1451 po*ur* iij pok*es* lane q*ue* po*ise* cu*m* t*are*:

| | | |
|---|---|---|
| N° | 363 | lb 263 |
| 3 | 353 | lb 272 |
| | 358 | lb 279 |

S*um*ma de po*ise* cu*m* t*are*: lb 814
T*are* po*ur* uso et macaȝoni et sup*ra*più de sachi et sup*ra*più de pezo et po*ur* umido,[60] *sum*ma de tar*e*: lb 56
Rest*e* net lb 758, a fl. 24 le C. q*ue* fa fl. 181 s.18 a or*o*
S*um*ma fl. 181 s. 26 d. -, argent *con*tent

The mark*e* j° manip*u*lo de quinq*ue* popeis cu*m* j sc*ri*ptura que dicit Laus Deo.

**e)** It*em* le dyd Thom*aso* de Urbertino, doit le dyd jo*ur* po*ur* j pok*e* lane q*ue* po*ise* cu*m* t*are*:

| | | |
|---|---|---|
| N° | 379 | lb 299 |
| j | | |

T*are* po*ur* uso et sup*ra*più de sach*i* et sup*ra*più de pezo et po*ur* umido: lb 17
Rest*e* net lb 282, a fl. 18 le C. q*ue* fa fl. 50 s.15 a or*o*
S*um*ma fl. 50 s. 21 d. 9, argent *con*tent

The mark*e* uno manip*u*lo de quinq*ue* popeis et de una M.

**f)** Pero de Soldo et Antonio Baldoveny et *compagni*a, doit le dyd jo*ur* po*ur* ij pok*es* lane que po*ise* cu*m* t*are*:

| | | |
|---|---|---|
| N° | 410 | lb 272 |
| 2 | 409 | lb 269 |

S*um*ma de po*ise* cu*m* t*are*: lb 541
T*ara* po*ur* uso lb 11 po*ur* pok*e*: lb 22
Et po*ur* sup*ra*più de sach*i*: lb 4

[60] The amount per poke is not mentioned here.

Et sup*ra*più de pezo: lb 2
Et po*ur* umido: lb 2
S*um*ma de tar*e*: lb 30
Rest*e* n*e*t lb 511, a fl. 18 le C. q*ue* fa fl. 91 s.19 a or*o*
S*um*ma fl. 91 s. - d. -, argent *con*tent

The mark*e* una jaye cu*m* erba in ore.

**g)** Matheo de Nycholao Lachy et *compagni*a, doit le xxviij jo*ur* de jun*e* po*ur* vj pok*es* lane q*ue* po*ise* cu*m* *tare*:

| | | |
|---|---|---|
| N° | 285 | lb 276 |
| | 278 | lb 270 |
| | 281 | lb 265 |
| | 274 | lb 278 |
| | 276 | lb 280 |
| 6 | 279 | lb 277 |

S*um*ma de po*ise* cu*m* *tare*: lb 1646
T*ara* po*ur* uso: lb 11 po*ur* pok*e*, lb 66
Et po*ur* macaʒoni: lb 20
Et po*ur* sup*ra*più de sach*i*: lb 8
Et sup*ra*più de pezo: lb 7
Et po*ur* umido: lb 6
S*um*ma de tar*e*: lb 107
Rest*e* n*e*t lb 1539, a fl. 24 le C. q*ue* fa fl. 369 s.7 a or*o*
S*um*ma: fl. 369 s.10 d. -, argent *con*tent

The mark*e* una mitra cu*m* cruce de sup*ra*.

Pok*es* 29

**Page 22 [70r.]**

fl.70

**a)** Francisco de C*hris*toforo Aleoti et *compagni*a, doit le xxviij jo*ur* de june 1451 po*ur* vij pok*es* lane q*ue* po*ise* *cum* *tare*:

| | | | | | |
|---|---|---|---|---|---|
| N° | 99 | lb 283 | N° | 97 | lb 283 |
| | 93 | lb 265 | | 94 | lb 258 |
| | 98 | lb 259 | | 96 | lb 278 |
| 7 | 95 | lb 276 | | | |

S*um*ma de po*ise* *cum* *tare*: lb 1902
T*ara* po*ur* uso: lb 11 po*ur* pok*e*, lb 77
Et po*ur* sup*ra*più de sach*i*: lb 9 unc*e* 6
Et sup*ra*più de pezo: lb 7
Et po*ur* umido: lb 7
Et po*ur* fradisch*o*: lb 1 unc*e* 6
S*um*ma de tar*e*: lb 102
Rest*e* net lb 1800, a fl. 18 le C. q*ue* fa fl. 324 s. - d. -
S*um*ma: fl. 324 s. - d. -, argent *con*tent

The mark*e* una peccora coronat*a* quod h*ab*et in ore suo modicum de una erba.

**b)** It*em* le dyd Francisco, doit le dyd jo*ur* po*ur* ix pok*es* lane q*ue* po*ise* cu*m* *tare*:

| | | | | | |
|---|---|---|---|---|---|
| N° | 272 | lb 273 | N° | 267 | lb 275 |
| | 265 | lb 265 | | 270 | lb 280 |
| | 266 | lb 261 | | 268 | lb 260 |
| | 271 | lb 270 | | 273 | lb 247 |
| 9 | 269 | lb 273 | | | |

S*um*ma de po*ise* cu*m* *tare*: lb 2404
T*ara* po*ur* uso: lb 11 po*ur* pok*e*, lb 99
Et po*ur* sup*ra*più de sach*i*: lb 13
Et sup*ra*più de pezo: lb 6
Et po*ur* fradisch*o*: lb 2
S*um*ma de tar*e*: lb 102
Rest*e* net lb 2284, a fl. 18 le C. q*ue* fa fl. 411 s. 2 a or*o*
S*um*ma: fl. 411 s. 2 d.10, argent *con*tent

The mark*e* u*no* garland asure blod*e* *cum* t*ri*b*us* florib*us* et in medio garland*o* una stella rubia et in medio stelle uno O.

**c)** Pero de Cosimo de Medeci et *compagnia*, doit le dyd jo*ur* po*ur* ix pok*es* lane q*ue* po*ise* cu*m* t*are*:

| | | | | | |
|---|---|---|---|---|---|
| N° | 42 | lb 268 | N° | 61 | lb 266 |
| | 59 | lb 266 | | 65 | lb 274 |
| | 55 | lb 260 | | 67 | lb 258 |
| | 62 | lb 261 | | 49 | lb 227 |
| 9 | | | | 60 | lb 255 |

S*um*ma de po*ise* cu*m* t*are*: lb 2365
T*are* po*ur* uso et macaȝoni et po*ur* sup*ra*più de sack*es* et sup*ra*più de pezo et po*ur* umido: lb 18 po*ur* pok*e*: lb 162
Et più po*ur* fradisch*o*: lb 9
S*um*ma de tar*e*: lb 171
Rest*e* net lb 2194, a fl. 24 le C. q*ue* fa fl. 526 s.11 a or*o*
S*um*ma: fl. 526 s. 15 d. 11, argent *con*tent

The mark*e* una manu cu*m* j manip*u*lo de rosis de trib*us* foliis.

**d)** It*em* le dyd Pero de Cosimo, doit le dyd jo*ur* po*ur* j pok*e* lane q*ue* po*ise* cu*m* t*are*:

| | | |
|---|---|---|
| N° | 436 | lb 252 |
| j | | |

T*are* po*ur* uso et sup*ra*più de sach*i* et sup*ra*più de pezo et po*ur* umido: lb 18
Rest*e* net lb 234, a fl. 24 le C. q*ue* fa fl. 56 s.3 a or*o*
S*um*ma: fl. 56 s. 4 d. 4, argent *con*tent

The mark*e* una sole.

**e)** It*em* le dyd Pero de Cosimo, doit le dyd jour po*ur* j pok*e* lane q*ue* po*ise* cu*m* t*are*:

| | | |
|---|---|---|
| N° | 372 | lb 272 |
| j | | |

T*are* po*ur* uso et sup*ra*più de sach*i* et sup*ra*più de pezo et po*ur* umido: lb 18
Reste net lb 254, a fl. 24 le C. q*ue* fa fl. 60 s.19 a or*o*
S*um*ma fl. 60 s. 27 d. 4, argent *con*tent

The mark*e* j° manip*u*lo de quinq*ue* popeis cu*m* una sc*ri*ptura que dicit Laus Deo

**f)** Item le dyd Pero de Cosimo, doit le dyd jour pour j poke lane que poise cum tare:

| | | |
|---|---|---|
| N° | 378 | lb 280 |
| j | | |

Tara pour uso et pour toti altri tare: lb 15
Reste net lb 265
Et lb 154 pour lana juvene, a fl. 18 le C.
Et lb 111 de lana bona, a fl. 24 le C. que fa in toti fl. 54 s.7 a oro
Summa: fl. 54 s. 10 d. -, argent content

The marke j manipulo de quinque popeis cum j scriptura que dicit Laus Deo.

**g)** A Bernardo de Genotzo Manetti et compagnia, doit le dyd jour pour iiij pokes lane que poise cum tare:

| | | |
|---|---|---|
| N° | 201 | lb 268 |
| | 207 | lb 266 |
| | 200 | lb 272 |
| 4 | 212 | lb 263 |

Summa de poise cum tare: lb 1069
Tare pour uso et suprapiù de pezo et suprapiù de sachi et pour umido: lb 18 unce 6 pour poke
Summa de tare: lb 74
Reste net lb 995, a fl. 24 le C. que fa fl. 238 s.16 a oro
Summa: fl. 238 s. 23 d. 2, argent content

The marke uno pavo.

Pokes 32

**Page 23 [70v.]**

**a)** Matheo de Nicholas Lachy et compagnia doit le xxx jour de june 1451 pour vj pokes lane que poise cum tare:

| | | | | | |
|---|---|---|---|---|---|
| N° | 275 | lb 278 | N° | 282 | lb 282 |
| 6 | 283 | lb 286 | | 280 | lb 277 |
| | 284 | lb 271 | | 277 | lb 276 |

Summa de poise cum tare: lb 1670
Tara pour uso: 11 pour poke, lb 66

Et po*ur* macaȝoni: lb 19
Et po*ur* sup*ra*più de sach*i*: lb 9
Et sup*ra*più de pezo: lb 8
Et po*ur* umido: lb 6
S*um*ma de tar*e*: lb 108
Rest*e* net lb 1562, a fl. 24 le C. q*ue* fa fl. 374 s.17 a or*o*
S*um*ma: fl. 374 s. 24 d. 7, argent *con*tent.

The mark*e* una mitra cu*m* cruce sup*ra.*

**b)** It*em* le dyd Matheo, doit le dyd jo*ur* po*ur* vj pok*es* lane q*ue* po*ise* cu*m* *tare*:

| | | | | | |
|---|---|---|---|---|---|
| N° | 243 | lb 267 | N° | 237 | lb 270 |
| 6 | 247 | lb 268 | | 248 | lb 247 |
| | 236 | lb 272 | | 249 | lb 263 |

S*um*ma de po*ise* cu*m* *tare*: lb 1587
T*ara* pour uso: 11 po*ur* pok*e*, lb 66
Et po*ur* sup*ra*più de sach*i*: lb 9
Et sup*ra*più de pezo: lb 4
Et po*ur* fradisch*o*: lb 8
Et po*ur* umido: lb 6
S*um*ma de tar*e*: lb 93
Rest*e* net lb 1494, a fl. 18 le C. q*ue* fa fl. 268 s.18 a or*o*
S*um*ma: fl. 268 s. 26 d. -, argent *con*tent

The mark*e* u*no* garland*o* vir*i*de duplic*e* et in medio dic*ti* garlandi una rosa.

**c)** Antonio Lensy et *compagni*a, doit le dyd jour po*ur* v pok*es* lane q*ue* po*ise* cu*m* *tare*:

| | | |
|---|---|---|
| N° | 215 | lb 264 |
| | 196 | lb 262 |
| | 205 | lb 255 |
| | 219 | lb 280 |
| 5 | 208 | lb 266 |

S*um*ma de po*ise* cu*m* *tare*: lb 1327
T*are* pour uso et pou*r* macaȝoni et po*ur* sup*ra*più de sack*es* et sup*ra*più de pezo et po*ur* umido: lb 18 pou*r* pok*e*
Et più lb u*no* pou*r* lochy
S*um*ma de tar*e*: lb 91

Reste net lb 1236, a fl. 24 le C. q*ue* fa fl. 296 s.12 a or*o*
S*um*ma: fl. 296 s. 17 d. 4, argent *con*tent.

The mark*e* uno pavo.

**d)** Antonio Chambini et *compagni*a, doit le dyd jo*ur* po*ur* iij pok*es* lane q*ue* po*ise* cu*m* *tare*:

| | | |
|---|---|---|
| N° | 28 | lb 264 |
| 3 | 35 | lb 268 |
| | 4 | lb 266 |

S*um*ma de po*ise* cu*m* *tare*: lb 798
T*ara* po*ur* uso: lb 11 po*ur* pok*e*, lb 33
Et po*ur* maca3oni: lb 9 unc*e* 6
Et po*ur* sup*ra*più de sach*i*: lb 2 unc*e* 6
Et sup*ra*più de pezo: lb 2
Et po*ur* umido: lb 3
Et[61] più lb 2 po*ur* pok*es* d'achordo
Et po*ur* intyngim*en*to: lb 15
S*um*ma de tar*e*: lb 71
Rest*e* net lb 727, a fl. 26 le C. q*ue* fa fl. 189 s. - d. -
S*um*ma: fl.189 s. - d. -, argent *con*tent

The mark*e* una ancella cum humer*is* de capite v*ir*ginis.

**e)** Jacobo d'Orsino Lanfredini et Francisco Guydotti et *compagni*a, doit le dyd jo*ur* po*ur* v pok*es* lane q*ue* po*ise* cu*m* *tare*:

| | | |
|---|---|---|
| N° | 30 | lb 271 |
| | 15 | lb 279 |
| | 9 | lb 275 |
| | 5 | lb 265 |
| 5 | 11 | lb 261 |

S*um*ma de po*ise* *cum* *tare*: lb 1351
T*ara* po*ur* uso: lb 11 po*ur* pok*e*, lb 55
Et po*ur* maca3oni: lb 16
Et po*ur* sup*ra*più de sach*i*: lb 5

[61] The scribe writes *Et et* in the MS.

Et sup*ra*più de pezo: lb 4
Et po*ur* umido: lb 5
Et po*ur* intyngim*en*to: lb 8
Et più lb 2 po*ur* pok*es* d'achordo
S*um*ma de tar*e*: lb 103
Rest*e* net lb 1248, a fl. 26 s.10 a oro le C. q*ue* fa fl. 330 s.14 a or*o*
S*um*ma: fl.330 s. ~~14~~ 20 d. 3, argent *con*tent

The mark*e* una ancilla cu*m* humeris de capite virginis.

**f)** Matheo de Nycholao Lachy et *compagni*a, doit le dyd jo*ur* po*ur* ij pok*es* lane q*ue* poi*se* cu*m* *tare*:

| | | |
|---|---|---|
| N° | 19 | lb 282 |
| 2 | 33 | lb 276 |

S*um*ma de poi*se* cu*m* *tare*: lb 558
T*ara* pou*r* uso: lb 11 pou*r* pok*e*, lb 22
Et po*ur* macaʒoni: lb 6 unc*e* 6
Et po*ur* sup*ra*più de sachi: lb 2 unc*e* 6
Et sup*ra*più de pezo: lb 3
Et po*ur* umido: lb 2
Et po*ur* intingim*en*to: lb 10
Et più lb 2 po*ur* pok*es* d'achordo
S*um*ma de tar*e*: lb 50
Rest*e* net lb 508, a fl. 26 le C. q*ue* fa fl. 132 s. j a or*o*
S*um*ma: fl.132 s. 1 d. 5, argent *con*tent

The mark*e* una donzella.

**g)** It*em* le dyd Matheo, doit le dyd jo*ur* po*ur* viij pok*es* lane q*ue* poi*se* cu*m* *tare*:

| | | | | | |
|---|---|---|---|---|---|
| N° | 416 | lb 272 | N° | 418 | lb 231 |
| | 414 | lb 265 | | 415 | lb 268 |
| | 412 | lb 270 | | 411 | lb 240 |
| 8 | 413 | lb 258 | | 417 | lb 257 |

S*um*ma de poi*se* cu*m* *tare*: lb 2061
T*ara* pou*r* uso: lb 11 pou*r* pok*e*, lb 88
Et po*ur* macaʒoni: lb 33
Et po*ur* sup*ra*più de sachi: lb 12

Et sup*ra*più de pezo: lb 3
Et po*ur* umido: lb 8
Et po*ur* fradysch*o*: lb 6
S*um*ma de tar*e*: lb 150
Rest*e* net lb 1911, a fl. 24 le C. q*ue* fa fl. 458 s. 12 a or*o*
S*um*ma: fl.458 s. 17 20 d. 4, argent *con*tent

The mark*e* a abbot ys crowysse.

Pok*es* 35

**Page 24 [71r.]**

fl.71

**a)** Matheo de Nycholao Lachy et *compagnia*, doit le xxx jo*ur* de jun*e* 1451 po*ur* v pok*es* lane q*ue* po*ise* cum t*are*:

| | | |
|---|---|---|
| N° | 239 | lb 270 |
| | 242 | lb 259 |
| | 240 | lb 276 |
| | 252 | lb 277 |
| (5) | 235 | lb 268 |

S*um*ma de po*ise* cu*m* t*are*: lb 1350
T*ara* pour uso: lb 11 po*ur* pok*e*, lb 55
Et po*ur* sup*ra*più de sachi: lb 8 unc*e* 6
Et po*ur* fradisch*o*: lb 5
Et po*ur* umido: lb 5
S*um*ma de tar*e*: lb 78
Rest*a* netta: lb 1272, a fl. 18 le C. q*ue* fa fl. 228 s. 19 a or*o*
S*um*ma: fl. 228 s. 27 d. 6, argent *con*tent

The mark*e* j garland*o* v*ir*id*e* duplic*e* et in medio dict*i* garland*i* una rosa.

**b)** It*em* le dyd Matheo doit le dyd jour po*ur* ij pok*es* lane q*ue* po*ise* cu*m* t*are*:

| | | |
|---|---|---|
| N° | 287 | lb 271 |
| 2 | 286 | lb 270 |

S*um*ma de po*ise* cu*m* t*are*: lb 541
T*ara* pour uso: lb 11 po*ur* pok*e*, lb 22
Et po*ur* sup*ra*più de sachi: lb 3
Et po*ur* umido: lb 2

Et po*ur* sup*ra*più de pezo: lb 2
S*um*ma: lb 29
Rest*e* net lb 512, a fl. 18 le C. q*ue* fa fl. 92 s.3 a or*o*
S*um*ma: fl. 92 s. 4 d. 4, argent *con*tent

The mark*e* una mitra sine cruce.

**c)** Andrea de Loteryncho de la Stuffa et *compagni*a, doit le dyd jo*ur* pou*r* vij pok*es* lane q*ue* po*is*e cu*m* t*are*:

| | | | | | |
|---|---|---|---|---|---|
| N° | 293 | lb 257 | N° | 301 | lb 268 |
| | 297 | lb 275 | | 329 | lb 280 |
| | 322 | lb 268 | | 315 | lb 269 |
| 7 | | | | 325 | lb 270 |

S*um*ma de po*is*e cu*m* t*are*: lb 1887
T*are* pou*r* uso et macaȝoni et sup*ra*più de sach*i* et sup*ra*più de pezo et po*ur* umido: lb 18 po*ur* pok*e*
Et più lb 2 de tar*e* pour sachy de canevas q*ue* era duply
S*um*ma de tar*e*: lb 128
Rest*e* net lb 1751, a fl. 24 le C. q*ue* fa fl. 420 s. 4 a oro
S*um*ma: fl. 420 s.5 d. 9, argent *con*tent

The mark*e* una Agn*us* Dei cu*m* cruce in vexilla.

**d)** It*em* le dyd Andrea doit le dyd jo*ur* pou*r* v pok*es* lane q*ue* po*is*e cu*m* t*are*:

| | | |
|---|---|---|
| N° | 449 | lb 263 |
| | 450[62] | lb 270 |
| | 451 | lb 252 |
| | 452 | lb 229 |
| 5 | 454 | lb 253 |

S*um*ma de po*is*e cu*m* t*are*: lb 1237
T*are* pou*r* uso et macaȝoni et sup*ra*più de sach*i* et sup*ra*più de pezo et po*ur* umido: lb 17 po*ur* poke,
S*um*ma de tar*e*: lb 85
Rest*e* net lb 1152, a fl. 25 le C. q*ue* fa fl. 288 s. - d. -
S*um*ma: fl. 288 s. - d. -, argent *con*tent

62 Poke no. 450 is possibly mixed up with no. 453 (see 24f below) as it is recorded in the opening section as having a sun mark, not a *storo* label.

The mark*e* una sc*ri*ptura sup*ra*scripto storo.

**e)** It*em* le dyd Andrea, doit le dyd jour po*ur* iiij pok*es* lane q*ue* po*ise* cu*m* *tare*:

| | | |
|---|---|---|
| N° | 225 | lb 272 |
| | 223 | lb 261 |
| | 233 | lb 252 |
| 4 | 232 | lb 254 |

S*um*ma de po*ise* cu*m* *tare*: lb 1044
T*ara* pou*r* uso: 11 po*ur* poke, lb 44
Et po*ur* fradysch*o*: lb 12
Et po*ur* sach*i*: lb 7
Et sup*ra*più de pezo: lb 2
S*um*ma de tar*e*: lb 65
Rest*e* net lb 979, a fl. 18 le C. q*ue* fa fl. 176 s.4 a or*o*
S*um*ma fl. 176 s. 5 d. 9, argent *con*tent

The mark*e* uno pavo cu*m* j campana ad pedem sinistrum.

**f)** It*em* le dyd Andrea doit le dyd jo*ur* pou*r* xij pok*es* lane q*ue* po*ise* cu*m* *tare*:

| | | | | | |
|---|---|---|---|---|---|
| N° | 425 | lb 258 | N° | 424 | lb 271 |
| | 427 | lb 282 | | 443 | lb 239 |
| | 423 | lb 259 | | 433 | lb 260 |
| | 422 | lb 269 | | 428 | lb 260 |
| | 436 | lb 259 | | 444 | lb 252 |
| 12 | 453 | lb 258 | | 445 | lb 247 |

S*um*ma de po*ise* cu*m* *tare*: lb 3114
T*are* pou*r* uso et macaȝoni et sup*ra*più de sachi et sup*ra*più de pezo et po*ur* umido: lb 18 po*ur* poke
S*um*ma: lb [216][63]
Rest*e* net lb 2898, a fl. 24 le C. q*ue* fa fl. 695 s. 10 a or*o*
S*um*ma: fl. 695 s. 14 d. 6, argent *con*tent

The mark*e* uno sole.

Pok*es* 35

[63] The scribe has not written a number here.

**Page 25 [71v.]**

**a)** Laurenxo de Larione de Bardy et *compagnia*, doit le 3 jo*ur* de julio[64] 1451 po*ur* v pok*es* lane q*ue* po*ise* cu*m* *tare*:

| | | |
|---|---|---|
| N° | 3 | lb 274 |
| | 17 | lb 259 |
| | 20 | lb 282 |
| | 7 | lb 270 |
| 5 | 13 | lb 263 |

S*um*ma de po*ise* cu*m* *tare*: lb 1348
T*ara* po*ur* uso: 11 po*ur* pok*e*, lb 55
Et po*ur* macaʒoni: lb 16
Et po*ur* sach*i*: lb 4 unc*e* 6
Et sup*ra*più de pezo lb 4 unc*e* 6
Et po*ur* umido lb 5
Et po*ur* entyngim*en*to: lb 17
Et più lb 2 po*ur* poch*e* d'achordo
S*um*ma de tar*e*: lb 112
Rest*e* net lb 1236, a fl. 26 s.10 a oro le C. q*ue* fa fl. 327 s.10 a or*o*
S*um*ma: fl. 327 s. 14 d. 6, argent *con*tent

The marke una ancilla cu*m* humeris de capite v*ir*ginis.

**b)** Laurenxo de Paris Chorbenelli et *compagnia* doit le dyd jo*ur* po*ur* v pok*es* lane q*ue* po*ise* cu*m* *tare*:

| | | |
|---|---|---|
| N° | 32 | lb 272 |
| | 10 | lb 272 |
| | 1 | lb 277 |
| | 16 | lb 278 |
| 5 | 23 | lb 260 |

S*um*ma de po*ise* cu*m* *tare*: lb 1355
T*ara* po*ur* uso: 11 po*ur* pok*e*, lb 55
Et po*ur* macaʒoni et sup*ra*più de sach*i*: lb 20
Et po*ur* umido: lb 5

[64] Along with *magio* (20d / 30g), *julio* is a rare example of Balmayn using a clearly Italian month. It also appears in entries 25e, 26a and 30j.

Et po*ur* intyngim*en*to: lb 11 unc*e* 6
Et più lb 2 po*ur* poch*e* d'achordo
S*um*ma de tar*e*: lb 101 unc*e* 6
Rest*e* n*e*t lb 1253 unc*e* 6, a fl. 26 s.10 a or*o* le C. q*ue* fa fl. 332 s.3 a or*o*
S*um*ma: fl. 332 s. 4 d. 4, argent *con*tent

The mark*e* una ancilla cu*m* humeris de capite v*ir*ginis.

**c)** Nicholao de Zuane de Sandro Barbigia et *compagni*a, lanaiuoli, doit le dyd jo*ur* po*ur* v pok*es* lane q*ue* po*ise* cu*m* *tare*:

| | | |
|---|---|---|
| N° | 129 | lb 262 |
| | 128 | lb 268 |
| | 130 | lb 282 |
| | 122 | lb 265 |
| 5 | 123 | lb 269 |

S*um*ma de po*ise* cu*m* *tare*: lb 1346
T*ara* po*ur* uso: 11 po*ur* pok*e*, lb 55
Et po*ur* sup*ra*più de sach*i*: lb 7
Et sup*ra*più de pezo: lb 4 unc*e* 6
Et po*ur* lochy: lb 2 unc*e* 6
S*um*ma: lb 69
Rest*e* n*e*t lb 1277, a fl. 17 s.5 a or*o* le C. q*ue* fa fl. 220 s.5 a or*o*
S*um*ma: fl. 220 s. 7 d. 3, argent *con*tent

The mark*e* una peccora coronat*a* cu*m* suo agnello et pecus h*ab*et modicum de erba in ore.

**d)** Simone de Zuane de Sandro Barbigia et *compagni*a, lanaiuoli, doit le dyd jo*ur* po*ur* iiij pok*es* lane q*ue* po*ise* cu*m* *tare*:

| | | |
|---|---|---|
| N° | 127 | lb 275 |
| | 125 | lb 272 |
| | 126 | lb 289 |
| 4 | 124 | lb 260 |

S*um*ma de po*ise* cu*m* *tare*: lb 1096
T*ara* po*ur* uso: 11 po*ur* pok*e*, lb 44
Et po*ur* sup*ra*più de sach*i*: lb 6
Et sup*ra*più de pezo: lb 4
Et po*ur* fradischi*o*: lb j

S*um*ma: lb 55
Rest*e* net lb 1041, a fl. 17 s.5 a or*o* le C. q*ue* fa fl. 179 s.11 a or*o*
S*um*ma: fl. 179 s. 15 d. 11, argent *con*tent

The mark*e* una peccora coronat*a* cu*m* suo agnello et pec*us* h*ab*et modicum de[65] erba in ore.

**e)** Lorenxo de Paris Corbenelli et *compagni*a, doit le xxvij de julio 1451 po*ur* iij pok*es* lane q*ue* po*ise* cu*m* *tare*:

| | | |
|---|---|---|
| N° | 14 | lb 270 |
| 3 | 34 | lb 262 |
| | 8 | lb 257 |

S*um*ma de po*ise* cu*m* *tare*: lb 789
T*ara* po*ur* uso: 11 po*ur* pok*e*, lb 33
Et po*ur* macaȝoni et sup*ra*più de sach*i*: lb 12
Et sup*ra*più de pezo: lb 2
Et po*ur* umido: lb 3
Et po*ur* intyngime*n*to: lb 10
S*um*ma de tar*e*: lb 60
Rest*e* net lb 729, a fl. 24 le C. q*ue* fa fl. 174 s.19 a or*o*
S*um*ma: fl. 174 s. 27 d. 6, argent *con*tent

The mark*e* una donzella.

Pok*es* 22

**Page 26 [72r.]**

fl. 72

**a)** Antonio de Chambino Chambini et *compagni*a, doit le xxix jo*ur* de julio 1451 po*ur* iij pok*es* lane q*ue* po*ise* cu*m* *tare*:

| | | |
|---|---|---|
| N° | 24 | lb 271 |
| 3 | 22 | lb 265 |
| | 26 | lb 258 |

S*um*ma de po*ise* cu*m* *tare*: lb 794
T*ara* po*ur* uso: 11 po*ur* pok*e* lb 33
Et po*ur* macaȝoni: lb 9 unc*e* 6

[65] *de:* scribal insertion.

Et po*ur* sup*ra*più de sach*i*: lb 2 unc*e* 6
Et sup*ra*più de pezo: lb 2
Et po*ur* umido: lb 3
Et po*ur* intyngim*en*to: lb 15
S*um*ma de tar*e*: lb 65
Rest*e* net lb 729, a fl. 24 le C. q*ue* fa fl. 174 s.19 a or*o*
S*um*ma: fl. 174 s. 27 d. 6, argent *con*tent

The mark*e* una donzella.

**b)** Laurenxo de Laryon*e* de Bardy et *compagni*a, doit le vij jo*ur* de august*e* po*ur* ij pok*es* lane q*ue* poi*se* cu*m* t*are*:

| | | |
|---|---|---|
| N° | 31 | lb 274 |
| 2 | 27 | lb 272 |

S*um*ma de po*ise* cu*m* t*are*: lb 546
T*ara* po*ur* uso: 11 po*ur* pok*e*, lb 22
Et po*ur* macaȝoni: lb 6 unc*e* 6
Et po*ur* sup*ra*più de sach*i*: lb 3
Et sup*ra*più de pezo: lb 2 unc*e* 6
Et po*ur* umido: lb 2
Et po*ur* intyngimento: lb 10
S*um*ma de tar*e*: lb 46
Rest*e* net lb 500, a fl. 24 le C. q*ue* fa fl. 120 s. - d. -, argent *con*tent[66]

The mark*e* una donzella.

**c)** De Jachobo Federicy et *compagni*a, doit le xij jour de august*e* po*ur* ij pok*es* lane q*ue* po*ise* cu*m* t*are*:

| | | |
|---|---|---|
| N° | 6 | lb 260 |
| 2 | 18 | lb 263 |

S*um*ma de po*ise* cu*m* t*are*: lb 523
T*ara* pou*r* uso: 11 po*ur* pok*e* lb 22
Et po*ur* macaȝoni: lb 6 unc*e* 6
Et po*ur* sach*i*: lb 2
Et po*ur* intyngim*en*to: lb 10

[66] There is no final total in this entry.

S*um*ma: lb 44
Rest*e* n*e*t lb 479, a fl. 24 le C. q*ue* fa fl. 114 s.19 a or*o*
S*um*ma fl. 114 s. 27 d. 6, argent *con*tent

The mark*e* una donzella.

**d)** Jachobo d'Orsino Lamfredini et Francysco Guydotti et *compagni*a, doit le xxvij de august*e* po*ur* ij pok*es* lane q*ue* po*ise* cu*m* t*are*:

| | | |
|---|---|---|
| N° | 12 | lb 266 |
| 2 | 29 | lb 265 |

S*um*ma de po*ise* cu*m* t*are*: lb 531
T*ara* po*ur* uso: 11 po*ur* pok*e*, lb 22
Et po*ur* maca3oni: lb 6 unc*e* 6
Et po*ur* sup*ra*più de sach*i*: lb 2
Et po*ur* sup*ra*più de pezo: lb 1 unc*e* 6
Et po*ur* intyngim*en*to: lb 7
Et po*ur* umido: lb 2
S*um*ma: lb 41
Rest*e* n*e*t lb 490, a fl. 24 le C. q*ue* fa fl. 117 s.12 a or*o*
S*um*ma fl. 117 s. 17 d. 4, argent *con*tent

The mark*e* una donzella.

**e)** Matheo de Nycholao Lachy et *compagni*a, doit le xxv jo*ur* de septembr*e* 1451 po*ur* j pok*e* de lana q*ue* po*ise* cu*m* t*are*:

| | | |
|---|---|---|
| N° | 455 | lb 250 |
| j | | |

T*ara* po*ur* uso: 11 po*ur* pok*e*,
Et po*ur* sup*ra*più de sach*i*: lb 2
Et po*ur* umido: lb j
S*um*ma de tar*e*: lb 14
Rest*e* n*e*t lb 236, a fl. 18 le C. q*ue* fa fl. 42 s.9 a or*o*
S*um*ma: fl. 42 s. 13 d. -, argent *con*tent

The mark*e* signo *con*trasigno.

Pok*es* 10

**Page 27 [72v.]**

**a)** It*em* le dyd Matheo de Nycholao Lachy et *compagni*a, doit le dyd jo*ur* de xxv de septembr*e* po*ur* iij pok*es* lane q*ue* po*ise* cu*m* tare:

| | | |
|---|---|---|
| N° | 421 | lb 280 |
| | 419 | lb 278 |
| (3) | 420 | lb 281 |

S*um*ma de po*ise* cu*m* t*are*: lb 839
T*ara* po*ur* uso: 11 po*ur* pok*e*, lb 33
Et po*ur* sup*ra*più de sach*i*: lb 5
Et po*ur* umido: lb 3
Et po*ur* sup*ra*più de pezo: lb 4
S*um*ma de tar*e*: lb 45
Rest*e* net lb 794, a fl. 18 le C. q*ue* fa fl. 142 s.18 a or*o*
S*um*ma: fl. 142 s. 26 d. -, argent *con*tent

The mark*e* una pye.

Pok*es* 3

**b)** Thys ys the s*um*ma of all the pok*es* þat ben*e* solde, *con*taynyng in this boke viij levys, the whych*e* leffe bygynnyth wi*th* fl. 65. The s*um*ma ys iiij$^{c}$ xlviij pok*es*,[67] the whych*e* drawyth to the s*um*ma of money in Florens as in florinys: S*umma* fl. 25524. 12. 5

**c)** And this rekenyng ys made in Florens the xxviij daye of Septembr*e* 1451 by Alaman Salviati, for he solde all*e* the woll*e* and send the money by exch*a*unge.

**d)** Thys ys the rate þat *con*taynyth in this viij levys, what in pok*es* and what in florynys:

Cart*a* p*ri*ma þe whyche ys fl. 65 de ceste c*ontaynth*[68] in pok*es* 45 and in fl.[69]

| | |
|---|---|
| Cart*a* 2 | þe whych*e* ys fl. 66 de ceste c*ontaynth* in pok*es* 60 and in fl. |
| Cart*a* 3 | þe whych*e* ys fl. 67 de ceste c*ontaynth* in pok*es* 92 and in fl. |

[67] Here we have 448 pokes; there are another 17 below in 28a but there is still one sack missing.
[68] It is impossible to know for sure the language of expansion for the 'ct' abbreviations in the main body of this paragraph. ME *contaynyth* has been chosen as it is clearly written out in full in the opening and closing lines of this section but it should be recognised that we do not know which language Balmayn had in mind, if indeed, he had one all. This is a typical example of a translingual business short-hand.
[69] It seems that Balmayn meant to insert the total price in florins on each folio here but then failed to complete the task.

| | |
|---|---|
| Cart*a* 4 | þe whych*e* ys fl. 68 de ceste *contaynth* in pok*es* 45 and in fl. |
| Cart*a* 5 | þe whych*e* ys fl. 69 de ceste c*ontaynth* in pok*es* 69 and in fl. |
| Cart*a* 6 | þe whych*e* ys fl. 70 de ceste c*ontaynth* in pok*es* 67 and in fl. |
| Cart*a* 7 | þe whych*e* ys fl. 71 de ceste c*ontaynth* in pok*es* 57 and in fl. |
| Cart*a* 8 | þe whych*e* ys fl. 72 de ceste c*ontaynth* in pok*es* 13 and in fl. |

S*um*ma of this viij levys þat *con*taynyth in pokes ys 448 and in fl.

**e)** The s*um*ma of all*e* the cost*es* of iiij^c lxvi pok*es* as aforewretyn*e* in to the xxviij° daye of septembr*e* 1451 don*e* at Pyse and at Florens as hit apperyth by the p*ar*cell*e* wretyn*e* in this boke in the cart*a* of 41. The s*um*ma ys in florinys: fl. 3165. 5. 8

**f)** And so the rest*e* ys þat ys o*ure* solde of the s*um*ma aboveseyd, xviij pok*es* of the which vj pok*es* ys yong*e* March*e* and viij pok*es* yong*e*, I markyd w*ith* borage and iij pok*es*, I markyd w*ith* signo *con*tr*a*signo of the marke of all*e* the balys and j pok*e*, I markyd w*ith* j pecora coronat*a* cu*m* *e*rba in ore. The s*um*ma ys xviij pok*es*.

**g)** S*um*ma tot*a*l*e* of the 448 solde as aforeseyd,[70] all*e* thyng ys rekenyd and abatyd the daye aboveseyd, the s*um*ma ys clere: fl. 22359. 6. 9

**h)** Of the whych*e* s*um*ma was send by exch*a*unge fro Florens to Venic*e* and to London, as hit apperyth by the p*ar*cell*e* wretyn*e* in this boke, carta 130. The s*um*ma ys: fl. 15292. 24.4

**i)** It*em* the seyd Alaman Salviati owyth le dyd jo*ur* po*ur* £10 de gr. de Venec*ia*, the whych*e* he send to Joh*an* Russelaye et *compagni*a de V*e*necia in the s*um*ma anext[71] aforeseyd, the whych*e* was ret*or*nyd agayn*e* to Florens le xxvij jo*ur* de septembr*e*, a £16 s. j d. 6 a fl. po*ur* libra de gr. de V*enec*ia: fl. 110. 25. -

**j)** And so the s*um*ma of the 448 pok*es* ys clere rest*e* at this daye, the whych*e* ys the vj daye of octobr*e* 1451 p*er* *con*to assignato G: fl. 7177.7. 5

**Page 28 [73r.]**

fl. 73

**a)** Nicola*o* de Barbigia et *compagni*a, lanaiuoli, doit le xj jo*ur* de octobr*e* 1451 po*ur* xvij pok*es* lane, the whych*e* ben*e* the rest*e* of 466 pok*es* *contra*scritto *que* po*ise* cu*m* t*are*:

[70] *as aforeseyd*: scribal insertion above the line.
[71] *anext*: scribal insertion above line.

| | | | | | |
|---|---|---|---|---|---|
| N° | 3 | lb 262 | N° | 458 | lb 273 |
| | 5 | lb 252 | | 457 | lb 255 |
| | 7 | lb 261 | | signo † *contra*signo | |
| | 8 | lb 247 | | | |
| | 4 | lb 249 | | | |
| | 6 | lb 259 | | | |
| | j | lb 268 | | | |
| | ij | lb 257 | | | |
| | 8 de borage | | lb 264 | the whych*e* hathe neyther marke nor nombyr | |
| N° | 40 | lb 275 | | | |
| | 36 | lb 281 | | | |
| | 39 | lb 275 | | | |
| | 41 | lb 270 | | | |
| | 38 | lb 270 | | | |
| | 37 | lb 278 | | | |
| | vi de March*e* yonge | | | | |

S*umm*a tot*a*l*e* de po*ise* cu*m* *tare* of the xvij pok*es*: lb 4496
T*are* po*ur* uso: 11 po*ur* pok*e*, lb 187
Et po*ur* sup*ra*più de sach*i*: lb 28
Et po*ur* sup*ra*più de pezo: lb 10
Et po*ur* umido: lb 17
Et po*ur* fradysch*o* et intyngim*en*to: lb 60
Et più lb 2 po*ur* pok*es* d'achordo: lb 34
S*umm*a de tar*e*: lb 336
Rest*e* net lb 4160, a fl. 17 le C. q*ue* fa fl. 707 s. 4 d. 5 a or*o*
S*umm*a: fl. 707 s. 5 d. 9, argent *con*tent

**b)** The mark*e* firste viij pok*es* w*ith* a hand of borage, vj pok*es* yong*e* March*e* w*ith* a maydyn*e* his head w*ith* a peyr of corall*e* bedis abowte her neke, ij pok*es* w*ith* signo † *contra*signo and anothir pok*e* þat hadd*e* neyther nombyr nor marke.[72]

[72] As mentioned above, there is some confusion here. In the previous folio, Balmayn lists the 18 remaining pokes: 6 of young March wool, 8 marked with borage, 2 with Cantelowe's mark and one with a crowned sheep. In this corresponding final entry, there are only 17 pokes listed, one with the *signo contrasigno* and another with no mark at all.

## [Bills of exchange]

**Page 29 [130r.]**

fl. 130

1450

**a)** M*emorandum* that this ys the money send by exch*a*unge fro Florens by Alaman Salviati to Venic*e* and to London for the p*ar*te of the *con*to de G,[73] for the whych*e* the seyd Alaman Salviati hathe wretyn*e* to Joh*an* Russelay et Vanni Francisco de Strossy[74] et *compagni*a de Venec*ia* for to rescyve of div*ers per*sonis as folewyth. And that the seyd Joh*anne* Russelay et Vanni Francisco de Strossy *et compagni*a de Venec*ia* scholde send the same money by exch*a*unge to Jacob Salviati *et compagni*a de Londra p*er con*to de G and of this mark*e* †.

**b)** Firste Alaman Salviati of Florens send by ech*a*unge for the p*ar*t*e* of the *con*to aboveseyd signato G le xxx jo*ur* de janev*er* 1450,[75] at usaunce po*ur* £100 de Grossy de Venec*ia* to Joh*an* Russelay et Vanni Francisco de Strossy *et compagnia* de Venec*ia*, for to resceyve of Antonio de la Luna et Francischo de Strossy *et compagni*a, a £15 s. 19 d. 6 a fl. po*ur* una libra de Grossy de Ve*neci*a, for hit was delyv*er*d here to Lucha Chapponi *et compagni*a: fl. 1101 s. 21 d. -

**c)** It*em* le dyd jo*ur* po*ur* £20 de gr. send to Ve*neci*a at usaunce to the seyd Russelay and Strossy, for to resceyve of Joh*an* Portenary et *compagni*a a £15 s. 19. d. 4 a fl. po*ur* una libra de gr.*,* for hit was delyv*er*d here to the seyd Portenar*i*: fl. 220 s. 6 d.8

**d)** It*em* le 4[76]de fev*er*ell*e* po*ur* £30 de gr. send to Ve*neci*a to the seyd Russelay et Strossy a d*ì* 20 ditto, for to resceyve hit of Cosmo de Medici et *compagni*a a £15 s.18 a fl. po*ur* lb, for the seyd Cosmo hadd*e* hit here: fl. 328 s. 28. d -

**e)** It*em* le vj jo*ur* ditto po*ur* £100 de gr. r*icevuto*[77] a Ve*neci*a to þe seyd Russelay for to ressc*eyve* of Cosmo de Medici *et compagni*a, a usaunce a £15 s. 18 a fl. po*ur* libra de gr., for hit was delyv*er*d here to the seyd Cosmo: fl. 1096 s. 16 d. -

**f)** It*em* a d*ì* 13 ditto po*ur* £80 s. 4 d. - p*ez*. 12 de gr. send by usaunce a Venec*ia* a ditti da lloro midesimi, a £15 st .17 d.10 a fl. po*ur* libra de gr., for hit was delyv*er*d here to the seyd *compagni*a de le dyd Russelay et Strossy: fl. 878 s. 28 d. 7

[73] The same reference to the account labelled 'G' also appears in the Salviati Florentine accounts (Holmes, 'Anglo-Florentine Trade', 375).

[74] = Giovanni Rucellai and Giovanfrancesco Strozzi, partners of a wealthy Venetian bank (cf. Holmes, 'Anglo-Florentine Trade', 376).

[75] 30 January 1451 in modern calendar usage.

[76] Sic – there is no *jour* or *dì* here.

[77] This is an unusual abbreviation: a capital 'R' with a superscript 'o'. I am grateful to Dr Ignazio Del Punta of the Università di San Marino for his advice on its expansion.

| | | |
|---|---|---|
| **g)** | It*em* le xxvij ditto po*ur* £28 de gr. send to Ve*neci*a a ditti Russelay et Strossy for to ress*ceyve* of Lowes Pig[o],[78] a £15 s. 18 d. 4 a fl. po*ur* £ de gr., for her*e* hadd*e* hit Cornelio de M*ysser* Carlo et *compagni*a: | fl. 307. s. 10. d. 4 |
| **h)** | It*em* le dyd jo*ur* po*ur* £70 de gr. send to Ve*neci*a a ditti Russelay, for to ress*ceyve* of Antonio P*ar*tini, a £15 s. 18 d. 4 a fl. po*ur* £ de gr., for her*e* hadd*e* hit Pero et herede de P*ar*tino P*ar*tini: | fl. 768 s. 11. d. 4 |
| **i)** | It*em* le xx jo*ur* de march*e* po*ur* £30 de gr., for I have wretyn*e* to the Russelay et Strossy po*ur* Ser Jachobo Salviati et com*p*agni*a* de Londra, creditori, et debitore, Salviati de Pisa, a £15 s. 19 d. - a fl. po*ur* £ de gr.: | fl. 330 s. - d. - |
| **j)** | It*em* le 3 jo*ur* de ap*r*ell*e* 1451 po*ur* £10 de gr. send to Ve*neci*a a le dyd Russelay et Strossy upon*e* them*e*selffe, a £15 s.19 d. 6 a fl. po*ur* libra de gr., for here hadd*e* hit *compagni*a de le dyd Russelaye: | fl. 110 s. 5 d. - |
| **k)** | It*em* a d*ì* ditto po*ur* £20 de gr. send to Ve*neci*a a le dyd Russelay, for to ress*ceyve* of Michaell*e* Rondenelly, a £15 s.19 d. 8 a fl. po*ur* £ de gr., for her*e* hadd*e* hit: | fl. 220 s. 13 d. 4 |
| **l)** | It*em* a d*ì* ditto po*ur* £15 de gr. send to Ve*neci*a a le dyd Russelay, for to ress*ceyve* of Phelyppe Inggorani, a £15 s. 19 d. 8 a fl. po*ur* £ de gr., for her*e* hadd*e* hit: | fl. 165 s. 15 d. - |
| **m)** | It*em* a d*ì* ditto po*ur* £30 de gr. send to Ve*neci*a a le dyd Russelaye, for to ress*ceyve* of Joha*n* Portenary et *compagni*a de Ve*neci*a, a £15 s.19 d. 8 a fl. po*ur* £ de gr., for her*e* hadd*e* hit the seyd Joh*an* Portenary et *compagni*a: | fl. 330 s. 20 d. - |
| **n)** | It*em* a d*ì* ditto po*ur* £15 de gr., I have wretyn*e* to the seyd Russelay et Strossy for to make Jacob Salviati et *compagni*a de Londra creditori, and dettours, Salviati de Pisa, a £16 a fl. po*ur* £ de gr., and rekyne to us: | fl. 165 s. 15 d. - |
| **o)** | It*em* a d*ì* 9 ditto po*ur* £15 de gr. send a Ve*neci*a a le dyd Russelaye et Strossy, for to ress*ceyve* of Jacob de Benzy et *compagni*a, a £16 a fl. po*ur* £ de gr., for her*e* hadd*e* hit.....[79] Mirabelly: | fl. 165 s. 15 d. - |
| **p)** | It*em* a d*ì* ditto po*ur* £100 de gr. send to Ve*neci*a a le dyd Russelay et Strossy da lloro midesimi, a £16 s. - d. uno a fl. po*ur* libra, for her*e* hadd*e* hit the seyd *compagni*a de le dyd Russelaye et Strossy: | fl. 1103 s. 21 d. 4 |
| **q)** | S*um*ma fl.:[80] | |

**Page 30 [130v.]**

**a)** P*er* *con*to signato G for money send by exch*a*unge to Joh*an* Russelaye and Vanni Francisco de Strossy et *compagni*a de Ve*neci*a p*er* Alaman Salviati in Florens, as hit apperyth in the tothyr syde of this leve.

[78] This could be *Lowes Pige.*
[79] The scribe has left a blank space.
[80] The sum total is left blank in the MS.

| | | |
|---|---|---|
| **b)** | It*em* a d*ì* 30 de ap*relle* 1451 po*ur* £20 de gr., a £16 a fl. po*ur* libra de gr., send by the seyd Russelay and Strossy of Ve*necia* to Alaman Salviati in Florens, to paye by a l*ettre* of the ix daye of ap*relle*, at usaunce, to Benet de Fransisco de Strossy in Flore*ns*: | fl. 220 s. 20 d. - |
| **c)** | It*em* a d*ì* ditto po*ur* £58 de gr., a £16 a fl. po*ur* £ de gr., send by the seyd Russelay and Strossy of Ve*necia* to Alaman Salviati by a l*ettre* of the ix daye of ap*relle*, at usaunce, to paye to Antonio de Branocha: | fl. 640 s. 0 d. - |
| **d)** | It*em* a d*ì* ditto po*ur* £24 s.16 d. uno de gr., a £16 a fl. po*ur* libra de gr., send by the seyd Russelay and Strossy of Ve*necia* to Alaman*o* Salviati by a l*ettre* of this ix daye of ap*relle*, at usaunce, to paye to Cosmo: | fl. 273 s. 20 d. 4 |
| **e)** | It*em* a d*ì* ditto po*ur* £37 s. 3 d. 11 de gr., a £16 a fl. po*ur* libra de gr., send by the seyd Russelay and Strossy of Ve*necia* to Alaman Salviati by a l*ettre* of þe ix daye of ap*relle*, at usaunce, to paye to Pero de Galiano: d.4[81] | fl. 410 s.12 d.8 |
| **f)** | It*em* a d*ì* 30 ditto po*ur* £60 de gr., a £16 a fl. po*ur* libra de gr.,send by the seyd Russelaye and Strossy of Ve*necia* to Alaman Salviati by a l*ettre* of the x daye of ap*relle*, at usaunce, to paye to Pero de Galyano: | fl. 662 s. 22 d. - |
| **g)** | It*em* a d*ì* 18 de magio 1451 po*ur* £50 de gr. send to Venic*e* to the seyd Russelaye et Strossy, for to resceyve of Lowes Thechyatzy et *compagni*a in Ve*neci*a, a £16 s. - d. 7 a fl. po*ur* £ de gr., for here hadd*e* hit the seyd Lowes: | fl. 552 s. 2 d. 2 |
| **h)** | It*em* fl. 1500, I write to you þat ye write to Jacob Salviati *et compagni*a de Londra, creditori in p*ri*mo *con*to and dettours: | fl. 1500 s. - d. - |
| **i)** | It*em* a d*ì* 22 ditto po*ur* £50 de gr. send to Ve*neci*a a ditti Russelay et Strossy, for to resceyve of Pero de Francisco de Medici *et compagni*a in Ve*neci*a, a £16 a fl. p*ro* libra de gr., for here hadd*e* hit Joh*an* et Pero Francisco de Medici *et compagni*a: | fl. 551 s. 21. d. - |
| **j)** | It*em* a d*ì* 14 julio 1451 po*ur* £37 s. 4 d. 10 de sterl.[82] send to Jacob Salviati et *compagni*a de Londra at xv dayes aft*er* the seyth of the l*ett*re, for to resceyve of Pero de Medici et Jerezzo de Pili et *compagni*a in Londra, po*ur* fl. 222 s. 26. d. 2, a fl., for here hadde hit Joh*an* del Pulesse: | fl. 222 s. 26 d. 2 |

[81] The amount *d.4* appears on its own in the middle of the line. It is unclear to what it refers and it does not appear to be a superscript insertion relating to the line below.

[82] Written as *sterl-* in the text, we cannot know if Balmayn meant *sterling* or *sterlini*. Subsequently, in the following entries, he uses an even simpler abbreviation: *st*.

**k)** Item a d*ì* ditto po*ur* £32 s. 18 d. - de st. send to Jacob Salviati *et compagni*a de Londra, a d*ì* 15 a vista da l*ette*ra,[83] for to resceyve of Alysandyr Beremey de Mys*ser* Antonio, po*ur* fl. 196 s. 26 d 2, a fl., for here hadd*e* hit Jorge Luke: fl. 196 s. 26 d.2

**l)** It*em* a d*ì* ditto po*ur* £148 s. 1 d. 7 de st. send to Jacob Salviati et *compagni*a de Londra, a pagare a d*ì* 15 da vista da l*ette*ra, for to resceyve of Pero de Medici and Jeros de Pili po*ur* fl. 886 s. 7 d. 3., for here hadd*e* hit Joh*anne* and Pero Francisco de Medici *et compagni*a: fl. 886 s. 7 d. 3

**m)** It*em* a d*ì* ditto po*ur* £182 s. 15 d. 9 de st. send to Jacob Salviati *et compagni*a de Londra, for to resceyve a d*ì* 15 da vista a Pero de Medyci et Jerozzo de Pili *et compagni*a in Londra, po*ur* fl. 1094. For here hadd*e* hit Joh*an* and Pero Francischo de Medici et *compagni*a: fl. 1094 s. - d. -

**n)** It*em* le dyd for a savacondyd po*ur* le[84] robe de Will*ia*m Cantelowe durynge a yere: fl. 30 s. 19 d. 4

**o)** It*em* p*er* senceria de ditt*i* d*e*nari cambiati p*er* sencyale: fl.3 s. 16 d.4

**p)** It*em* le vj jour de octobr*e* 1451, Joh*an* Balmay*n*, s*er*vaunt of Will*ia*m Cantelowe: fl. 200 s. -d. -[85]

**q)** S*um*ma fl. fl. 15292. 24. 4.
S*um*ma to*tale* what of this syde and of the tothyr:

**Page 31 [131r.]**

fl.131

**a)** Money send by exch*a*unge fro Venic*e* to London and to Bruges p*er con*to de G.

**b)** M*emorandum* that this ys the rekenyng*e* of the money send by exch*a*unge fro Venic*e* by Joh*an* Russelay and Vanni Francescho de Strossy et *compagni*a de Venec*ia* for the *con*to assignato G, send all*e* this p*a*rcell*es* as folowyth to Jacob Salviati et *compagni*a de Londra et de Brugis po*ur* le dyd *con*to. The whych*e* money was send to us fro Florens by Alaman Salviati, as hit apperyth by the p*a*rcell*es* in this book, carta 130.

**c)** Firste le vj jo*ur* de fev*er*elle, send by usaunce to Lo*n*do*n* a st. 45¼ po*ur* le doc.[86] a Umfrido Justyan*e*, for here hadd*e* hit Pancras Justyan*e*: £15 - -

**d)** It*em* le 11 ditto, send by usaunce to Londo*n* a st. 45 le doc., a Sebestyan*e* et Jerolimis Bawdwere, for here hadd*e* hit Vittor*e* Capell*e* and his brotherys: £10 - -

[83] This abbreviation clearly ends in an *a*, rather than an *e* as in *lettre* above.
[84] I am assuming that this definite article is the Italian feminine plural, *le*, and not AF plural, *lé*.
[85] Presumably these 200 florins are for Balmayn's salary?
[86] = Venetian ducat (*docato*). Balmayn never writes the coin name in full in the accounts.

**e)** It*em* le 13 ditto, send by usaunce to Lo*n*do*n* a st. 44½ a Lowes Strossy, for her*e* hadd*e* hit Antonio P*ar*tini: £225 - -

**f)** It*em* le 17 ditto, send by usaunce to Lo*n*do*n* a 44 st. a Lowes Strossy, for her*e* hadd*e* hit the seyd P*ar*tini: £50 - -

**g)** It*em* le 8 de march*e*, send by usaunce a st. 44 ⅙ a Filice de Fagniano, for here hadd*e* hit our*e*selffe: £26. 18. 6

**h)** It*em* a d*ì* 11 ditto, send by usaunce to Bruges a gr. 52 ⅓ a Lorenxo Banbo, for here hadd*e* hit Jacobo Pissamano: £10 - -

**i)** It*em* le dyd jo*ur*, send by usaunce to Bruges a gr. 52 ⅓ a Damiano Ruffini, for here hadd*e* hit Pero Bassato: £10 - -

**j)** It*em* le dyd jo*ur*, send by usaunce to Brugens[87] a gr. 52 ½ a Antonio de Rabatta et Bernard Cambi, for her*e* hadd*e* hit Vinceguerra Justynyan*e*: £10 - -

**k)** It*em* le dyd jo*ur*, send by usaunce a gr. 52 ⅛ a Strossys, po*ur* *con*to a no*str*i: £47 - -

**l)** It*em* le 18 de le dyd, send by usaunce to London, a st. 44 ⅙ a Leonard Cattano po*ur* *con*ti a nostri: £23. 3. j

1451

**m)** It*em* le vj de aprell*e* send by usaunce to Londo*n* a st. 45 a Leonard*o* Cattano po*ur* *con*ti a no*str*i: £30- -

**n)** It*em* le x de le dyd, send by usaunce to Brugens a gr. 52 ¾ a Lomelini,[88] for her*e* hadd*e* hit Rondenelli: £60 - -

**o)** It*em* le xij de le dyd, send by usaunce to Brugens a le dyd p*re*cio a Antonio de Rabata et Bernard*o* Cambi, for her*e* hadd*e* hit Lowes Techiassy: £17- -

**p)** It*em* le 4 jour de Maye, send to Brugens for x days leng*th* pa*st* the usaunce a gr. 52 ½ a le Strossy, for her*e* hadd*e* hit Antonio de la Luna: £64 - -

**q)** It*em* le dyd jo*ur*, send by usaunce to Brugens a gr. 52 ½ da lloro midesimi. For her*e* hadd*e* hit Antonio de la Luna: £100 - -

**r)** It*em* le dyd jo*ur*, send by usaunce to Brugens a gr. 52 ⅔ a Jacobo Dario, for here hadd*e* hit M*esser* Antonio Beremay: £40. 2. 8

**s)** It*em* le dyd jo*ur*, send by usaunce to Brugens a le dyd p*re*cio a Francischo Jerolimo [...]nynysy, for her*e* hadd*e* hit Joh*an* Beremay et *compagnia*: £10. - 7

**t)** It*em* le 17 de le dyd, send to Brugens a gr. 52 ¾ a le Strossy. For her*e* hadd*e* hit Joh*an* de Matheo Gryty: £10 - -

[87] It is unclear why Balmayn switched at times to this unusual variant for Bruges. My thanks to Dr Angelo Nicolini for pointing out the differences in the toponyms.
[88] No forename is given.

| | | |
|---|---|---|
| **u)** | It*em* le 19 de le dyd, we have wretyn*e* to them*e*selfe to make credens for ij days leng*th* pa*st* the usaunce at Brugens a gr.52 ¾ and to make us dettours: | £33 - - |
| **v)** | It*em* le 24 de le dyd, send by usaunce to Bruges to them*e*selffe a gr. 52 ¾ a Francisco et Joh*an* Salviati *et compagni*a in Pisa, for her*e* hadd*e* hit Antonio P*ar*tini: | £22. 5. 3 |
| **w)** | It*em* le prim*er* jour de jun*e*, *w*e have wretyn*e* to them*e*selffe at Bruges to make creditours a gr. 52 ¾ and us dettours: | £50 - - |
| **x)** | It*em* le 5 ditto, we have wretyn*e* to them*e*selffe at Bruges a gr. 54 to make creditours and us dettours: | £55 - - |
| **y)** | It*em* le 9 de le dyd, we have wreytn*e* to them*e*selffe at Bruges þat at usaunce and of the same p*recio* scholde make them*e* creditours and us dettours: | £70 - - |
| **z)** | It*em* we write to them*e*selffe at Londo*n* þat of the v daye of this monyth at usaunce scholde make us dettours in theyr rekenyng a st. 46 po*ur* le doc. and us creditours: | £22 |
| **aa)** | Item po*ur* sensaria de denari cambiati a questo *con*to a sensiale: | £ -. 8. 4 |
| **bb)** | It*em* po*ur* nostra p*ro*visione a doc. ij po*ur* m*i*ll*e* et po*ur con*solatico, doc. ij po*ur* m*i*ll*e*: | £2. 2. 0. 12 |
| **cc)** | It*em* the seyd *compagni*a owyth for as much*e* as we have sette hit in his rekenyng*e*: | £ - . 3. 7 |

S*um*ma: £1013 s. 4 d. 0 *pez.* 12

## [Miscellaneous documents]

**Page 32 [5v.]**

1451

**a)** By the g*ra*ce of God*e* this ys the weyȝth of a Ciiij pok*es* wolle, aft*er* the weyȝths of H*a*mpton*e*, of my mayst*er* Will*ia*m Cantelowe ys and Jacob Salviat*i* et c*ompagni*a de Londra, p*or*tabylle[89] to them boþe.

**b)** The whyche Ciiij pok*es* was schippyd at H*a*mptone ~~the~~ in the monyth of aprell*e* 1451 upon a caryk of Jene, patron*e* Morys Catane, by Joha*n* de Albycys et c*ompagni*a de Londra, for to be delyv*er*ed by the g*ra*ce of God at Port*e* Pysan*e* to Frances et Joh*an* Salviati, or to suche as ben*e* þ*ere* for them at Pyse.

[89] = 'attributable'. Both Cantelowe and the Salviati are equally liable for any charges incurred in this joint business venture, cf. the Scottish 'portable charge: a payment or service that is to be, or must be, rendered by every person or corporation liable for it' (OED3 sub **portable**, att. c. 1450; see also AND2 sub **portable**[2], att. 1334).

| Nº | Pokes | Cloves | Nº | Pokes | Cloves[90] |
|---|---|---|---|---|---|
| 71 | 1 | 5 ÷ | 76 | 1 | 3 ÷ |
| 31 | 1 | 3 ÷ | 87 | 1 | 3 |
| 43 | 1 | 3 | 84 | 1 | 5 |
| 42 | 1 | 2 ÷ | 85 | 1 | 3 |
| 55 | 1 | 4 | 32 | 1 | 6 |
| 39 | 1 | 3 | 35 | 1 | 3 ÷ |
| 51 | 1 | 4 | 88 | 1 | 4 |
| 48 | 1 | 4 ÷ | 23 | 1 | 1 |
| 64 | 1 | 3 ÷ | 28 | 1 | 0 |
| 73 | 1 | 5 | 9 | 1 | 0 |
| 37 | 1 | 6 | 7 | 1 | 1 |
| 38 | 1 | 2 ÷ | 15 | 1 | 2 |
| 66 | 1 | 4 | 25 | 1 | 1 |
| 44 | 1 | 3 ÷ | 80 | 1 | 6 |
| 67 | 1 | 4 ÷ | 17 | 1 | 1 |
| 69 | 1 | 4 ÷ | 31 | 1 | 0 |
| 59 | 1 | 5 | 30 | 1 | 0 |
| 61 | 1 | 2 ÷ | 33 | 1 | 4 |
| 62 | 1 | 5 | 91 | 1 | 3 ÷ |
| 46 | 1 | 4 ÷ | 20 | 1 | 1 ÷ |
| 57 | 1 | 3 | 11 | 1 | 2 |
| 49 | 1 | 3 ÷ | 26 | 1 | 0 ÷ |
| 74 | 1 | 4 | 22 | 1 | 1 ÷ |
| 60 | 1 | 4 ÷ | 8 | 1 | 1 ÷ |
| 52 | 1 | 3 | 36 | 1 | 6 ÷ |
| 58 | 1 | 4 | 27 | 1 | 0 |
| 72 | 1 | 4 ÷ | 13 | 1 | 0 |
| 40 | 1 | 3 ÷ | 4 | 1 | 2 ÷ |
| 45 | 1 | 1 | 18 | 1 | 0 ÷ |
| 70 | 1 | 4 ½ | 12 | 1 | 1 ÷ |
| 53 | 1 | 3 ÷ | 14 | 1 | 0 |

[90] This list of figures gives the exact weight of each of the 104 pokes of wool in a separate shipment sent out to Tuscany by Cantelowe and the Salviati in April 1451. As before, the labels 'pokes' and 'cloves' have been added (in bold) to the original to explain the figures. The subsequent pages in the accounts are missing so we have no tallies, details of marks used or wool types. This is the not the most accurate of records: there are only 103 pokes in the list and several numbers (e.g. no. 68 and no. 31) appear twice.

| | | | | | |
|---|---|---|---|---|---|
| 54 | 1 | 3 ÷ | 19 | 1 | 3 |
| 41 | 1 | 3 | 3 | 1 | 2 ÷ |
| 68 | 1 | 3 ÷ | 21 | 1 | 0 |
| 50 | 1 | 4 | 2 | 1 | 2 ÷ |
| 47 | 1 | 3 | 6 | 1 | 2 |
| 55 | 1 | 4 ÷ | 16 | 1 | 2 |
| 95 | 1 | 3 ÷ | 75 | 1 | 3 |
| 81 | 1 | 3 ÷ | 24 | 1 | 1 |
| 79 | 1 | 5 | 5 | 1 | 2 |
| 92 | 1 | 2 ÷ | 29 | 1 | 1 |
| 86 | 1 | 3 ÷ | 10 | 1 | 1 ½ |
| 77 | 1 | 5 | 99 | 1 | 3 ½ |
| 78 | 1 | 1 ÷ | 97 | 1 | 2 ½ |
| 83 | 1 | 3 | 104 | 1 | 2 |
| 68 | 1 | 3 | 95 | 1 | 2 ½ |
| 90 | 1 | 3 ÷ | 96 | 1 | 2 |
| 93 | 1 | 2 | 102 | 1 | 4 |
| 34 | 1 | 1 ÷ | 100 | 1 | 3 ½ |
| 82 | 1 | 3 ÷ | 94 | 1 | 2 ½ |
| | | | 98 | 1 | 3 ½ |
| | | | 103 | 1 | 5 |
| | | | 101 | 1 | 3 ½ |

**Page 33** [64r.][91]

fl.64

**a)** A d*i*[92] 27 august*o* in Ferens

**b)** And s*o*[93] ther*e* ben*e* x pok*es* of þe mark*es* of þe sage I solde for redy money at xxv fl. le C. Et ij pok*es* of them*e* ben*e* delyv*er*ed and S*er* Jacob woll*e* avyse you, and s*o* he woll*e* send to you a le*ttre* þ*at* ye scholde by a C or ijC sack*es* woll*e*, but ye moste bye of þe beste and sorte ev*ery* colour by hymselffe; for x flysse in a pok*e* schall*e* distroye þe remenaunt as in þe sale. And s*o* the [~~S~~*er*][94] Strossys and the Medyc*is* hathe not solde as yet past*e* lx pok*es*, and yet ther w[oll*e*] ys ryȝth gode, and they selle hit for xxiiij fl. le C., the best*e*.

[91] This is a copy or draft of a letter, cancelled by Balmayn but inserted into the main accounts on a loose piece of paper (f. 64r.).

[92] Balmayn switches from his usual AF date form of *le xxvij jo-* to the standard Italian equivalent: *a d- 27.*, which stood for *a dì* (or *addì*). He also frequently uses this Italian abbreviation in the buyers' entries and lists of bills of exchange.

[93] This is simply 's' and appears five times in the letter, always after 'and'. Holmes ('Anglo-Florentine Trade', 385) transcribes it as 'so'.

[94] The same *S* symbol appears here just before *Strossy*, even though it seems to have been written over. It is possible that the scribe was using the abbreviation to stand for an Italian title such as *signori*.

**c)** And s*o* I dowȝt not of the otterawnce[95] w*ith* that þat there com*e* no quantite but yo*urs*, and so yf ye make þe graunt w*ith* any patron*e*, we sopose þat the woll*e* come to Port*e* Pysan*e*; w*ith* þat he may be sewr of ij$^{C}$ sack*es* and so ye may have lx naylle*e*[96] of woll*e* upo*n* a caryk for xxviij s. st. and of the days, as ye can*e* acorde.

**d)** Also ye schall*e* undyrstand howe that the le*ttr*es þat were made at London the xvij and xviij daye of J*une* were send fro Bruges to Venic*e*,[97] and theyr the le*ttr*es of þe Medyc*is* Anton de Rabatt*is* and the Salviatys were et ben*e* taryed, and so as yet we have them*e* not.

**e)** And yf the lett*res* þat I browȝth w*ith* me to Bruges hadd*e* not com*e* to Florens we scholde hadde a [able] t*ur*ne[98] but they cam*e* not by the waye of Venic*e*, and yf ye send my le*tt*re w*ith* Jacob ys le*tt*re þ*en* ben*e* they at Venic*e*, for I have no let*tr*es fro you synce the xx daye of Maye.

**f)** And s*o* if ye have to do w*ith* any Venysyan*s*, yet may thanke them for Jacob ys sake and for yo*ur* owen. And S*er* Alman hathe take iij pok*es* of þe mark*e* w*ith* þe myter w*ith* the croyse.

Sc*rito*[99]

**Page 34 [f.64 bis]**

1451

**a)** Joh*an* Bertrem doit le xi jo*ur* de auguste po*ur* amont p*re*sté a xliiij d. le doc., ster. xiiij s. viij d. to resseyve of Ric*hard*[100] Boltone of Eryth.[101]

**b)** May*ster* Thom*as* Bedford, p*ar*son of Lubbenh*am*[102] i*n* Lestetyrschyre, doit le iiij jo*ur* de octob*re* po*ur* 80 doc. de cam*era*[103] remisse a [Pe]rogia[104], a iiij moys a pagar*e* a gr. 52 ½ po*ur* doc. and to rescyve hit of Nycholas Bedford,[105] march*aun*te of Caleys.

By iij l*ett*res of payement

[95] See OED2 sub **utterance** 1a, 'The disposal of goods, commodities, etc., by sale or barter' and MED sub **outrance** 'the marketing (of goods), sale'.
[96] i.e. a clove of wool or 7-8lb (see OED3 sub **nail, 9a**).
[97] This could be Venice or Venic*ia*.
[98] The meaning of these two words is unclear.
[99] *Scrito*, written in Balmayn's hand at a later date, confirms that the letter had been copied out.
[100] This could equally be Ric*ardus* or Ric*ardo*.
[101] Erith is a small town in Kent on the south bank of the Thames.
[102] Lubenham in south Leicestershire.
[103] *I ducati de camera* (i.e. from the Camera Apostolica) were minted by the Vatican.
[104] Perugia (central Italy) was a papal possession and so would make sense here but it should be noted that the placename in question is not entirely clear.
[105] *Ser Nicholas Beddeford, merchante di Stapola* is recorded in several exchange transactions in the Salviati London book e.g. AS Serie I: 336 carte 45, 66, 191.

**Page 35** [64v.][106]

| | | | |
|---|---|---|---|
| 3 | | 8 | |
| po*ur* | 848. 10. - | C.6 | 324 - - |
| | 230. 11. 7. | | 411. 2.10. |
| | 236. 17. 4. | | 526.15.11. |
| | 234. 5. 9. | | 56. 4. 4. |
| | 89. 17. 4. | | 60. 27. 6. |
| | 293. - - | | 54. 10 - |
| | **1932. 4. 0** | | 238. 23. 2. |
| po*ur* | 99. 15. 11. | | **1671. 25. 9.** |
| | 298. 20. 3. | C.6 | 374.24.7 |
| | 232. 1. 5. | | 268.26 |
| | 235. 26. - | | 296.17.4 |
| | 355. 1. 5. | | 189 |
| | 284. 24. 7. | | 330.20.3 |
| | 587. 7. 3. | | 132.1.5 |
| | **2093. 9.10.** | | 458.17.4 |
| | 1932. 4. 0 | | **2050.19.11** |
| S*umm*a | **4025.13. 10.** | | 1671.25.9 |
| | 226. 11. 7. | C.6 | **3722.16.8** |
| | 474. 14. 6. | C.7 | 228.27.6 |
| | 1297. 5. 9. | | 92.4.4 |
| | 588. - - | | 420.5.9 |
| | 173. - - | | 288 - - |
| | 356. 11. 7. | | 176.5.9 |
| | **3115. 14. 5.** | | 695.14.6 |
| C. 5 | 567. 17. 4. | | **1900.28.10** |
| | 466. - - | C.7 | 327.14.6 |
| | 756. 20. 3. | | 332.4.4 |
| | 91. 23. 2. | | 220.7.3 |
| | 201. 18.10. | | 179.15.11 |

[106] Once again, this scrap of paper has been inserted into the main folder and the rough list of figures has been cancelled with a line. It seems to be a list of prices in pounds sterling, shillings and pence for various hundred weights of wool. The C- abbreviation is the same as that one that appears in *le C.*, found throughout the accounts. In bold, we see the totals which Balmayn places between two lines in the MS.

| | | | |
|---|---|---|---|
| | 94. 18.10. | | 174.27.6 |
| | 2178. 11. 5. | | **1234.11.6** |
| C.5 | 179. 17. 4. | | 1900.28.10 |
| | 45. 26. - | C.7 st. | **3135.11.4** |
| | 735. 10. - | C.8 | 174.27.6 |
| | 181. 26. - | | 120 |
| | 50. 21. 9 | | 114.27.6 |
| | 91. - - | | 117.17.4 |
| | 369. 10. - | | 42.13 |
| | 1653. 24.1. | | |
| C.5 | 2178. 11.1. | | 569.27.4 |
| | 822. 6. 2. | | 192.26 |
| | | 8 | 3155 |
| | | | 712.94 |
| | | | **3705.9.8** |

# Glossary

## Balmayn's vocabulary: a multilingual glossary

As we have seen, it can be challenging to categorise the languages Balmayn uses, with Latin / Italian and Anglo-French / Middle English lexis being especially difficult to separate. In some cases, the languages assigned below give only a speculative idea of a lexeme's most likely language category based on its appearance(s) within the source text. The main historical dictionaries used to determine senses are the *Middle English Dictionary* (MED), *Oxford English Dictionary* (OED), *Anglo-Norman Dictionary* (AND), *Dictionary of Medieval Latin from British Sources* (DMLBS), *Lessico etimologico italiano* (LEI) and the *Tesoro della Lingua Italiana delle Origini* (TLIO).

Words of particular interest are followed by references to footnotes elsewhere in the edition where the reader can find further discussion and details of relevant lexicographical and lexical sources.

Underlined vocabulary in the glossary only appears in merchant mark descriptions within the accounts.

The following abbreviations are used to refer to parts of speech:

adj. = adjective
n. = noun
phr. = phrase
pl. = plural
v. = verb

*abatyd* (ME, adj.): deducted (from a sum total)
*<u>abbots croyse / crowysse</u>* (ME, n.): crosier, pastoral staff; *see also* pastorale
*<u>agnus</u>* (Lat., n.) / *<u>agnello</u>* (It., n.): a lamb
*<u>agnus Dei</u>* (Lat., n.): the Lamb of God (usually carrying a banner with a red cross)
*argent content* (AF, phr.): money in cash / coins [cf. 34n28]
*amont presté* (AF, phr.): amount borrowed [cf. 35n35-6]
*arsinà* (It., n.): dockyard [cf. 38n44]

*averia* (It., n.) / *avery* (ME, n.): insurance tax to cover damage to cargo / ship at sea [cf. 38n45; 49n1-2]
ancilla (Lat. / It., n.) / ancella (It., n.): handmaiden [cf. 76n14]
baner (ME, n.): banner or flag; *see also* vexilla
bedis (ME, n.): beads
*berynge* (ME, n.): transport of the wool from the docks to the warehouse
blode (ME, adj.): dark blue colour [cf. 75n2]
borage (ME, n.): borage (flowers)
*botega* (It., n.): merchant's shop or studio [cf. 42n59)
*botte* (ME, n.): boat
*cambiati* (It., adj.): exchanged (money)
campana (Lat. / It., n.): a bell
*carraca* (It. / Lat., n.) / *caryk* (ME, n.): large, armed merchant sailing vessel with three or four masts [cf. 31n20]
*carta* (It., n): page (of account book)
chapleta (? It., n.): chaplet; a wreath or crown of flowers [cf. 108n14]
*c(h)omperatore* (It., n.): buyer
*clerkys* (ME, n. pl.): clerks, scribes
*clove* (ME, n.): unit of weight for wool, 7-8lb; *see also* naylle [cf. 19n1]
*consare* (It., v.): to adjust / repair
*consely de mare* (It., phr.): Sea Consuls; Florentine officials who specialised in maritime law; *see also* Offysyalle of the See [cf. 112n39]
*consolatico* (It., n.): Consul office in medieval Florence [cf. 42n65]
*contento* (It., n.): contents (of the pokes of wool)
*conto* (It., n.): set of accounts
*conto (as)signato G / conto de G* (It., phr.): the Salviati accounts labelled 'G' [cf. 156n73]
*contrasignata* (It., adj.): (of wool sack), labelled with a second merchant mark or countermark
*contrascritto* (It., adj.): 'written as follows'
coralle vermoille (AF, phr.): red coral [cf. 107n13]
coronato /*a* (It. / Lat., adj.): crowned (referring to a sheep)
*credens* (ME, n.): credit
*creditore* (It., n.) / *creditour* (ME, n.): creditor; a person who gives credit and to whom a debt is owing
cruce (Lat. / It., n.): cross
*custome* (ME, n.): duty to be paid on merchandise
*damno* (It, n.): damage (i.e. a financial loss)
*debitore* (It., n.) / *dettour* (ME, n.): debtor; a person who owes a debt to another
degito ariculare (Lat., phr.): little finger
*deminucione* (It., n.): reduction, decrease

*denari* (It., n. pl.) coins worth 1/240 of a florin
*depincta* (It. / Lat., adj.): painted / daubed (onto a woolsack)
*ditto* (It., adj. / n.) / *dyd* (AF, adj. / n.): aforementioned (month)] [cf. 50n3]
*doc(ato)* (It., n.): gold coin of Venice [cf. 89n4]
—*doc(ato) de camera* (It., phr.): ducat from the Papal mint (Camera Apostolica) [cf. 164n103]
*donzella* (It., n.): maiden, young girl [cf. 76n14]
*duodesimo* (It., n.): twelfth (some form of Florentine custom duty) [cf. 38n46]
*duplice* (Lat. / It., adj.): double, dual
*(by) exchaunge* (ME, n.): (by) a bill of exchange; *see also* lettre / lettera [cf. 2n4, 52n1]
*felyschip* (ME, n.): fellowship, guild (presumably the Mercers' Company of London) [cf. 110n24]
*flese wolle* (ME, phr.): wool shorn from a living sheep (rather than pulled from a sheepskin) [cf. 45n75]
*florino* (It., n.) / *floryne* (ME, n.): gold coin of Florence, worth 20 soldi or 240 denari [cf. 31n19, 89n2]
*fradischo* (It. adj.): soaked / sodden (wool) [cf. 39n50]
*freyȝth* (ME, n.): freight, hire of a vessel to transport goods
*garlando* (Lat. / It., n.): a garland
*graunt* (ME, n.): agreement
*grossy* (It., n. pl.): silver Venetian coins worth 26 denari parvi each [cf. 50n4, 89n3]
*harneys* (ME, n.): equipment; in this case presumably used to unload the wool off the ship [cf. 111n28]
*(et) herede* (It. / Lat., phr.): 'and sons'
*intingimento* (It., n.): soaking (of wool) [cf. 40n51]
*jaye* (ME, n.): a jay
*lana* (Lat. / It., n.) / *lane* (It., n. pl.) / *lane* (AF, n.): wool
—*Abbathie*: 'abbey' wool from monastic estate, exact provenance unknown
—*de Cotiswolde*: wool from the Cotswolds
—*de la Marche*: wool from the Welsh Marches
—*fine:* fine, smooth wool (i.e. not coarse or rough-textured)
—*juvene / younge:* wool from younger animals [cf. 107n12]
—*rubie / vermoile*: wool dyed red for identification [cf. 45n74]
*lanaiuoli* (It., n. pl.): merchants in the Florentine guild known as the *Arte della Lana.* They purchased raw wool and oversaw the numerous stages in its transformation to cloth before selling the finished product.
*leffe / levys* (ME, n. pl.): leaves, pages of the account book
*lettre* (ME, n.) / *lettera* (It., n.): letter (in general sense) / a bill of exchange; *see also* exchaunge [cf. 2n4, 52n1]

*libra* (It., n.): a pound in weight or money
*lloro midesimi* (It., phr.): themselves
*lokes* (ME, n. pl.) / *lochy* (It., n. pl.): lowest-quality English wool from the belly of the sheep [cf. 32n23]
*macaȝoni* (It, n.): imperfection / damage (to wool) [cf. 39n49]
*magasino* (It., n.) / *magasyne* (ME, n.): merchant's warehouse [cf. 50n5]
*maiore* (It., n.): the greater part
*manipulo* (Lat. / It., n.) / *mazzo* (It., n.): a bunch
*maydyne* (ME, n.): maiden, young girl
*mitra* (Lat. /It., n.) / *mytre* (ME, n.): a bishop's mitre
*mo(w)nta* (It., n.): (money) amounting to
*naylle* (ME, n.): unit of weight for wool, 7-8lb; *see also* clove [cf. 163n96]
*netta* (It., adj.) / *net* (ME, adj.): amount of weight / money remaining after deductions [cf. 52n2]
*Offysyalle of the See* (ME, phr.): Florentine maritime officials; *see also* consely de mare [cf. 112n39]
*onlading / ladynge* (ME, n.): loading (of cargo)
*ospytalle* (ME, n.): hostel for travellers / merchants
*oste* (ME, n.): host, receiver of goods who stores them temporarily [52n3]
*ostelage* (ME, n.): fee paid to host for receiving and storing goods [52n4]
*otterawnce* (ME, n.): utterance, the selling and marketing of goods [cf. 163n95]
*papavery* (It., n. pl.) / *popeis* (ME, n. pl.): poppies
*parcelle* (ME, n.): an item or entry in a financial account [cf. 34n30]
*partita* (It., n.): entry (in account book)
*pastorale* (It., n.): a crosier (pastoral staff); *see also* abbots croyse
*patrone* (ME, n.): captain or master of an Italian ship [cf. 31n21]
*pavo* (Lat. / It., n.) / *pecoke* (ME): peacock
*pecore* (It., n.) / *pecus* (Lat., n.): sheep
*pere precius* (AF, phr.): precious stone [cf. 35n34]
*pezo* (It., n.) weight (of wool)
*pezoly* (It., n. pl.): small, low value coins of variable worth, minted from a copper-silver mix [cf. 50n6, 89n5]
—*s(oldi) de pezoly: soldi* that are denominations of a silver *lira* (pound) and not of a gold florin [cf. 89n5]
*pisare* (It., v.): to weigh (wool)
*plee* (ME, n.): plea, a formal written allegation or claim
*po(c)ke* (ME, n.) / *poccha* (It., n.): unit of weight for wool, equivalent to roughly half a sack (182lb) although this could vary [cf. 19n1, 32n22]
*portare* (It., v.): to carry / transport (wool)
*pylynge* (ME, n.): piling up / storing (wool) in warehouse

*portabylle* (ME, adj.): liable for payment [cf. 161n89]
*portours* (ME, n. pl.): porters, men employed to carry the wool
*precio* (It., n.): price
*provisione* (It., n.) / *provysyon* (ME, n.): commission paid to a host, agent or official [cf. 52n5]
*pye* (ME, n.): a magpie
*racione* (? It., n.): type / quality (of wool) (?) [cf. 45n76]
*remenaunt* (ME, n.): remainder, remaining part [cf. 37n40]
*rebatyd* (ME, adj.): deducted (from a sum total)
*retencione* (It., n.): deduction of a fixed percentage from a sale or purchase price [cf, 42n62]
*rekyn* (ME, v.): to reckon; to calculate, work out
*rekenyd* (ME, adj.): reckoned; calculated / tallied up
*rekenyng* (ME, n.): reckoning; an account / set of calculations / tally
*restivare* (It., v.): to re-stow cargo
*ryȝth* (ME, n.): tax or duty to be paid; or (in 33b) adverb meaning 'entirely, completely'
*robe* (It., n. pl.): goods / possessions [cf. 39n47]
*rosa* (Lat. / It., n.): a rose
*savacondyd* (ME, n.): safe-conduct (of goods on a ship) [cf. 35n38]
*sackes* (ME, n. pl.) / *sachi* (It., n. pl.): unit of weight for wool, 364lb [cf. 19n1]
*sensaria* / *senceria* (It., n.): broker's fee [cf. 42n63]
*salle* (ME, n.): sale
*semis* (Lat., n.): a half (of a sack / clove of wool)
*sensiale* / *sencyale* (It., n.): a broker [cf. 42n64]
*signo contrasigno* (It, phr.): William Cantelowe's personal merchant mark
*sole* (Lat. / It., n.) / *sonne* (ME, n.): a sun
*spago* (It., n.): *string*
*stella* (Lat. / It., n.): a star
*stone* (ME, n.): unit of weight (of wool), 14lb
*storo* (It., n.): 'stock wool' i.e. wool from a single estate [cf. 45n77, 46n78]
*styvare* (It., v.): to stow cargo
*suprapiù de pezo* (It., phr.): surplus weight
*tara* (It., n.) / *tare* (It., n. pl.) / *tare* (ME, n.): amount deducted from the gross weight of the packed wool for the purpose of calculating the net weight [cf. 50n7]
—*tara pour uso*: standardised fee of 11lb per poke to cover 'wear and tear' [cf. 41n55]
*taratura* (It., n.): calibration or adjustment of tare to be deducted from the gross weight [cf. 42n60]

*taryed* (ME, adj.): tarried, delayed
*(at) usaunce* (ME, n.): within an agreed period of time (to pay a bill of exchange) [52n6]
*umido* (It., n.): dampness (of wool)
*unlading* (ME, n.): unloading (of cargo)
*valueta* (It., n.) / *valewe* (ME, n.): value, worth
*vexilla* (Lat., n.): a banner, flag; *see also* baner
*victura* (It., n.): a cart or wagon [cf. 37n43]
*(a) vista da lettera* (It., phr.): 'from seeing the bill (of exchange)' [cf. 52n1]
*viride / veride* (Lat, adj.): green

# Bibliography


Beale, Philip, Adrian Almond and Mike Scott Archer. *The Corsini Letters* (Stroud, Amberly, 2011).

Bell, Adrian R., Chris Brooks and Paul R. Dryburgh. *Advance Contracts of the Sale of Wool, c. 1200-c. 1327* (Chippenham, List and Index Society, 2006).

Bell, Adrian R., Chris Brooks and Paul R. Dryburgh. *The English Wool Market: c. 1230–1327* (Cambridge, Cambridge University Press, 2007).

Bell, Adrian R., Chris Brooks and Tony K. Moore. *Accounts of the English Crown with the Italian Merchant Societies, 1272–1345* (London, List and Index Society, 2009).

Bigwood, Georges, and Armand Grunzweig. *Les livres des comptes des Gallerani* (Bruxelles, Palais des Académies, 1961).

Bolton, James. *The Medieval English Economy, 1150–1500* (London, Dent, 1980).

Bond, Edward A. *Extracts from the Liberate Rolls relative to Loans Supplied by Italian Merchants to the Kings of England in the 13th and 14th Centuries* (London, The Society of Antiquaries of London, 1840).

Boyer, Carl. *A History of Mathematics* (New York, John Wiley & Sons, 1968).

Boyns Trevor, and John R. Edwards. A *History of Management Accounting: the British Experience* (Abingdon, Routledge, 2013).

Bradley, Helen. 'Italian Merchants in London c1350–1450', Ph.D. thesis (Royal Holloway and Bedford New College, University of London, 1992).

Bradley, Helen. *The Views of the Hosts of Alien Merchants, 1440–1444* (London, London Record Society, 46, 2012).

Bradley, Helen. 'Southampton's Trading Partners: London', in Michael Hicks (ed), *English Inland Trade, Southampton and its region* (Oxford, Oxbow, 2015), pp. 65–80.

Bradley, Helen. ' "Saluti da Londra": Italian Merchants in the City of London in the Late Fourteenth and Early Fifteenth Centuries', in Michele Campopiano and Helen Fulton (eds), *Anglo-Italian Cultural Relations in the Later Middle Ages* (Woodbridge, York Medieval Press, 2018), pp. 103–27.

Burnett, Charles. *Numerals and Arithmetic in the Middle Ages* (Aldershot, Ashgate Variorum, 2010).

Cajori, Florian. *A History of Mathematical Notations*, 6th edn (New York, Dover Publications Inc., 1993).

Cappelli, Adriano. *Lexicon abbreviaturarum: dizionario delle abbreviazioni latine e italiane*, 6th edn (Milano, Ulrico Hoepli, 1979).

Cappelletti, Luigi Alessandro. 'Un testo in volgare italo-romanzo in un rotolo della zecca di Canterbury (1291–1294)', *Studi linguistici italiani*, XLVI (2020), 163–200.

Carnicero, Jose Miguel Alcolado. 'The Dates of the Shift to English in the Financial Accounts of some London Livery Companies: A Reappraisal', *Multilingua*, 34 (2014), (De Gruyter Mouton), DOI: 10.1515/multi-2014-0068.

Carnicero, Jose Miguel Alcolado. 'Bridges of Innovation and Change: the English Language Around the Networks of the Mercery of London' in Esther-Miriam Wagner, Bettina Beinhoff and Ben Outhwaite (eds), *Merchants of Innovation: the Languages of Traders* (Berlin, De Gruyter Mouton, 2017), pp. 40–67.

Carus-Wilson, E. M., and Olive Coleman. *England's Export Trade 1275–1547* (Oxford, Clarendon Press, 1963).

Castellani, Arrigo. *Nuovi testi florentini del Dugento*, Volumes 1 and 2 (Firenze, G. C. Sansoni, 1952).

Castellani, Arrigo, and Ignazio Del Punta. *Lettere dei Ricciardi di Lucca ai loro compagni in Inghilterra (1295–1303)* (Roma, Salerno, 2005).

Cavallaro, Maura. 'La compagnia di Jacopo di Alamanno Salviati di Londra negli anni 1448–51', Undergraduate dissertation (Università di Pisa, 1969).

Cella, Roberta. *I Gallicismi nei testi dell'italiano antico (dalle origini alla fine del sec. XIV)* (Firenze, Accademia della Crusca, 2003).

Cella, Roberta. 'Anglismi e francesismi nel registro della filiale di Londra di una compagnia mercantile senese (1305–1308)', in Serge Vanvolsem *et al.* (eds), *Identità e diversità nella lingua e nella letteratura italiana. Atti del XVIII Congresso dell'A.I.S.L.L.I.* (Firenze, Cesati, 2007), pp. 189–204.

Cella, Roberta. *La documentazione Gallerani-Fini nell'Archivio di Stato di Gent (1304–1309)* (Firenze, SISMEL edizioni del Galluzzo, 2009).

Cella, Roberta. 'Prestiti nei testi mercantili toscani redatti di là dale Alpi. Saggio di glossario fino al 1350', *La Lingua Italiana: Storia, struttue, testi*, 6 (2010), 57–99.

De Roover, Raymond. *Money, Banking and Credit in Medieval Bruges* (Cambridge, MA, The Medieval Academy of America, 1948).

De Roover, Raymond. *Évolution de la lettre de change* (Paris, Colin, 1953).

De Roover, Raymond. *The Rise and Decline of the Medici Bank, 1397–1494* (New York, Norton, 1963).

Del Punta, Ignazio. 'Una lettera da Londra ad Avignone del 1313,' *Bollettino dell'Opera del Vocabolario Italiano*, 13 (2008), 351–69.

Del Punta, Ignazio. 'Italian Firms in Late Medieval England and their Bankruptcy: Re-reading an Old History of a Financial Crisis' in Michele

Campopiano and Helen Fulton (eds), *Anglo-Italian Cultural Relations in the Later Middle Ages* (Woodbridge, York Medieval Press, 2018), pp. 67–86.

Dietz, Klaus. 'Die frühen italienischen Lehnwörter des Englischen', *Anglia*, 123 (2005), 573–631.

Durham, John W. 'The Introduction of "Arabic" Numerals in European Accounting', *The Accounting Historians Journal*, 19 (1992), 25–55.

Edler, Florence. *Glossary of Mediaeval Terms of Business. Italian Series 1200–1600* (Cambridge, MA, The Mediaeval Academy of America, 1934).

Egan, Geoff. 'Provenanced Leaden Cloth Seals', Ph.D. thesis (University College, University of London, 1987).

Elton, Stuart F. *Cloth Seals: an Illustrated Guide to the Identification of Lead Seals Attached to Cloth* (Oxford, Archaeopress, 2017).

Endrei, Walter, and Geoff Egan. 'The Sealing of Cloth in Europe, with Special Reference of the English Evidence', *Textile History*, 13 (1982), 47–75.

Evans, Allan. *La Practica della Mercatura* (Cambridge, Medieval Academy of America, 1935).

Fennis, Jan. *Trésor du langage des galères: dictionnaire exhaustif, avec une introduction, des dessins originaux de René Burlet et des planches de Jean-Antoine de Barras de la Penne, un relevé onomasiologique et une bibliographie* (Tübingen, Niemeyer, 1995).

Fratianni, Michele, and Franco Spinelli. 'Italian City-States and Financial Evolution', *European Review of Economic History*, 10 (2006), 257–78.

Fryde, E. B. *Studies in Medieval Trade and Finance* (London, Hambledon Press, 1983).

Fryde, E. B. 'Italian Merchants in Medieval England c. 1270–1500', in *Aspetti della vita economica medievale: atti del Convegno di Studi nel X Anniversario della morte di Federigo Melis, Firenze-Pisa-Prato, 10–14 marzo 1984* (Firenze, Monte dei Paschi di Siena, 1984), pp. 215–32.

Gallagher, John. *Language Learning in Early Modern England* (Oxford, Oxford University Press, 2019).

Girling, Frank Aldous. *English Merchants' Marks: a Field Survey of Marks Made by Merchants and Tradesmen in England between 1400 and 1700* (London, Oxford University Press, 1964).

Goldthwaite, Richard. 'Italian Bankers in Medieval England', *Journal of European Economic History*, 2 (1973), 763–71.

Goldthwaite, Richard. *The Economy of Renaissance Florence* (Baltimore, Johns Hopkins University Press, 2009).

Guidi Bruscoli, Francesco. 'Un frammento inedito di un libro di conti di Domenico Villani e compagni di Londra, 1422–24', *Storia Economica*, 13 (2010), 375–409.

Guidi Bruscoli, Francesco. 'I mercanti italiani e le lingue straniere' in Isa Lori Sanfilippo and Giuliano Pinto (eds), *Comunicare nel Medioevo: La conoscenza e l'uso delle lingue nei secoli XII-XV* (Roma, Instituto Storico Italiano per il Medio Evo, 2015), pp. 105–31.

Guidi Bruscoli, Francesco, and James Bolton. 'The Borromei Bank Research Project' in Lawrin Armstrong, Ivana Elbl and Martin M. Elbl (eds), *Money, Markets and Trade in Late Medieval Europe: Essays in Honour of John H. A. Munro* (Boston, Brill, 2007), pp. 460–90.

Guidi Bruscoli, Francesco, and Jessica Lutkin. 'Perception, Identity and Culture: the Italian Communities in Fifteenth-Century London and Southampton Revisited', in W. Mark Ormrod, Nicola McDonald and Craig Taylor (eds), *Resident Aliens in Later Medieval England* (Turnhout, Brepols, 2017), pp. 89–104.

Guyotjeannin, Olivier. *Conseils pour l'édition des textes médiévaux, Vol II: Actes et documents d'archives* (Paris, Comité des travaux historiques et scientifiques, Librarie Droz, 2001).

Hanham, Alison. *The Celys and their World. An English Merchant Family of the Fifteenth Century*, 2nd edn (Cambridge, Cambridge University Press, 2002).

Harben, Henry A. *A Dictionary of London* (London, H Jenkins Ltd, 1918), https://www.british-history.ac.uk/no-series/dictionary-of-london.

Haspelmath, Martin, and Uri Tadmor. *Loanwords in the World's Languages: a Comparative Handbook* (Berlin, Walter de Gruyter, 2009).

Hayez, Jérôme. 'Un segno fra altri segni. Forme, significati e usi della marca mercantile verso il 1400', in Elena Cecchi (ed), *Di mio nome e segno. 'Marche' di mercanti nel carteggio Datini (sec. XIV-XV)* (Prato, Istituto di Studi Storici Postali, 2010), pp. ix–xlvi.

Hector, Leonard Charles. *The Handwriting of English Documents*, 2nd edn (Dorking, Kohler & Coombes Ltd, 1980).

Hill, Georges Francis. *The Development of Arabic Numerals in Europe* (Oxford, Clarendon Press, 1911).

Holmes, George. 'Anglo-Florentine Trade in 1451', *English Historical Review*, 108 (1993), 371–86.

Holmes, George. 'Florentine Merchants in England, 1346–1446', *Economic History Review*, 13 (1960), 193–208.

Hope, Thomas Edward. *Lexical Borrowing in the Romance Languages: a Critical Study of Italianisms in French and Gallicisms in Italian from 1100–1900* (Oxford, Blackwell, 1971).

Hsy, Jonathan. *Trading Tongues: Merchants, Multilingualism and Medieval Literature* (Columbus, The Ohio State University Press, 2013).

Hunt, Edwin S. 'A New Look at the Dealings of the Bardi and Peruzzi with Edward III', *Journal of Economic History*, 50 (1990), 149–62.

Hunt, Edwin S. *The Medieval Super-Companies: a Study of the Peruzzi Company of Florence* (Cambridge, Cambridge University Press, 1994).

Ingham, Richard. 'Code-Switching in the later Medieval English Lay Subsidy Rolls', in Herbert Schendl and Laura Wright (eds), *Codeswitching in Early English* (Berlin, De Gruyter, 2011), pp. 95–114.

Ingham, Richard. 'Language-mixing in Medieval Latin documents: Vernacular Articles and Nouns' in Judith A. Jefferson and Ad Putter (eds), *Multilingualism in Medieval Britain (c. 1066–1520), Sources and Analysis* (Turnhout, Brepols, 2013), pp. 105–21.

Ingham, Richard. 'Medieval Bilingualism in England: on the Rarity of Vernacular Code Switching' in Päivi Pahta, Janne Skaffari and Laura Wright (eds), *Multilingual Practices in Language History: English and Beyond* (Berlin, De Gruyter Mouton, 2018), pp. 319–37.

James, Tom Beaumont. 'The Town of Southampton and its Foreign Trade 1430–1540' in Michael Hicks (ed), *English Inland Trade* (Oxford, Oxbow Books, 2015), p. 11–25.

Jansen, Katherine L., Joanna H. Drell and Frances Andrews (eds), *Medieval Italy: Texts in Translation* (Philadelphia, University of Pennsylvania Press, 2009), pp. 77–110.

Jefferson, Lisa. *Wardens' Accounts and Court Minute Books of the Goldsmiths' Mistery of London, 1334–1446* (Woodbridge, Boydell and Brewer, 2003).

Jefferson, Lisa. *The Medieval Account Books of the Mercers of London: an Edition and Translation* (Farnham and Burlington, Ashgate, 2009).

Jenkinson, Hilary. 'The Use of Arabic and Roman Numerals in English Archives', *The Antiquaries Journal*, 6 (1926), 263–75.

Johnson, Arthur. *The History of the Worshipful Company of the Drapers of London* (Oxford, Clarendon Press, 1914).

Kaeuper, Richard. 'The Frescobaldi of Florence and the English Crown', in William M. Bowsky (ed), *Studies in Medieval and Renaissance History* Volume 10 (Lincoln, University of Nebraska Press, 1973), pp. 45–95.

Kaeuper, Richard. *Bankers to the Crown: the Riccardi of Lucca and Edward I* (Princeton, Princeton University Press, 1973).

Ladd, Roger. *Antimercantilism in Late Medieval English Literature* (New York, Palgrave Macmillan, 2010).

Lambert, Bart. '"Nostri fratelli da Londra": the Lucchese Community in Late Medieval England' in Michele Campopiano and Helen Fulton (eds), *Anglo-Italian Cultural Relations in the Later Middle Ages* (Woodbridge, York Medieval Press, 2018), pp. 87–102.

Lauwers, Luc, and Marleen Willekens. 'Five Hundred Years of Bookkeeping: A Portrait of Luca Pacioli', *Tijdschrift voor Economie en Management (Katholieke Universiteit Leuven)*, 39 (1994), 289–304.

Lawrence, Jason. *Who the Devil Taught Thee So Much Italian? Italian Language and Literary Imitation in Early Modern England* (Manchester, Manchester University Press, 2005).

Lepschy, Anna Laura, and Giulio Lepschy. *The Italian Language Today*, 2nd edn (London, Routledge, 1988).

Lloyd, Terence Henry. *The English Wool Trade in the Middle Ages* (Cambridge, Cambridge University Press, 1977).

Lloyd, Terence Henry. *Alien Merchants in England in the High Middle Ages* (Sussex, The Harvester Press, 1982).

Lopez, Robert, (ed), *The Dawn of Modern Banking* (New Haven, Yale University Press, 1979).

Mallet, Michael. 'The Sea Consuls of Florence in the Fifteenth Century', *Papers of the British School at Rome*, 27 (1959), 156–69.

Mallett, Michael. *The Florentine Galleys in the Fifteenth Century* (London, Oxford University Press, 1967).

Maiden, Martin. *A Linguistic History of Italian*, 2nd edn (Abingdon, Routledge, 2013).

Melis, Frederigo. *Documenti per la storia economica dei secoli XIII-XVI: con una nota di paleografia commerciale a cura di Elena Cecchi* (Firenze, Leo S. Olschki, 1972).

Marvin, Julia, (ed), *The Oldest Anglo-Norman Prose Brut Chronicle* (London, Boydell and Brewer, 2006).

Milroy, Jim. 'The Ideology of a Standard Language', in Laura Wright (ed), *The Development of Standard English, 1300–1800: Theories, Descriptions, Conflicts* (Cambridge, Cambridge University Press, 2006), pp. 11–28.

Murray, Alexander. *Reason and Society in the Middle Ages* (Oxford, Clarendon Press, 1978).

Nicolini, Angelo. 'Commercio marittimo genovese in Inghilterra nel Medioevo (1280–1495)', *Atti della Società Ligure di Storia Patria*, 47 (2007), 215–327.

Nightingale, Pamela. *A Medieval Mercantile Community: the Grocers' Company and the Politics & Trade of London, 1000–1485* (New Haven, Yale University Press, 1995).

Nightingale, Pamela. *Trade, Money and Power in Medieval England* (Aldershot, Ashgate Variorum, 2007).

Nightingale, Pamela. 'Alien Finance and the Development of the English economy, 1285–1311', *Economic History Review*, 66 (2013), 477–96.

Origo, Iris. *The Merchant of Prato: Francesco di Marco Datini* (Harmondsworth, Penguin Books, 1963).

Pagan, Heather, and Geert De Wilde. 'L'édition de texte et l'Anglo-Norman Dictionary' in Stephen Dörr and Yan Greub (eds), *Quelle philologie pour quelle lexicographie? Actes de la section 17 du XXVIIème Congrès International de Linguistique et de Philologie Romanes* (Heidelberg, Universitätsverlag Winter, 2016), pp. 107–16.

Pearsall, Derek. 'Strangers in Late Fourteenth-Century London' in F. R. P. Akehurst and Stephanie Cain Van D'Elden (eds), *The Stranger in Medieval Society*, (Minneapolis, University of Minnesota Press, 1997), pp. 46–62.

Poole, Reginald Lane. *The Exchequer in the Twelfth Century*, 2nd edn (London, Routledge, 2013).

Postan, Michael M. 'Italy and the Economic Development of England in the Middle Ages', *Journal of Economic History*, 11 (1951), 339–46.

Power, Eileen. *The Wool Trade in English Medieval History* (London, Oxford University Press, 1941).

Prestwich, Michael. 'Italian Merchants in Late Thirteenth and Early Fourteenth Century England', in Robert S. Lopez (ed), *The Dawn of Modern Banking* (New Haven, Yale University Press, 1979), pp. 77–104.

Rainer, Franz. 'Le rôle de l'italien dans la formation de la terminologie cambiale française', *Revue de linguistique romane*, 78 (2014), 57–86.

Re, Emilio. 'Archivi inglesi e storia italiana', *Archivio Storico Italiano*, 71 (1913), 249–81.

Re, Emilio. *La compagnia dei Riccardi in Inghilterra e il suo fallimento alla fine del secolo XIII.* (Roma, R. Società Romana di storia patria, 1914).

Repetti, Emanuele. *Dizionario Geografico, Fisico e Storico della Toscana*, Volume 1 (Firenze, A. Tofani, 1883).

Rickert, Edith. 'Extracts from a Fourteenth-Century Account Book', *Modern Philology*, 24 (1926), 111–19.

Rothwell, William. 'Lexical Borrowing in a Medieval Context', *Bulletin of the John Rylands University Library of Manchester*, 63 (1980), 118–43.

Rothwell, William. 'Ignorant Scribe and Learned Editor: Patterns of Textual Error in Editions of Anglo-French Texts', Anglo-Norman On-Line Hub, April 2004, http://www.anglo-norman.net/articlesA/scribe.xml

Rouse, Robert Allen. 'For King and Country? The Tension between National and Regional Identities in *Sir Bevis of Hampton*,' in Jennifer Fellows and Ivana Djordjevic (eds), *Sir Bevis of Hampton in Literary Tradition* (Cambridge, D. S. Brewer, 2008), pp. 114–26.

Ruddock, Alwyn. *Italian merchants and shipping in Southampton, 1270–1600* (Southampton, University College, 1951).

Russell, Ephraim. 'The Societies of the Bardi and the Peruzzi and their Dealings with Edward III, 1327–45', in George Unwin (ed), *Finance and Trade under Edward III: The London Lay Subsidy of 1332* (Manchester, The University Press, 1918), pp. 93–135.

Rylands, John Paul. 'Merchant Marks and Other Mediaeval Personal Marks', *Transactions of the Historic Society of Lancashire and Cheshire*, 62 (1911), 1–34.

Sapori, Armando. *La crisi delle compagnie mercantili dei Bardi e dei Peruzzi* (Firenze, Leo S. Olschki, 1926).

Sapori, Armando. *La compagnia dei Frescobaldi in Inghilterra* (Firenze, Leo S. Olschki, 1947).

Schendl, Herbert, and Laura Wright (eds), *Code-Switching in Early English* (Berlin, De Gruyter, 2011).

Scherman, Matthieu. 'Apprenticeship of Florentine Merchants-Bankers: the Example of the 15th century London Salviati Bank', paper given at the European Social Science History Conference, Vienna (2014), *Learning and Training Patterns of Skilled Labour Force in Preindustrial Europe (14th-18th Centuries*) session, https://salviati.hypotheses.org/315

Schofield, Phillipp (ed), *Seals and their Context in the Middle Ages* (Oxford, Oxbow, 2014).

Stahl, Alan M. *Zecca: The Mint of Venice in the Middle Ages* (Baltimore, John Hopkins University Press, 2000).

Steele, Robert. *The Earliest Arithmetics in English* (London, Early English Text Society, 1922).

Sutton, Anne F. *The Mercery of London: Trade, Goods and People, 1130–1578* (London, Ashgate, 2005).

Swetz, Frank. *Capitalisation and Arithmetic: the New Math of the 15th Century* (La Salle IL, Open Court, 1987).

Sylvester, Louise. 'Semantic Field and Text-Type Approach to Multilingualism' in Päivi Pahta, Janne Skaffari and Laura Wright (eds), *Multilingual Practices in Language History: English and Beyond* (Berlin, De Gruyter Mouton, 2018), pp. 77–96.

Thick, Anne. 'The Fifteenth-Century Stewards' Books of Southampton', Ph.D. thesis (King Alfred's College, University of Southampton, 1995).

Thomas, A.H. *Calendar of the Plea and Memoranda Rolls of the City of London: Volume 1, 1323–1364* (Cambridge, Cambridge University Press, 1926).

Tiddeman, Megan. 'Mercantile Multilingualism: Two Examples of Anglo-Norman and Italian Contact in the Fourteenth Century', in *Present and Future in Anglo-Norman: La Recherche Actuelle Et Future Sur L'Anglo-Normand* (The Anglo-Norman Online Hub, 2012), pp. 91–9.

Tiddeman, Megan. 'Early Anglo-Italian Contact: New Loanword Evidence from Two Mercantile Sources, 1440–1451', in Esther-Miriam Wagner, Bettina Beinhoff and Ben Outhwaite (eds), *Merchants of Innovation: The Languages of Traders* (Berlin, De Gruyter Mouton, 2017), pp. 217–34.

Tiddeman, Megan. 'Lexical Exchange with Italian in the Textile and Wool Trades in the Thirteenth to Fifteenth centuries', in Robin Netherton and Gale R. Owen-Crocker (eds), *Medieval Clothing and Textiles*, 14 (Woodbridge, Boydell & Brewer, 2018), pp. 113–40.

Tiddeman, Megan. 'Alum' and 'Southampton and the Later Medieval Textile Trade' in Gale R. Owen Crocker, Elizabeth Coatsworth and Maria Hayward (eds), *Encyclopedia of Dress and Textiles in the British Isles c. 450–1450*, Volume 2 (2018), https://referenceworks.brillonline.com/browse/encyclopedia-of-medieval-dress-and-textiles

Tiddeman, Megan. 'More Sugar and Spice: Revisiting Medieval Italian Influence on the Mercantile Lexis of England' in Laura Wright (ed), *The Multilingual Origins of Standard English* (Berlin, De Gruyter Mouton, 2020), pp. 381–410.

Tiddeman, Megan. '*Libri alienigeni*: Evidence of Anglo-Italian Language Contact from the Fifteenth-Century Port of Southampton' in Alessandra Petrocchi and Joshua Brown (eds), *Languages and Cross-Cultural Exchanges in Renaissance Italy* (Turnhout, Brepols, forthcoming).

Tommasin, Lorenzo. 'Sulla diffusione del lessico marinaresco italiano', *Studi Linguistici Italiani*, 36 (2010), 263–92.

Trotter, David. 'Bridging the Gap: the (Socio)linguistic Evidence of Some Medieval English Bridge Accounts', in Richard Ingham (ed), *The Anglo-Norman Language and its Contexts* (Woodbridge, York Medieval Press, 2010), pp. 52–62.

Trotter, David. 'Death, Taxes and Property: some Code-Switching Evidence from Dover, Southampton and York', in Herbert Schendl and Laura Wright (eds), *Code-Switching in Early English* (Berlin, De Gruyter, 2011), pp. 155–89.

Trotter, David. 'Italian Merchants in London and Paris: Evidence of Language Contact in the Gallerani Accounts, 1305–08', in Dominique Lagorgette and Tim Pooley (eds), *Le changement linguistique en français: études en homage au professeur R. Anthony Lodge* (Chambéry, Presses de l'Université de Savoie, 2011), pp. 209–26.

Trotter, David (ed), *Manuel de la philologie de l'édition* (Berlin, De Gruyter, 2015).

Trotter, David. 'Trop fidèle pour être belle: l'édition historique en anglo-normand' (Unpublished article, 2015).

Vanes, Jean. *The Ledger of John Smythe, 1538–1550: from the Transcript Made by John Angus* (London, Bristol Record Society, 1974).

Vidos, Benedek Elemér. *Storia delle parole marinaresche italiane passate in francese: contributo storico-linguistico all'espansione della lingua nautica italiana* (Firenze, Leo S. Olschki, 1939).

Vidos, Benedek Elemér. *Prestito, espansione e migrazione dei termini tecnici nelle lingue romanze e non romanze: problemi, metodo e risultati* (Firenze, Leo S. Olschki, 1965).

Whitwell, Robert J. 'Italian Bankers and the English Crown', *Transactions of the Royal Historical Society*, New Series 17 (1903), 175–233.

Wright, Laura. 'A Hypothesis on the Structure of Macaronic Business Writing' in Jacek Fisiak (ed), *Medieval Dialectology* (New York, De Gruyter Mouton, 1995), pp. 309–21.

Wright, Laura. *Sources of London English: Medieval Thames Vocabulary* (Oxford, Clarendon Press, 1996).

Wright, Laura. 'The Records of Hanseatic Merchants: Ignorant, Sleepy or Degenerate?', *Multilingua*, 16 (1997), 339–50.

Wright, Laura. 'Bills, Accounts, Inventories: Everyday Trilingual Activities in the Business World of Later Medieval England', in David Trotter (eds), *Multilingualism in Later Medieval Britain* (Woodbridge, D. S. Brewer, 2000), pp. 149–56.

Wright, Laura. 'Code Intermediate Phenomena in Medieval Mixed-Language Texts', *Language Sciences*, 24 (2002), 471–89.

Wright, Laura. 'Standard English and the Lexicon: why so Many Different Spellings?' in Mari C. Jones and Edith Esch (eds), *Language Change: the Interplay of Internal, External and Extra-linguistic Factors* (Berlin, De Gruyter, 2002), pp. 181–200.

Wright, Laura. 'A Pilot Study on the Singular Definite Articles *le* and *la* in Fifteenth-Century London Mixed-Language Business Writing', in Richard Ingham (ed), *The Anglo-Norman Language and its Contexts* (Woodbridge, York Medieval Press, 2010), pp. 130–142.

Wright, Laura. 'On variation and change in London medieval mixed-language business documents', in Merja Stenroos, Martti Mäkinen and Inge Særheim (eds), *Language Contact and Development around the North Sea* (Amsterdam, John Benjamins, 2012), pp. 99–115.

Wright, Laura. 'The Contact Origins of Standard English' in Daniel Schreier and Marianne Hundt (eds), *English as a Contact Language* (Cambridge, Cambridge University Press, 2013), pp.58–74.

Wright, Laura (ed), *The Multilingual Origins of Standard English* (Berlin, De Gruyter Mouton, 2020).

Zupko, Ronald Edward. *Italian Weights and Measures from the Middle Ages to the Nineteenth Century* (Philadelphia, American Philosophical Society, 1981).

# Index

This index comprises four separate parts: persons and places; commodities; languages; and other.

Those personal names marked with an asterisk are either unique to Balmayn's accounts (as far as I am aware) or his version is markedly different to the equivalent in the Salviati London records.

**Persons and places:**

## Commodities:

## Languages:



## Other

Printed and bound by CPI Group (UK) Ltd, Croydon, CR0 4YY
16/09/2026
14963460-0001